IMAGES
of Rail

KENOSHA ON THE GO

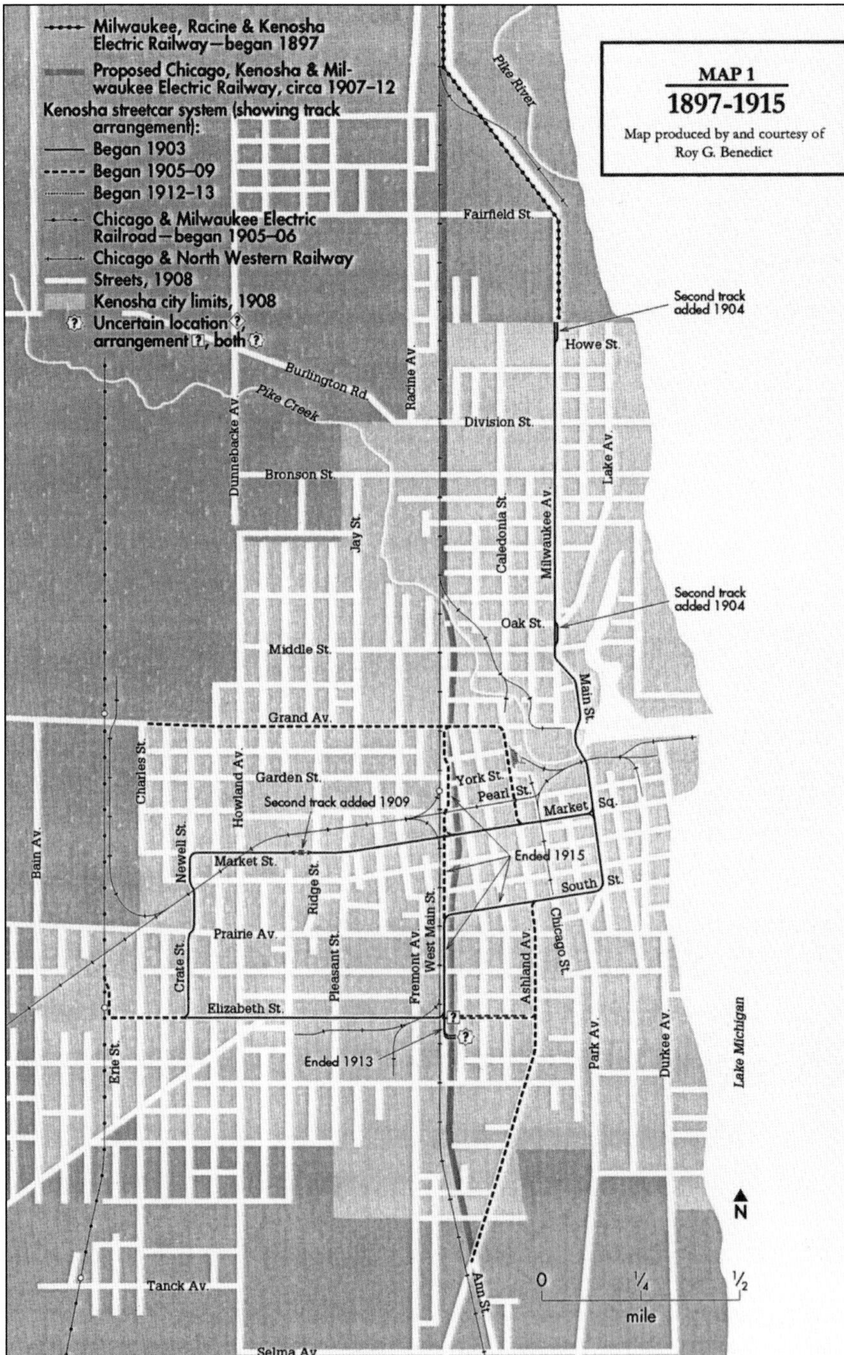

Map 1 shows the 1897–1915 era.

On the cover: Chicago, North Shore and Milwaukee Railway train No. 803 is northbound at the Kenosha North Shore station on Sunday, December 4, 1949. This articulated streamliner train, one of two operated by the North Shore, is seen here loading and unloading passengers on a sunny but cold winter day. (Photograph by John F. Humiston, courtesy of Richard Humiston.)

IMAGES
of Rail

KENOSHA ON THE GO

Kenosha Streetcar Society

ARCADIA
PUBLISHING

ISBN 978-0-7385-5098-5

Published by Arcadia Publishing
Charleston, South Carolina

Printed in the United States of America

Library of Congress Catalog Card Number: 2007928571

For all general information contact Arcadia Publishing at:
Telephone 843-853-2070
Fax 843-853-0044
E-mail sales@arcadiapublishing.com
For customer service and orders:
Toll-Free 1-888-313-2665

Visit us on the Internet at www.arcadiapublishing.com

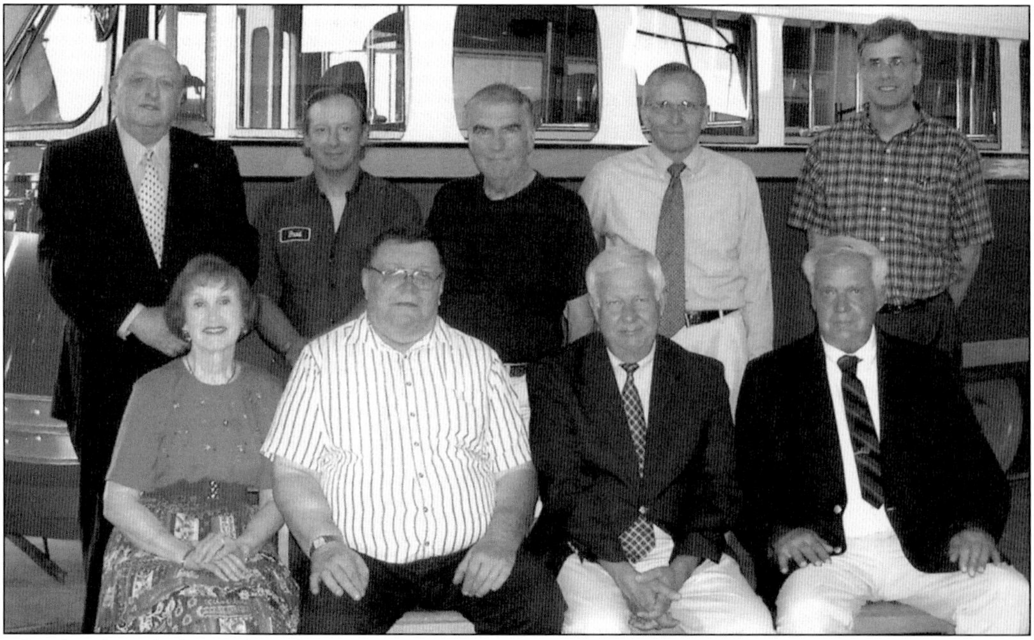

This book is dedicated to the train crews, streetcar crews, and to the trackless trolley and bus operators who served the citizens of Kenosha. They worked long hours and took riders to work and play while dutifully collecting fares along the way. Kenosha Streetcar Society Board members are pictured on July 5, 2007. They are, from left to right, (first row) Joyce Simons March, secretary; Edward Rosengren, chairman; Donald O. Ellison, vice chairman; and James E. Wolfe, treasurer; (second row) John F. Doyle, past chairman; and board members Bradley Preston, Louis Rugani, Roger A. Moddes, and John Bloner Jr. (Photograph by Diane J. Doyle.)

Contents

ACKNOWLEDGMENTS

We extend our thanks to John F. Doyle for writing the book, collecting the images, and writing the captions. Thanks to Kenneth C. Springirth for his financial assistance. Thanks to Diane J. Doyle for her many hours of editing and final layout. Thanks to Larry Godson for scanning and editing the images.

Acknowledgements are extended to the following individuals, for photographs, proofreading, and historical information, for without them, this book could not have been written: David Stanley (DS); Russell E. Schultz (RES); Thomas J. Jervan (TJJ); John E. Gervais (JEG); Robert Genack (RG); Donald O. Ellison (DOE), who also wrote his own captions; Philip A. Weibler (PAW); Joyce Simons March (JSM); George E. Kanary (GEK); William B. Becwar (WBB); Richard Kunz (RK); John F. Humiston (JFH); Richard Humiston (RH); Earlene Frederick (EF); Erik Bryant (EB); Diane J. Doyle (DJD); John F. Doyle (JFD); Milan Salek (MS); Robert W. Gibson (RWG); George Krambles (GK); Art Cox (AC); F. Knnecke (FK); A. F. Scholz (AFS); H. M. Pauly (HMP); Edward Montejano (EMO); John D. Horacheck (JDH), who also wrote his snow-scene caption; William Shapotkin (WS); Marty Hogan (MH); Larry Konsbruck (LK); Robert Konsbruck (RK); Richard Moseler (RM); Jeffery Wein (JW); Ernie Maragos (EM); Art Harnack (AH); Raymond E. DeGroote (RED); Ohio Brass (OB); General Electric (GE); Stone Consulting Company (SCC); Joseph Kline, Kenosha News (JK, KN); Paul Williams, Kenosha News (PW, KN); John Hill, Tiger Hill Aerial Photography (THAP); I. C. Scroggins (ICS); Walter R. Keevil (WRK); Richard Simons (RS); Robert Faelak (RF); James Kudla (JK); Mel Bernero (MB); John Hosmanek (JH); Bruce W. and Kenneth B. Rosenberg (BWR, KBR); James E. Wolfe (JEW); John J. Kelly Jr. (JJK); Kenosha Public Museum, H. L. Hastings (KPM, HLH); Kenosha County Historical Society (KCHS); Kenosha County Historical Museum (KCHM); Krambles-Peterson Archive (KPA); Joseph Piersen, Chicago and North Western Railroad Historical Society (JP, C&NWRHS); the Milwaukee Electric Railway and Transport Historical Society (TMER&THS); and Railroad Avenue Enterprises (RAE). Please note that initials are found in parentheses throughout the book for the appropriate image credits.

We also extend our appreciation to Michael E. Kehoe, Keith Kohlmann, Len Brandrup, and Albert E. Meier for proofreading and historical information. And thanks to Roy G. Benedict for the maps.

The following publications serve usefully for research: *First & Fastest* magazine, Autumn 2000; *Motor Coach Age* magazine, September 2004; *North Western Steam Power 1848–1956*, by C. T. Knudsen; *The KD Line* by P. L. Behrens; and Central Electric Railfans Association, bulletin numbers 106, 107, and 108.

Those interested in joining the Kenosha Streetcar Society can contact us at P. O. Box 2263, Kenosha, WI 53141-2263.

INTRODUCTION

Kenosha developed into a small industrial city on Lake Michigan, 48 miles north of Chicago and 37 miles south of Milwaukee. Originally named Pike and later Southport, Kenosha was home to many industries, such as Bain Wagon, Simmons Mattress, and Nash Motors, as well as tanneries and textile firms. Kenosha was well served with its local transportation system, two electric interurban lines and a mainline railway.

Local electric streetcar service started in Kenosha on February 1, 1903, under the name of Kenosha Electric Railway Company (KER) and was owned by its first president, Bion J. Arnold, until 1905. The second owner was Albert C. Frost. He sold KER to Investment Registry Limited of London in 1909. In April 1912, North American Company, a public utility, purchased KER and made it part of its holding company, Wisconsin Gas and Electric (WG&E). North American also owned The Milwaukee Electric Railway and Light Company (TMER&L), and over the years, both companies would share a close relationship.

In 1919, the first two gasoline buses were purchased to serve the ever-expanding residential areas of Kenosha. By 1925, the bus lines grew to four routes. The buses were garaged behind the streetcar barn at Fifty-fourth Street and Sheridan Road. In 1920, WG&E purchased 15 new single-truck Birney Safety Cars, a smaller-sized streetcar. In 1924, four double-truck cars were added to the fleet and along with three older refurbished cars made up the roster.

On February 15, 1932, electric trackless trolley service began in Kenosha. By the end of the year, all of Kenosha's streetcar lines and gas bus routes would be replaced by four trackless trolley lines. Kenosha became the first and only city in the United States to operate exclusively an entire trackless trolley fleet; that distinction would last a decade. Route destination signs introduced with the new fleet would designate the routes by color.

The fleet consisted of 22 coaches: 12 were built by Yellow Truck and Coach Manufacturing Company (GMC), and 10 were built by St. Louis Car Company.

In 1931, a former harness and sole tannery warehouse building, erected in 1912 for Allen Tannery, was purchased and converted to a trackless trolley garage. That building still stands today as a boathouse at Fifty-second Street and Sheridan Road.

In 1937, the U.S. Supreme Court upheld the Public Utility Act of 1935, reaffirming that electric utilities were a monopoly. This in turn led to those utilities transferring or selling off their electric transportation holdings. Such was the case when Henry P. Bruner, an experienced transportation manager and investor, purchased the Kenosha city lines from WG&E on September 7, 1942, renaming it Kenosha Motor Coach Lines.

In November 1942, KMCL took delivery of five new Ford transit gas buses, two of which replaced trackless trolley operations on the Twenty-second Avenue Crosstown Orange Line serving uptown. In 1943, the Office of Defense allocated five additional Ford transit buses to KMCL.

On December 1, 1946, Bruner sold his Kenosha city properties to Shore Line Transit of Hammond, Indiana. On February 8, 1948, Shore Line Transit sold the system to the Chicago, North Shore and Milwaukee Railway (CNS&M), and the name was changed to Kenosha Motor Coach Company. On February 14, 1949, the company took delivery of 15 new 32-passenger GMC transit diesel buses, followed by 8 more in January 1952.

Waukegan and North Chicago Transit, a subsidiary of the CNS&M, transferred 10 White gas buses to Kenosha and, along with the existing fleet of diesel buses, replaced trackless trolley operations on the Red and Green Lines on March 1, 1952, ending 49 years of local electric transportation in Kenosha.

After World War II, the automobile became the most popular mode of transportation for the average person. By 1961, Kenosha's bus system was carrying 2.3 million riders down from 9.5 million riders in 1947.

On November 12, 1962, Lake Shore Transit, owned by John Holcomb, purchased the Kenosha property. On February 18, 1969, he abandoned the bus system due to an employee strike, leaving the city without transit service.

Pathfinder City Transit Lines resumed bus operations in Kenosha, operating under subsidy from the city on August 4, 1969. Owner Gordon McAleer operated out of Lake Shore's former bus garage at Fifty-first Place and Eighth Avenue until he could no longer make payments on the property. That building still stands today as a Holsum Bakery bread route depot and thrift store.

Pathfinder City Transit Lines had a unique system of route identification for their 16 former Indianapolis Railways GMC transit diesel buses. They painted the bus in the color of the bus route—red for the Red Line, blue for the Blue Line, and so forth. Pathfinder City Transit Lines, lacking adequate subsidy, abandoned service on February 12, 1971. Again Kenosha was without bus service.

On September 7, 1971, the City of Kenosha restored bus service using six Highway Products Twin Coaches and seven used GMC transit diesels from the Milwaukee Transport Company. In April 1975, a new fleet of 24 GMC 45-passenger "fishbowl" diesel buses went into service. Over the years, there would be additional new buses. Today's modern fleet of Gillig buses, built in Hayward, California, provides excellent service for a $1 fare. City employees operate Kenosha's transit system (renamed Kenosha Area Transit on September 4, 2004) under the Kenosha Department of Transportation, which is governed by the Kenosha Transit Commission. The year 2000 would see the return of streetcars to the city on the lake—a second "first" for Kenosha.

The first interurban streetcar line to reach Kenosha was operated by the Milwaukee, Racine, and Kenosha Electric Railway (MRK); it started service to Kenosha's northern city limits on June 1, 1897. The line terminated on Milwaukee Avenue (Seventh Avenue) and what later would become Limit Street (Thirty-eighth Street) where riders could complete the trip via horse-drawn omnibus to downtown Kenosha.

By 1899, the line was absorbed into TMER&L. In 1903, city streetcars reached north to Limit Street becoming the transfer point for passengers riding into the city. Today the floor of the waiting station is still visible on the east side of Seventh Avenue at Thirty-eighth Street.

In 1912, the KER was sold to WG&E, a subsidiary of North American Company (owner of TMER&L). On May 4, 1912, the interurban cars were allowed to run over city streetcar tracks to downtown, south on Milwaukee Avenue (Seventh Avenue) into Main Street (Sixth Avenue) to Market Street (Fifty-sixth Street). Turning west to Chicago Street (Eighth Avenue), the cars changed ends and started their runs back to Milwaukee from the Kenosha Public Service Building located on Market Street.

New double track was installed on Seventh Avenue in three segments between 1924 and 1929. The new track gave the city streetcars, along with the rebuilt 1100 class interurbans, the best ride they ever had. The rebuilt interurbans were single-ended and required difficult maneuvers to turn them around in city traffic; therefore, a turning loop was built in 1925 behind the streetcar barn at Fifty-fourth Street and Sheridan Road.

The company realized that the old interurban operations were obsolete and opted to build a new rapid transit right-of-way; however, the Depression slowed progress on the reconstruction.

The rebuilt MRK line, the "Rapid Transit," entered Kenosha on private right-of-way; it was opened on April 18, 1932, along with a new rapid transit depot at Fifty-fifth Street and Eighth Avenue. The new MRK line was built to the highest standards but still had to navigate city street running through Milwaukee and Racine. During street reconstruction in August 2007, the expensive track long under asphalt on Seventh Avenue was removed.

In 1938, the MRK line was transferred to a new owner, The Milwaukee Electric Railway and Transport Company. Between 1943 and 1944, the MRK line was sold piecemeal to Henry P. Bruner and renamed Kenosha Motor Coach Lines (KMCL). The Racine–Kenosha segment was abandoned on September 13, 1947. After 50 years of interurban service, final closure took place on December 31, 1947, with the abandonment of the Racine to Milwaukee portion of the line.

The Kenosha terminal continued operations as the Union Bus Depot. The parallel bus route started by TMER&L in the 1920s between Kenosha and Milwaukee abandoned service five years after the KMCL purchase due to lack of patronage. The depot also served Cardinal, Greyhound, and the local Racine/Kenosha bus line and, by 1956, became Vena's Pizzeria. In 1965, the 33-year-old building was demolished.

In 1897, a small Waukegan, Illinois, streetcar line was purchased by Albert C. Frost and George Ball (promoter of the Mason jar) and eventually became the Chicago and Milwaukee Electric Railroad (C&ME). In 1899, service was completed south to Church Street in Evanston. On December 2, 1905, the line reached north to Kenosha where a grand celebration was held at the new station located at Elizabeth Street (Sixty-third Street) and Erie Street (Twenty-seventh Avenue). The first trains with their special guests were uncoupled and run over city streetcar tracks to Germania Hall where a gala celebration was held by Albert Frost.

Although the line was built to the highest standards, the panic of 1907 forced the company into receivership. Under receivers, the line reached Racine and finally connected with the Milwaukee Light, Heat, and Traction Company for through service into downtown Milwaukee on October 31, 1908. Additional interurban cars were purchased including parlor buffet cars. Limited trains, with Kenosha as a main stop, could now make the 73-mile run between Milwaukee and Evanston in 2 hours and 15 minutes.

Chicago utilities tycoon Samuel Insull purchased the C&ME on May 1, 1916, renaming it the Chicago, North Shore and Milwaukee Railroad and immediately implemented improvements. On August 6, 1919, interurban trains started operating over another Insull property, the North Western Elevated Railroad from Wilmette into the Chicago Loop. Soon thereafter the line became known as the "North Shore."

In 1922, a new station was built at Kenosha with plans drawn by Insull's staff architect Arthur U. Gerber. This striking building, influenced by the prairie-style architecture of Frank Lloyd Wright, still stands today at Sixty-third Street and Twenty-seventh Avenue. In 1926, a new route, the Skokie Valley Route, was opened as a second line to bypass the slower Shore Line route. The North Shore, second to none in both speed and equipment, had reached its zenith.

In September 1932, due to the stock market crash of 1929, the North Shore followed Insull's utilities empire into bankruptcy. Despite its financial difficulties, the North Shore continued to operate.

Traffic on the North Shore Line was still substantial in the years following World War II. In January 1963, however, a notice was posted in the Kenosha North Shore station announcing abandonment. Despite efforts to keep the railroad running, it was shut down. Riders were bewildered since the North Shore was their commuter train to work, pleasure, and shopping along its 85-mile route.

At 12:00 a.m. on a freezing winter night, train No. 437, originating at Roosevelt Road in Chicago slipped away into the dark night. While Kenosha slept, motorman Francis T. Murray of Cudahy, Wisconsin, and his collector, Charles Wussow of Appleton, Wisconsin, with their northbound train made the last scheduled stop at Kenosha on January 21, 1963. As only fate would have it, the train's conductor, Joe McGrath, was a citizen of Kenosha.

In 1851, the Green Bay, Milwaukee and Chicago Railroad Company was authorized to build a rail line north through Kenosha from the Illinois state line. By 1855, the railroad was renamed the Milwaukee and Chicago Railroad. The railroad was leased to and became part of the Chicago and North Western Railroad (known as the North Western), providing excellent service to Kenosha. Holding yards to turn steam engines and store commuter coaches were built at Kenosha and Waukegan.

In 1899, a new Queen Anne–style depot was built at West Main (Thirteenth Avenue) and York Street (Fifty-fourth Street). The North Western Kenosha train station was completely rebuilt in 1948, remodeled in 1984, and remains in use today.

In 1907, a freight bypass line (the New Line) running through Bain was built west of Kenosha, diverting through-route freight trains from the lakeshore communities. Bain station on the Kenosha Division (KD) Line became a junction and a coal and water stop.

The North Western ran through Kenosha at grade. Due to several accidents, the railway elevated the line through Kenosha with intermittent construction between 1930 and 1939.

By 1956, the Kenosha commuter line was a major route on the North Western suburban system that carried 72,000 riders each weekday. Limited trains from Chicago would average 1 hour and 30 minutes running time to Kenosha. After the government's takeover of passenger service (Amtrak) on May 1, 1971, through passenger trains were discontinued between Chicago, Kenosha, Milwaukee, Green Bay, and northern Wisconsin.

Since 1975, the Kenosha commuter line has been part of Metra, the suburban rail carrier of the Chicago Area Regional Transportation Authority. With equipment leased from the Regional Transportation Authority (RTA), the Kenosha commuter line is operated today by the Union Pacific Railroad.

Over the years, there have been many stories about why the North Western is operated on the left side of the right-of-way (the only United States railroad to have this distinction). The most commonly told story was that early British investment in the North Western led to building the railway to British operating standards, which use the left side; this is a good story but not true. The railway was first built as a single-track operation. Stations on the inbound track to the city were built east or north of the tracks. As business increased, a second track (outbound from the city) was built to the west or south of the existing track.

Kenosha also had a second railroad in general use by 1861 from the Kenosha Harbor to Rockford, Illinois. The 72-mile line created by Kenosha businessmen soon failed; it was acquired by the North Western in 1864 and became known as the KD Line. The line served Kenosha's industries and Kenosha County's two largest ice producers, Knickerbocker and Jefferson Ice, who used the railway to get their lake product to market. By 1920, the lakes were becoming popular resort areas resulting in increased passenger service to the Twin Lakes station near Lakes Elizabeth and Marie.

Most of the KD Line west of Bain was abandoned by 1939, and Kenosha's American Motors would eventually become the line's primary customer. The Kenosha section along with the North Western main line is operated today by the Union Pacific Railroad.

One

LOCAL TRANSPORTATION

Although streetcar track was initially installed in Kenosha by a Chicago firm between 1900 and 1901, it was never used. The Kenosha Electric Railway (KER) purchased the tracks on April 28, 1902, and completed the electric overhead wiring. The first carbarn, located in the middle of West Main at Elizabeth Street, was demolished and replaced in October 1903 by a new barn just south of the old structure (see solid lines on the map on page 2).

Using two former Waukegan city streetcars service was initiated on February 1, 1903. Additional secondhand streetcars were purchased, and by 1905, KER was expanding its service area (see dashed lines on the map on page 2). Kenosha's first new streetcars were a group of six cars built by the Kuhlman Car Company of Cleveland, Ohio, in 1907. The last new line built by KER in 1909 went north on Ashland Avenue (Sheridan Road) and west on Grand Avenue (Fifty-second Street). (See dotted lines on the map on page 2.)

The population of Kenosha in 1910 was 21,400 and by 1920, would expand to 40,500. In spite of the population growth, by 1915 fares only accounted for half of the revenue. The KER, now owned by Wisconsin Gas and Electric (WG&E), had to cut service and switch from two-man operation to one man. Due to the war effort in 1918, women were briefly employed as conductresses, and by 1921, the cars would become operated by one man again.

Over the years, new cars would be purchased with a new carbarn on the east side of Fifty-fourth Street and Sheridan Road.

From September 1, 1926, street names were changed to numbers (see the map on page 17). By 1932, streetcars would pass from the scene until their return in 2000. Kenosha's streetcars and gas buses would be replaced with trackless trolleys (see double lines on the map on page 23 showing the trackless trolley routes and new alignments).

With the retirement of trackless trolleys, in 1952 all of Kenosha's local transit lines would be serviced by transit buses. By 1971, the system would become city owned and operated.

In 2006, funding was approved for a study of streetcar expansion to uptown. It seems ironic that the west end would be in the same place as the original ending of the old Elizabeth Street line.

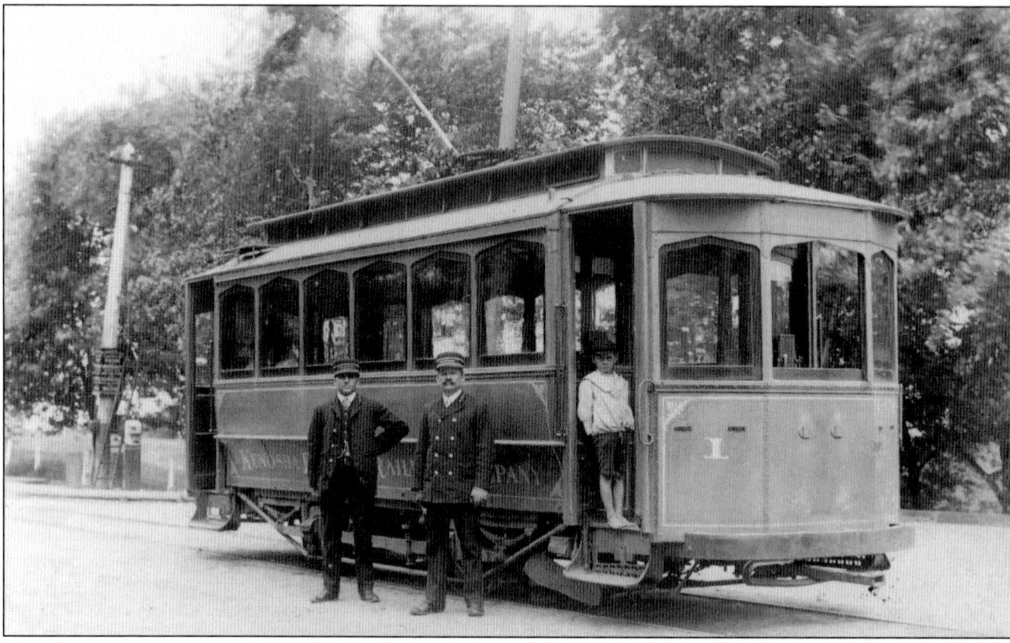

The first streetcars to run in Kenosha were two secondhand Waukegan city streetcars built by the J. G. Brill Company in 1895. Car No. 1 at Kenosha's northern city limits is seen here with its motorman John Fadgin to the right and his conductor Louis Schulte in the summer of 1903. Car No. 2 was demolished by a steam engine on the first day of streetcar service and was replaced with another Waukegan city streetcar. (Courtesy of JEG.)

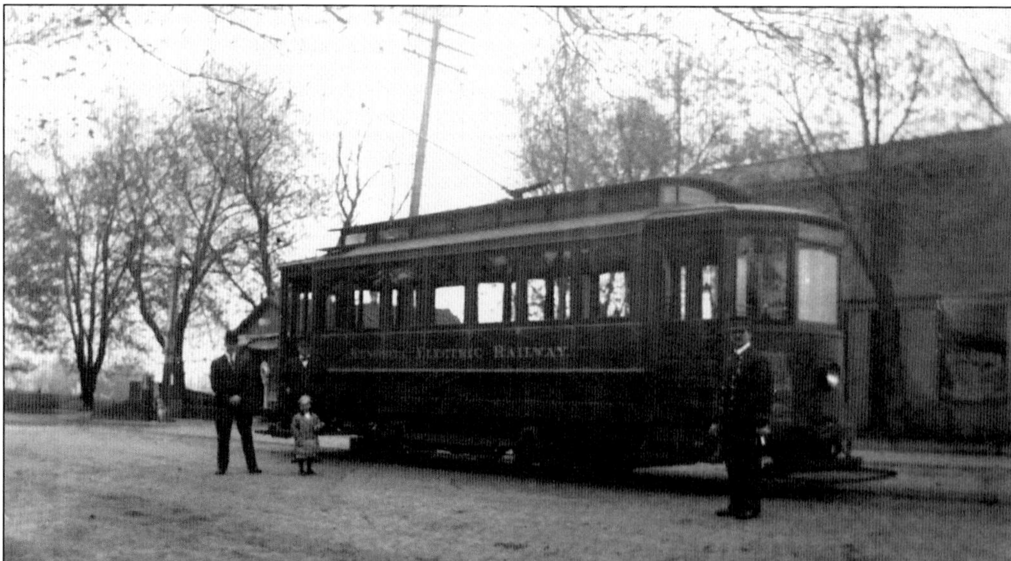

This KER single-truck streetcar is at the northern end of the Elizabeth streetcar line at Milwaukee Avenue (Seventh Avenue) and what would later become Limit Street (Thirty-eighth Street) around 1907. In the background to the left is the waiting station and terminal of the Milwaukee Racine and Kenosha (MRK) interurban line of The Milwaukee Electric Railway and Light Company (TMER&L). To the right is the Krisor family's saloon, liquor store, restaurant, and waiting room. (Courtesy of RES.)

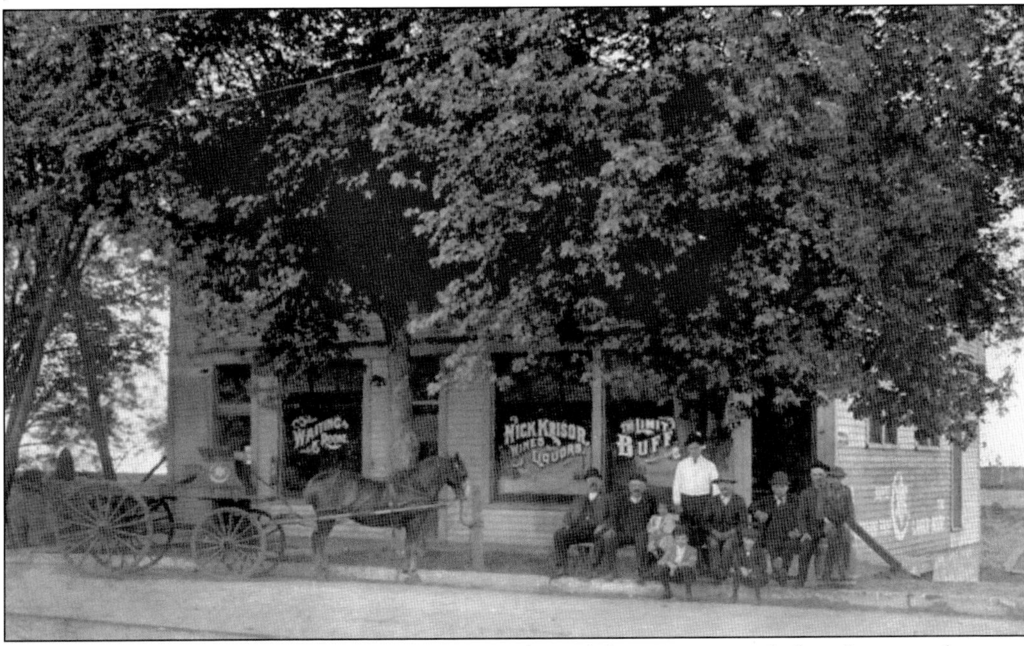

The Krisor family along with their Cream City beer delivery crew, including horse and wagon, pose for the camera in 1907. This combination saloon and liquor store also housed the Limit waiting room where sandwiches and coffee were served. Located at Kenosha's northern city limits, it was a transfer point between Kenosha City streetcars and interurbans of the MRK. This view is looking northeast to what would be Pennoyer Park today. (Courtesy of JSM, RS.)

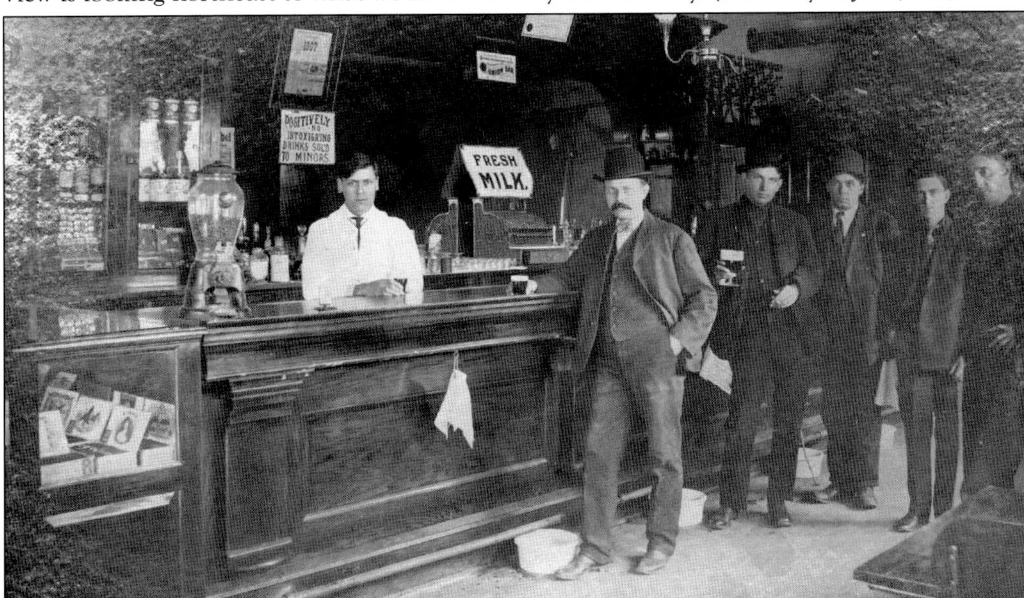

One can almost smell the effervescence of the Cream City beer in this interior view of Nick Krisor's saloon. The spittoon and cigars were all part of this 1907 scene. The brewery gave the loan to Krisor's father, Peter, to construct the building. This would assure the brewery of selling their product in what was a very competitive market. And yes, the good guys could drink fresh milk. (Courtesy of JSM, RS.)

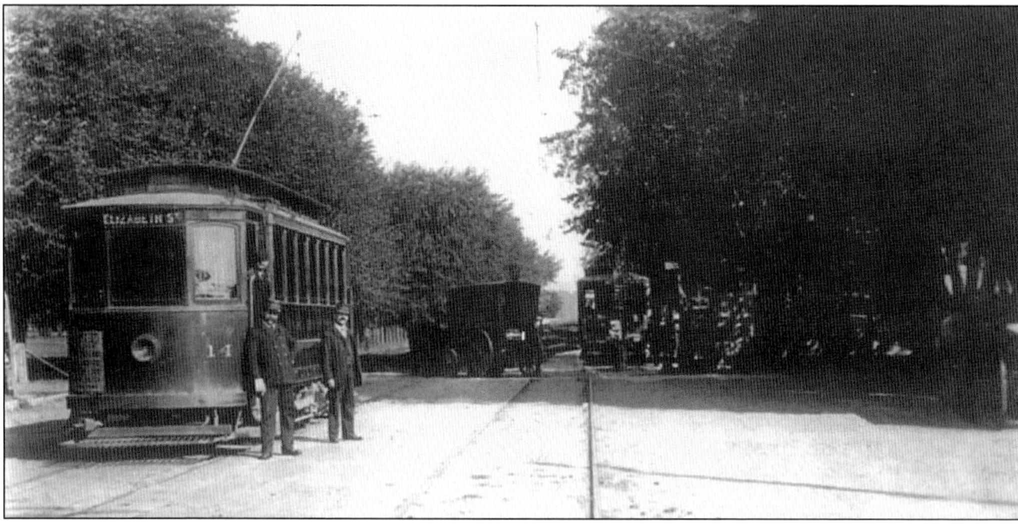

At Kenosha's northern city limits, city streetcar No. 14, built by the Kuhlman Car Company in 1907, along with its crew, is having its picture taken. To the right is a wagon delivering packages or newspapers that will be loaded onto the standing MRK interurban and delivered along its route. By May 1912, interurbans would be allowed to run over city streetcar tracks to downtown Kenosha. (Courtesy of RES.)

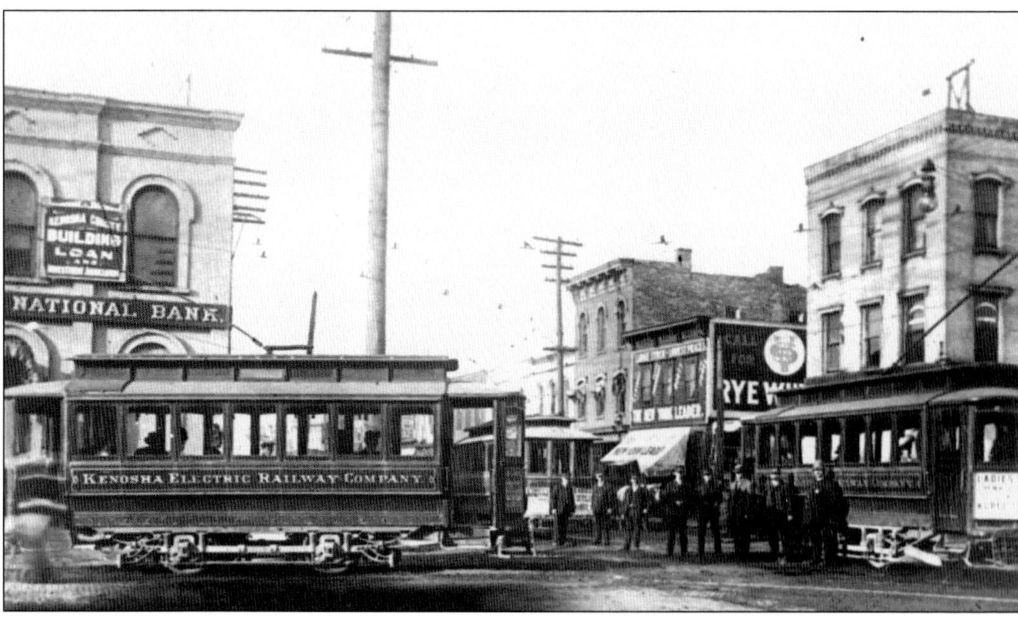

Kenosha used a variety of single truck streetcars and would not receive new cars of its own until 1907. Seen here at Market Square are three new semi-convertible streetcars built by the Kuhlman Car Company, looking northeast across Main Street (Sixth Avenue). (Courtesy of KCHM.)

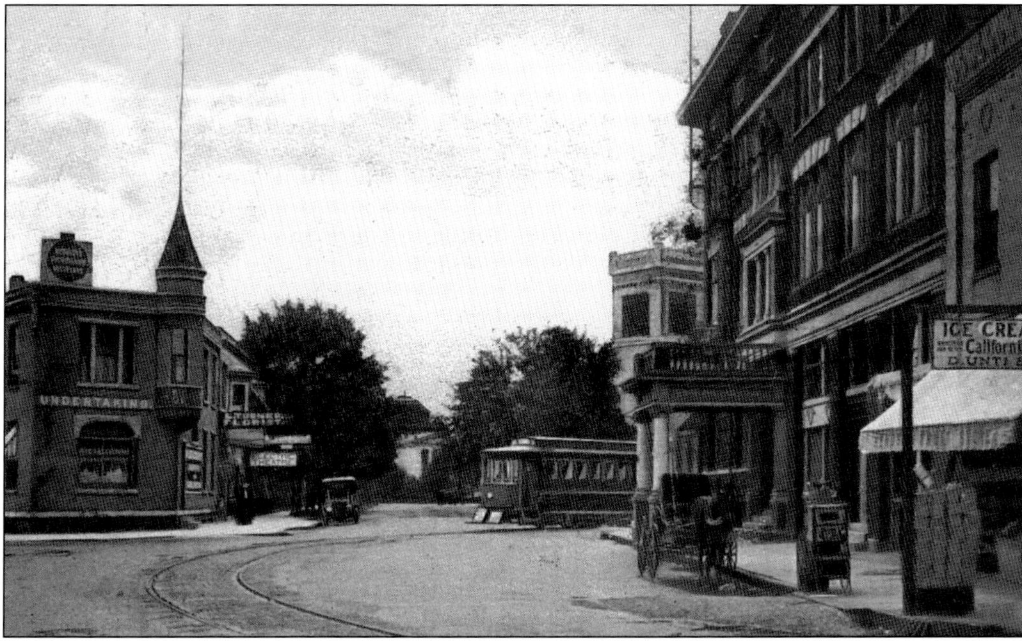

Looking south, a city streetcar of the KER can be seen, about to turn north into Main Street (Sixth Avenue) from South Street (Fifty-ninth Street) around 1909. The streetcar is probably operating on the Elizabeth/Milwaukee line. The two-way curved track would remain the same until 1927, when track was built on Fifty-eighth Street for westbound cars; however, Main Street would be double-tracked between 1912 and 1915 (see the map on page 17). (Courtesy of RES.)

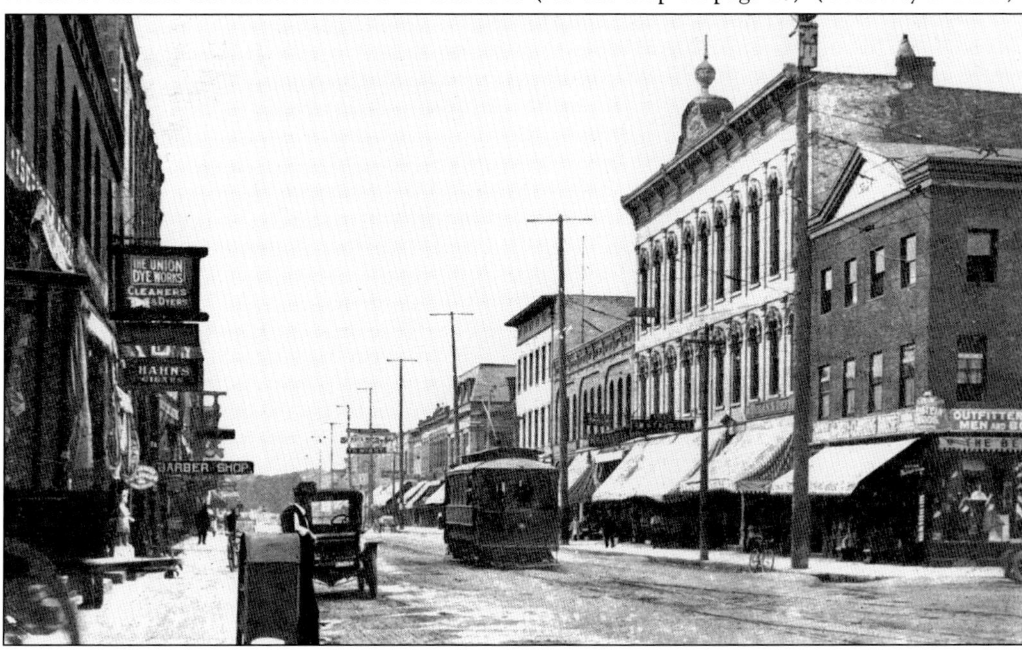

Looking south on Main Street, a KER streetcar is seen here at Market Street in 1909. The car is on the Elizabeth/Milwaukee line and will run north into Milwaukee Avenue (Seventh Avenue). Ending its run at city limits (Thirty-eighth Street) where there will be a transfer point to connect passengers to the MRK interurban to Racine and Milwaukee. (Courtesy of RES.)

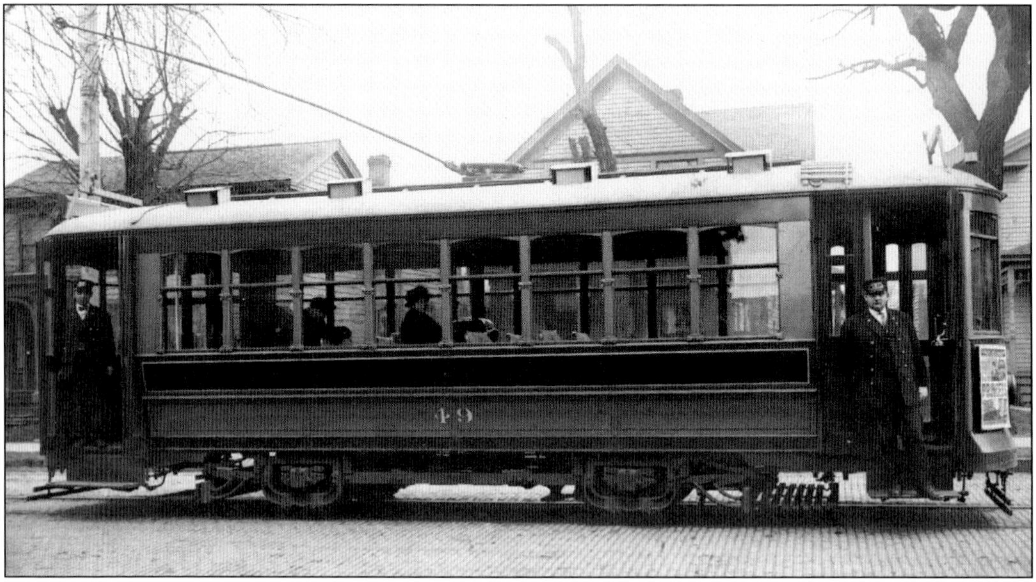

Pictured here is single-truck arch-roof Kenosha streetcar No. 49 built between 1912 and 1913 by TMER&L. This series of 11 cars were transferred back and forth between Kenosha and Racine and were converted to one-man operation in 1921. (Courtesy of KCHM.)

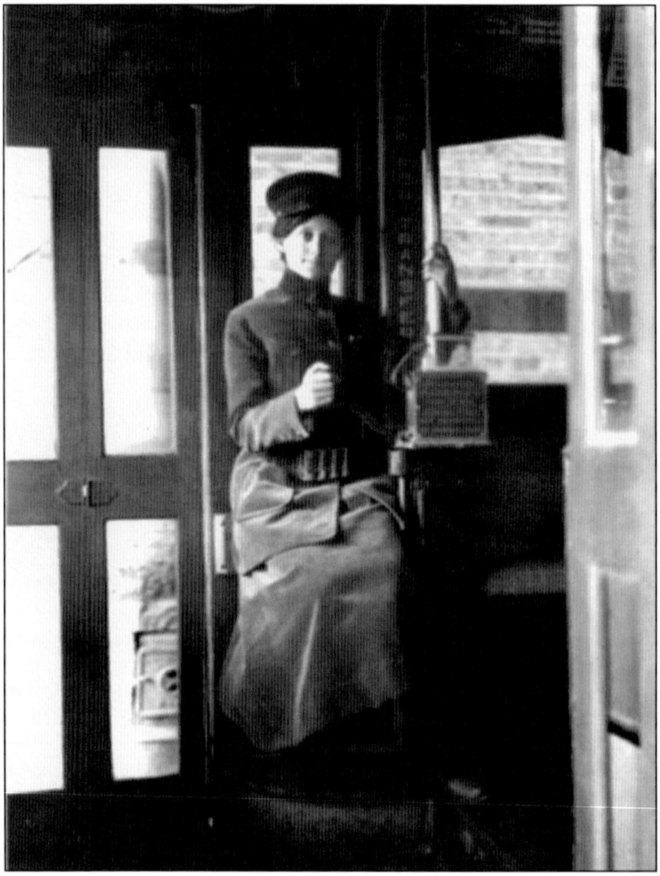

In late 1917 with war clouds gathering, conductors were brought back to handle the increased passenger traffic. In 1918, as America entered World War I, women were hired as "conductresses" due to a shortage of men who were needed in the military and Kenosha's factories. Seen here in this company photograph is a very pretty conductress on a Kenosha streetcar ready to collect fares. (Courtesy of TMER&THS.)

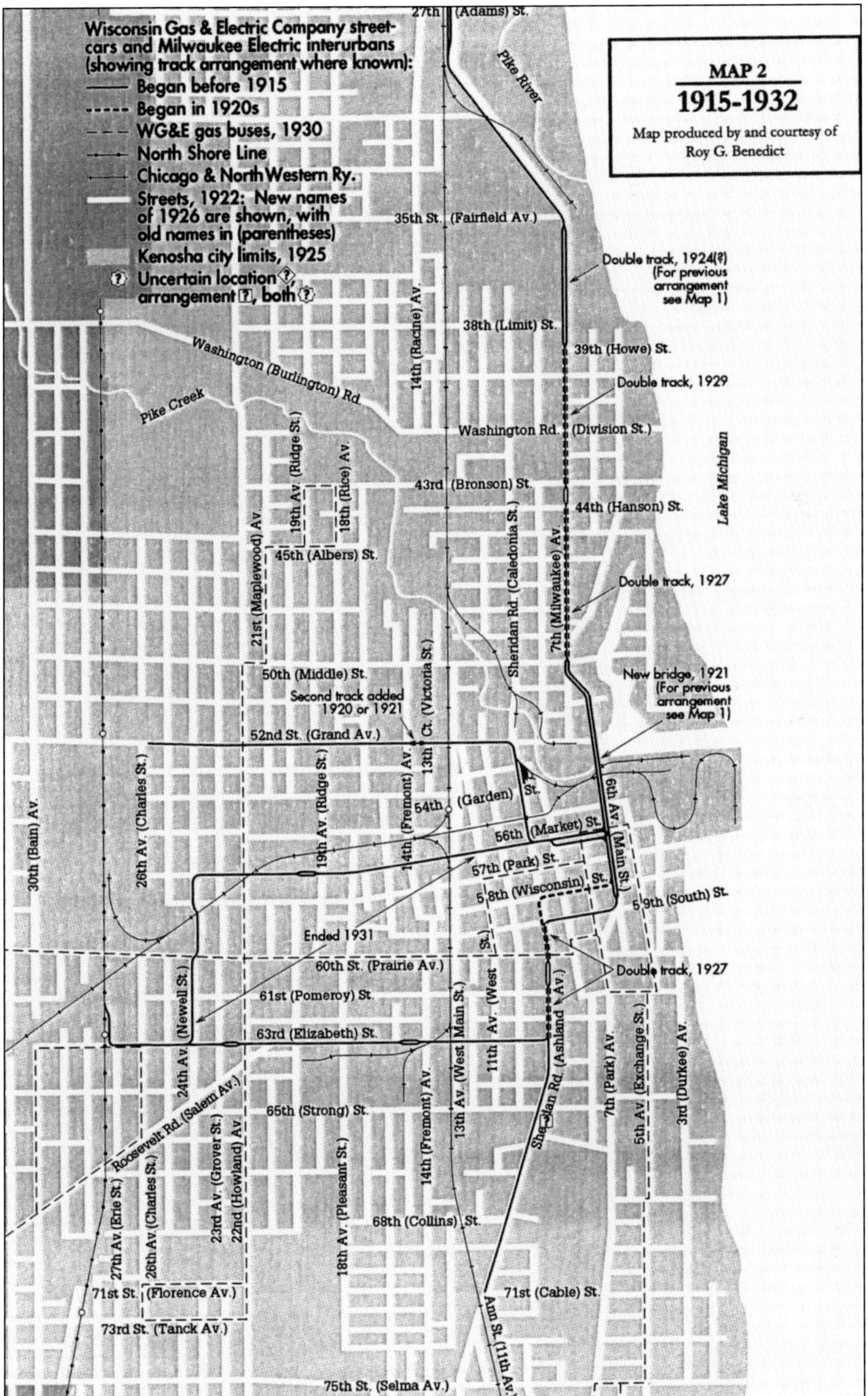

Map 2 shows the 1915–1932 era.

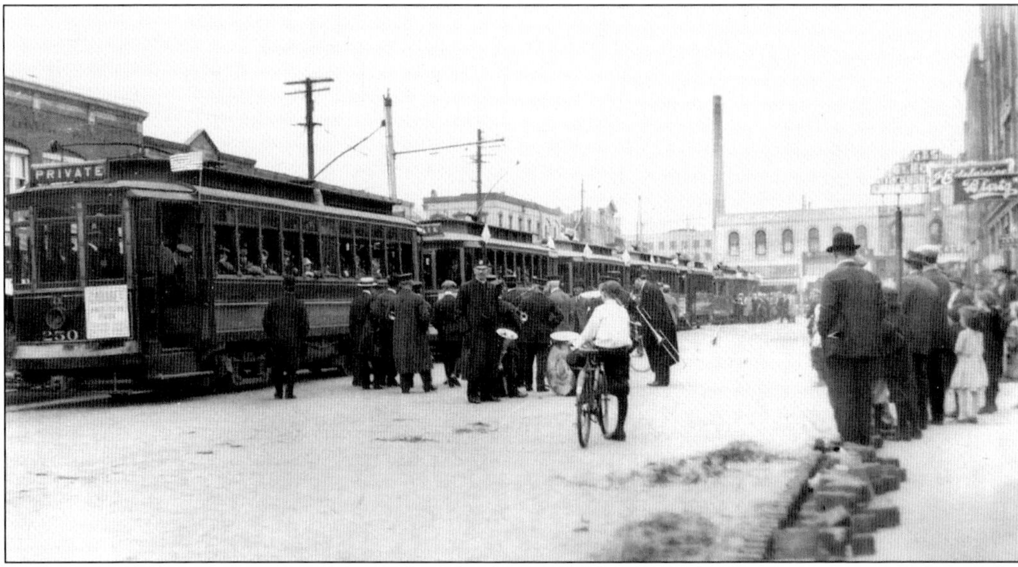

With American flags flying from the cars, former Milwaukee streetcar No. 250, borrowed from Racine, heads the lineup of special event streetcars around 1918. The sign on the streetcar advertises a cabaret at Anderson Park in Kenosha. The event, however, is still a mystery. This view is looking east to Main Street (Sixth Avenue) from Market Square (Fifty-sixth Street). (Courtesy of KCHS, JEG.)

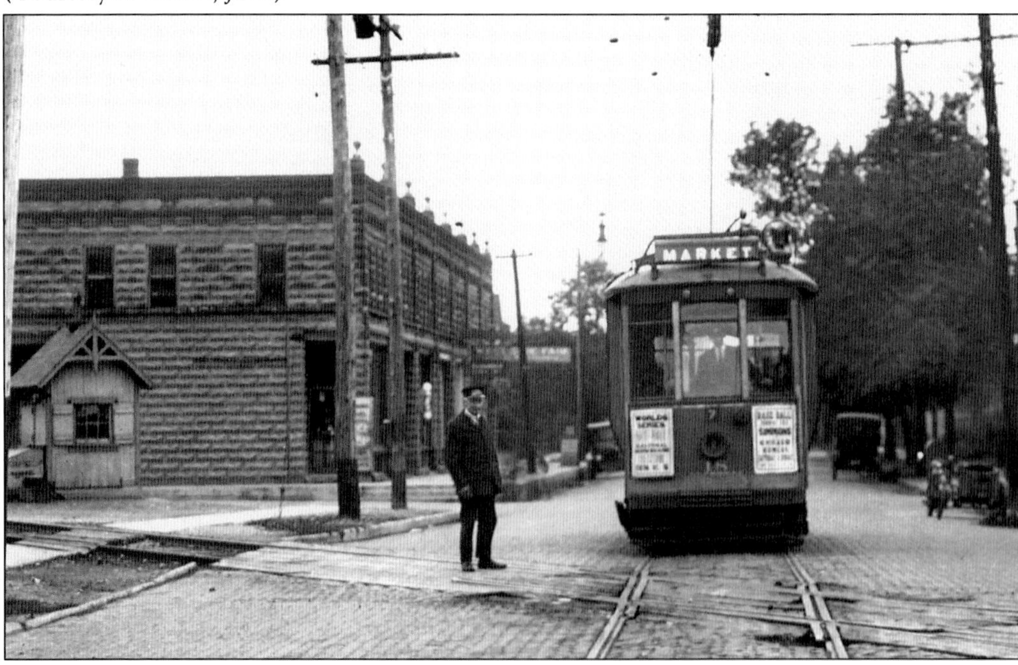

WG&E car No. 18, run No. 7, is being flagged over the Kenosha Division (KD) Line looking west on Market Street at Howland Avenue in the early 1920s (Fifty-sixth Street and Twenty-second Avenue). This streetcar was part of a six-car order built for KER by the Kuhlman Car Company in 1907. This photograph was part of a group of company photographs taken at Kenosha's Chicago and North Western Railroad (known as the North Western) grade crossings. (Courtesy of RES.)

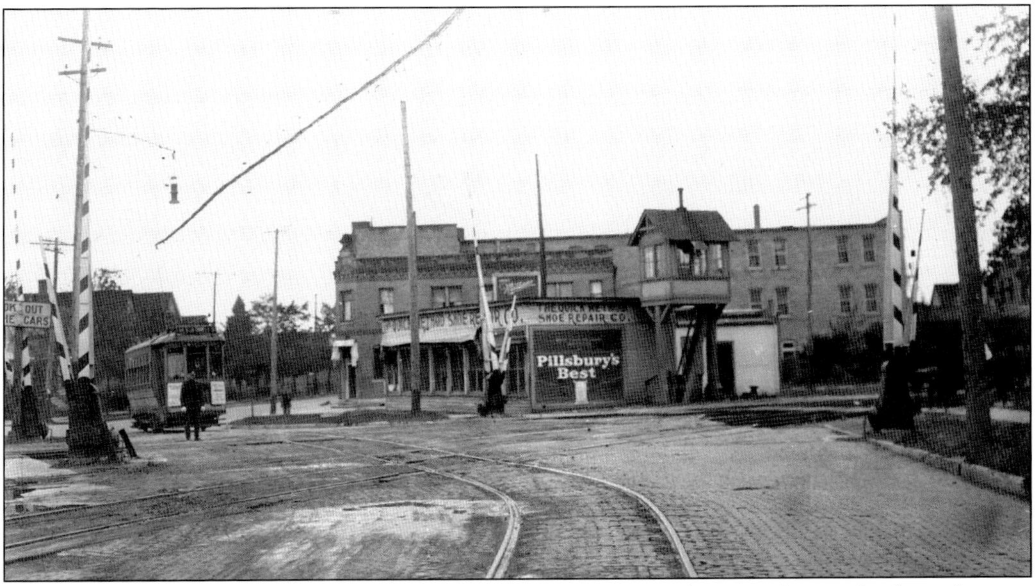

In this early-1920s company photograph, a WG&E streetcar can be seen about to be flagged across the KD Line on Newell Street (Twenty-fourth Avenue) just south of Park Street (Fifty-seventh Street). Today the buildings and street in this scene are gone, only the tracks of the KD Line remain and are owned by the Union Pacific Railroad. WG&E flagmen had no warming shelters. (Courtesy of RES.)

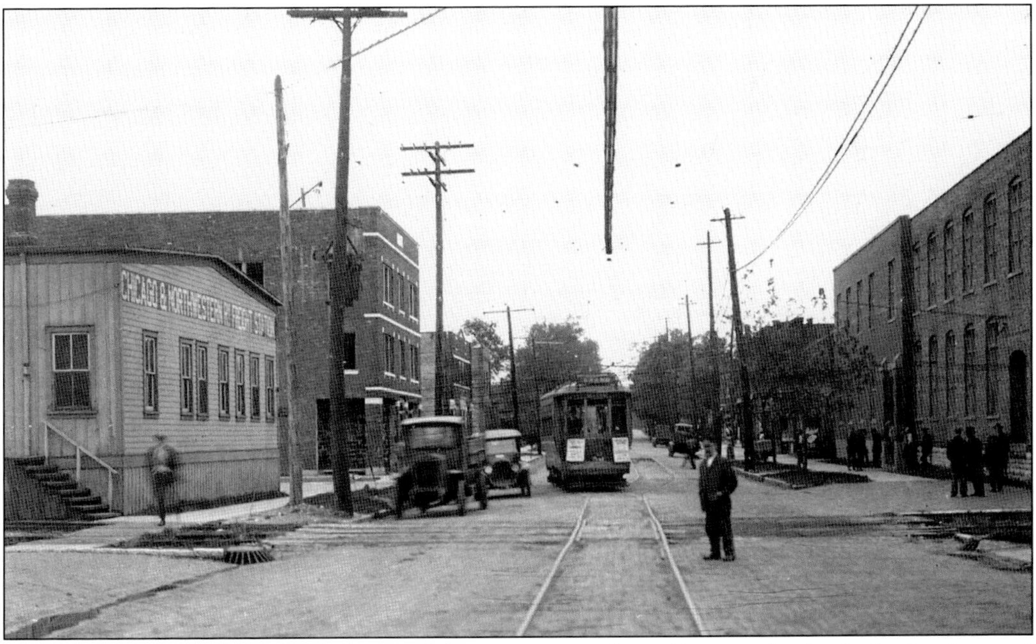

Car No. 50 is a single-truck streetcar that was part of an 11-car order built for Racine and Kenosha between 1912 and 1913 by TMER&L. The cars were converted to one-man operation in 1921. This early-1920s company photograph is looking west on Grand Avenue from West Main Street (Fifty-second Street and Thirteenth Avenue). Car No. 50 is about to cross the North Western Railroad tracks. (Courtesy of RES.)

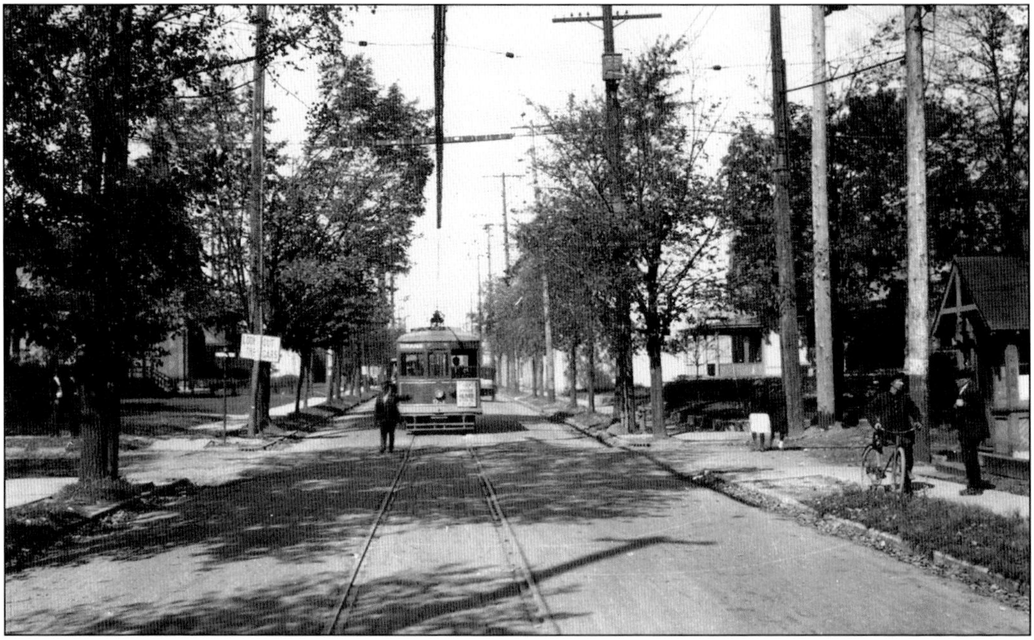

WG&E car No. 93, one of 15 new Birney Safety Cars built in 1920, is about to be flagged across the KD Line at Pearl Street (Fifty-fifth Street) in this early-1920s photograph. Looking north on Ashland Avenue (Sheridan Road), one can barely see (in the left of the photograph) the steeple and front of the Immanuel Methodist Church that would become a meeting place of the Kenosha Streetcar Society 73 years later. Note the KD Line's flagman shanty to the right. (Courtesy of MB.)

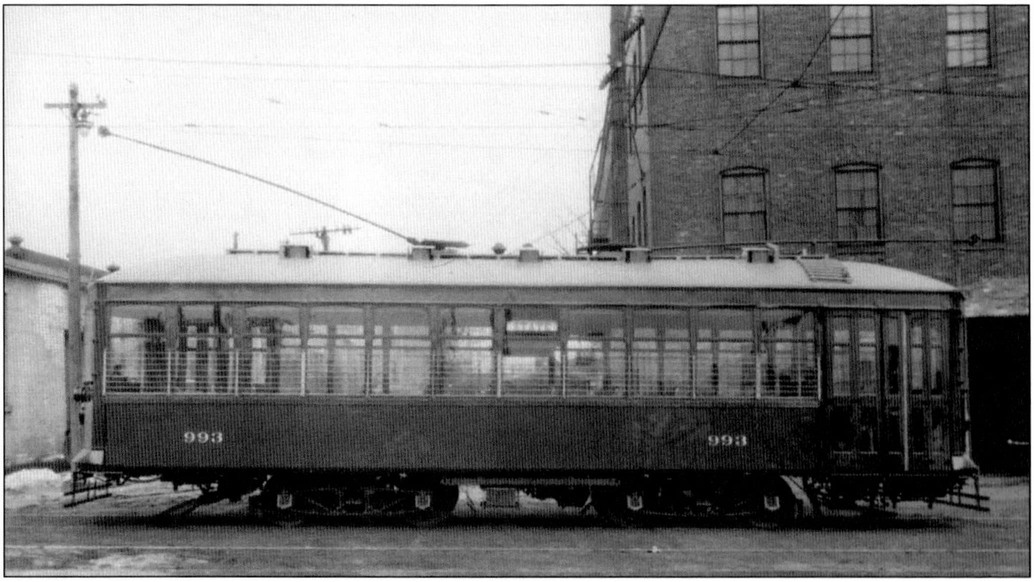

The double-truck, "990 Class" lightweight, one-man cars were used in both Racine and Kenosha service. Four of those cars, Nos. 990–993, would be the largest city streetcars to operate in Kenosha. Seen here new in 1924, the cars were designed by TMER&L and built by the St. Louis Car Company. When streetcar service ended in Kenosha, the cars were transferred to Racine and later to Milwaukee. (Courtesy of JEG.)

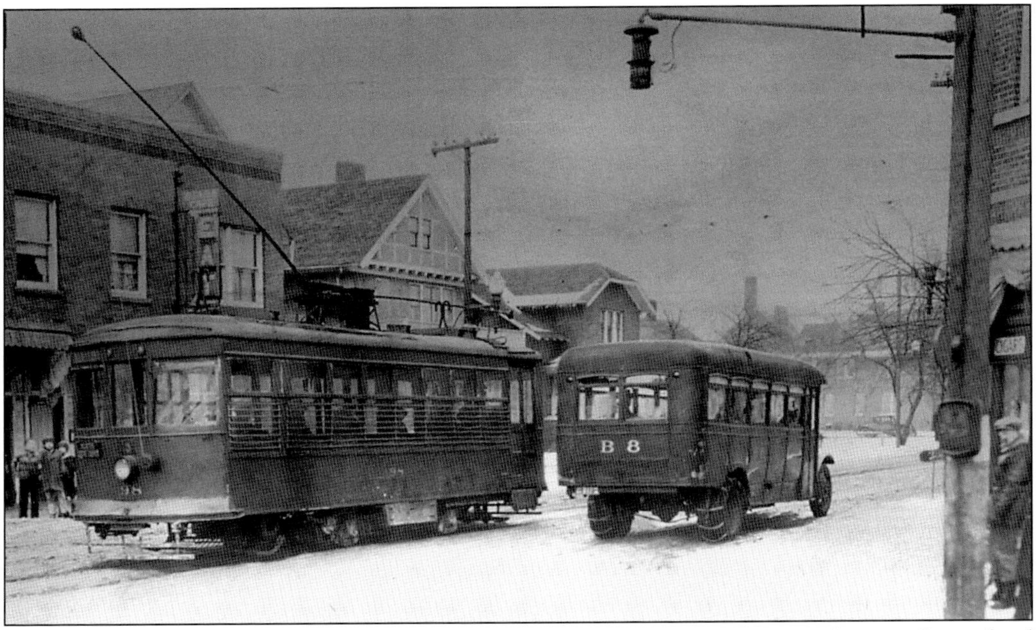

WG&E Birney Safety Car No. 98 and White-Ecklund gas bus No. B8 are seen here on Sixty-third Street at Twenty-seventh Avenue looking northeast in 1929. Car No. 98 has just changed ends and is about to depart from the west end of the car line; it will be going east, then north through downtown Kenosha and to the former city limits at Thirty-eighth Street and Seventh Avenue. The bus is serving the Roosevelt Road feeder route from this point to Seventy-fifth Street and Thirty-ninth Avenue. (Courtesy of RES.)

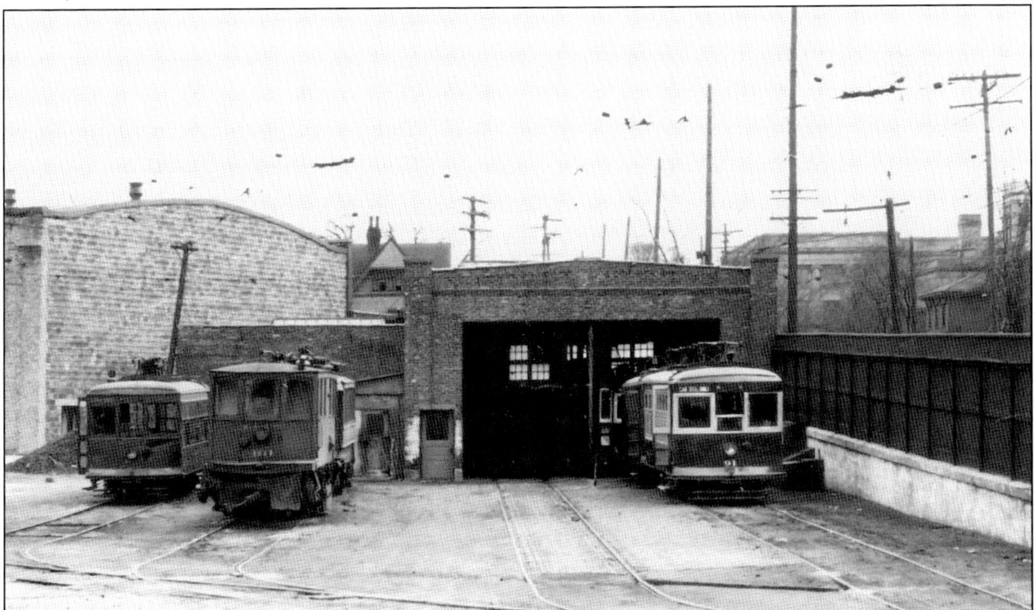

This carbarn scene is looking south next to Sheridan Road at Fifty-fourth Street in 1928. Note the Kenosha County Courthouse to the right. Birney Safety Car No. 88 (left) is still in the old maroon paint livery, while the other cars (right) are in the new orange and cream livery. Snow sweeper car No. B11 has an old KER streetcar used as a work car behind it. (Courtesy of JEG.)

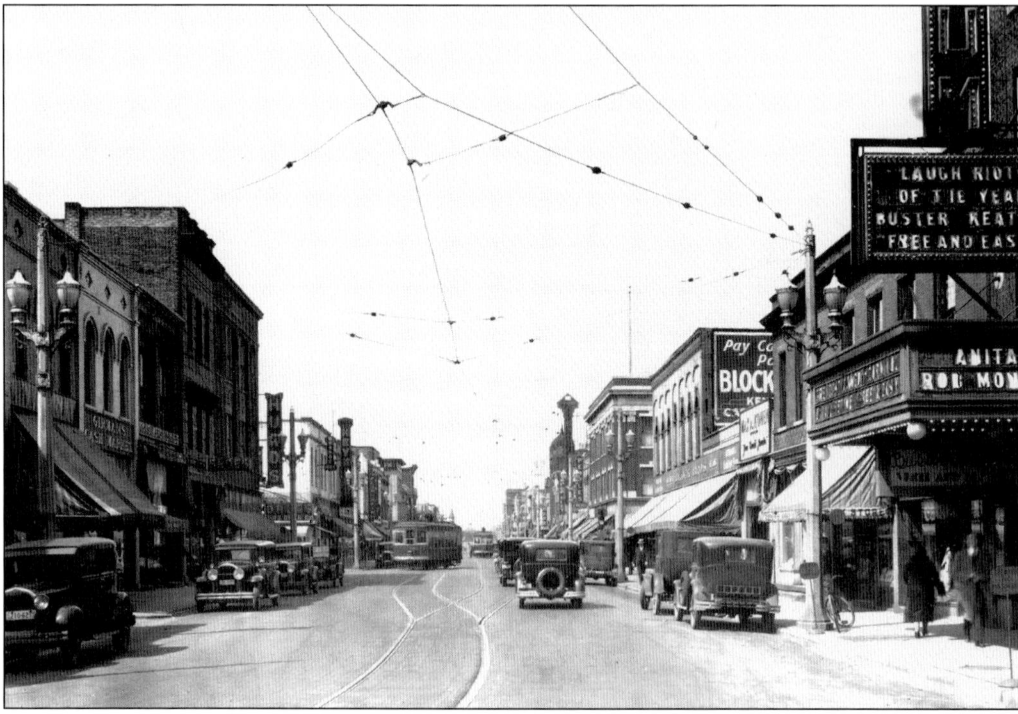

A southbound Birney Safety Car of the WG&E turns west from Sixth Avenue into Fifty-eighth Street in 1930. The car will operate three blocks to Sheridan Road on new streetcar tracks built in 1927. This new alignment eliminated two-way operations on the busy single-track Fifty-ninth Street. Note the streetcar tracks becoming double. (Courtesy of RES.)

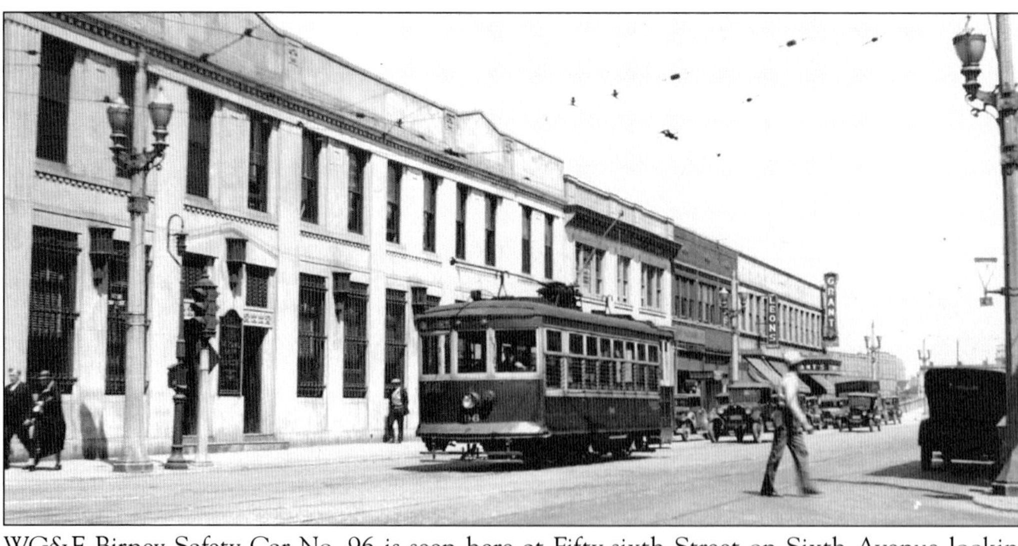

WG&E Birney Safety Car No. 96 is seen here at Fifty-sixth Street on Sixth Avenue looking northwest in the summer of 1930. The car is painted bright traction orange and cream with a salmon roof and dark olive-green trucks. During this time frame, Kenosha streetcars were painted in the same livery as Milwaukee city streetcars. (Courtesy of KCHM.)

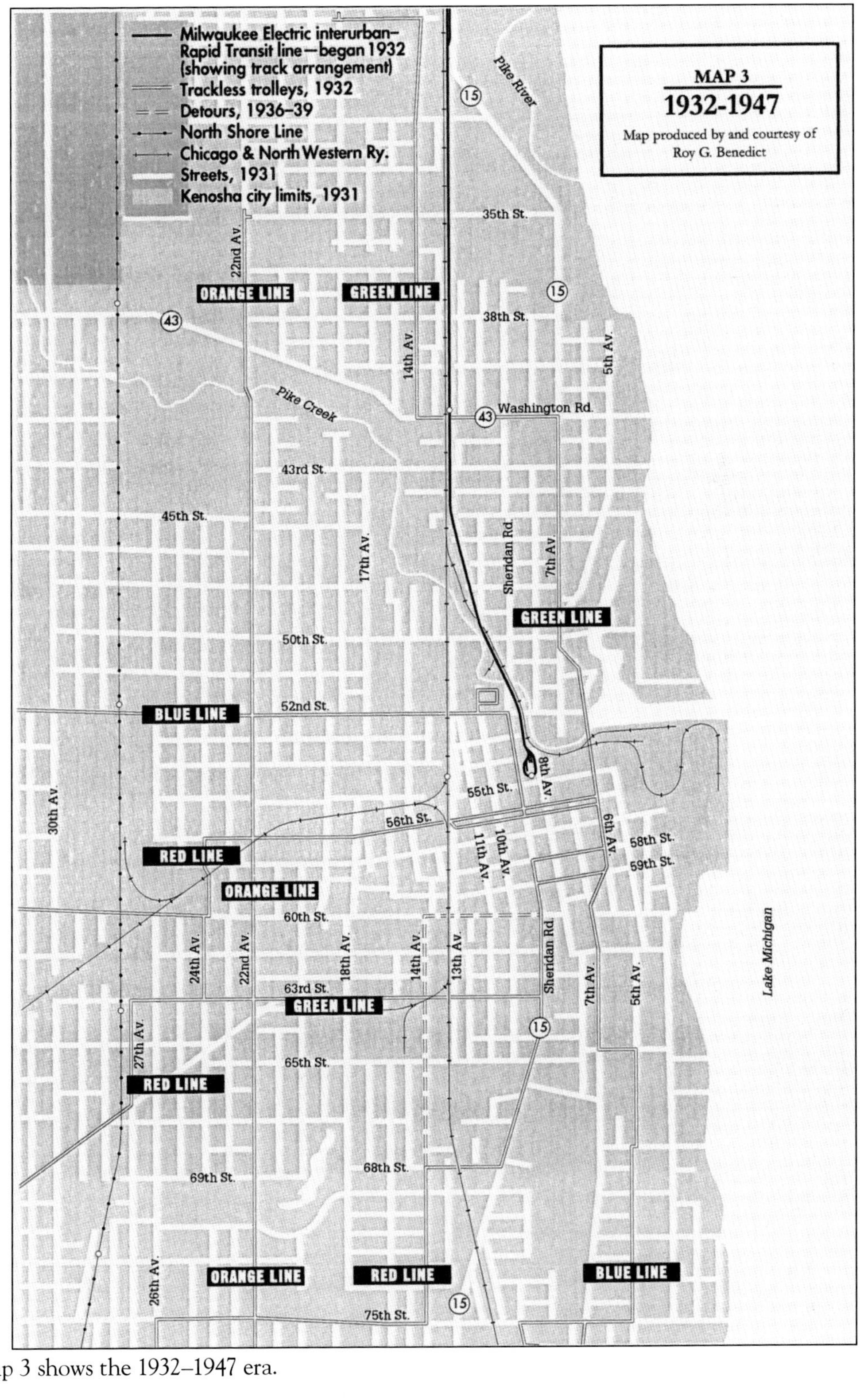

Map 3 shows the 1932–1947 era.

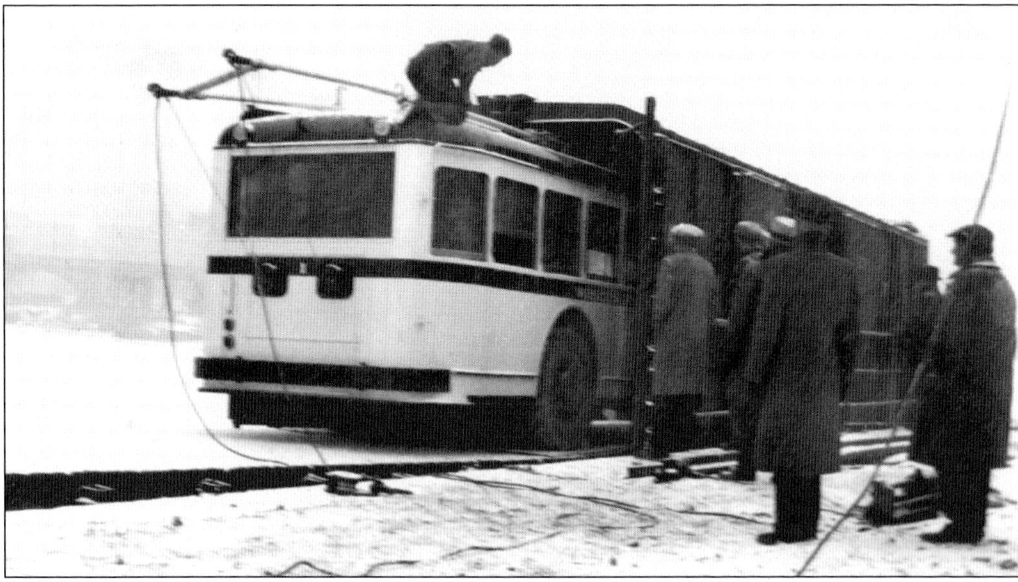

Kenosha's first trackless trolley coach No. 1 is being unloaded on a snowy winter day in February 1932 from an end-door boxcar at the Kenosha freight terminal of TMER&L. This series of 12 trackless trolleys delivered between February 1 and February 15, 1932, were built by Yellow Truck and Coach Division of General Motors at Pontiac, Michigan. To the left is the Sixth Avenue Bridge crossing Pike Creek. (Photograph by HMP.)

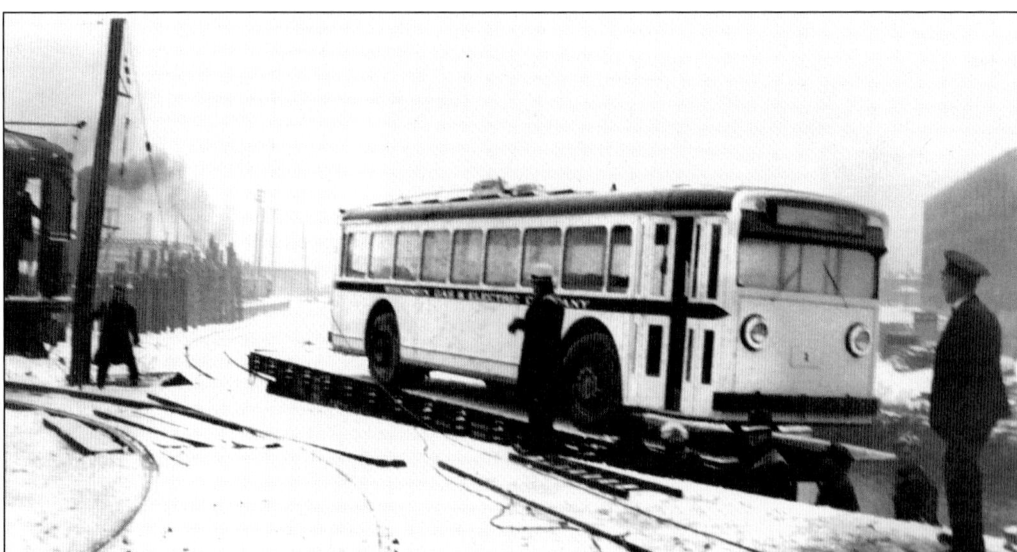

WG&E trackless trolley No. 1 is being unloaded in the second photograph at the MRK Kenosha freight terminal. Note the TMER&L 1100 interurban on the turning loop at the east side of Sheridan Road at Fifty-fourth Street. By April 18, 1932, the interurbans would be at their new depot at Fifty-fifth Street and Eighth Avenue. (Photograph by HMP.)

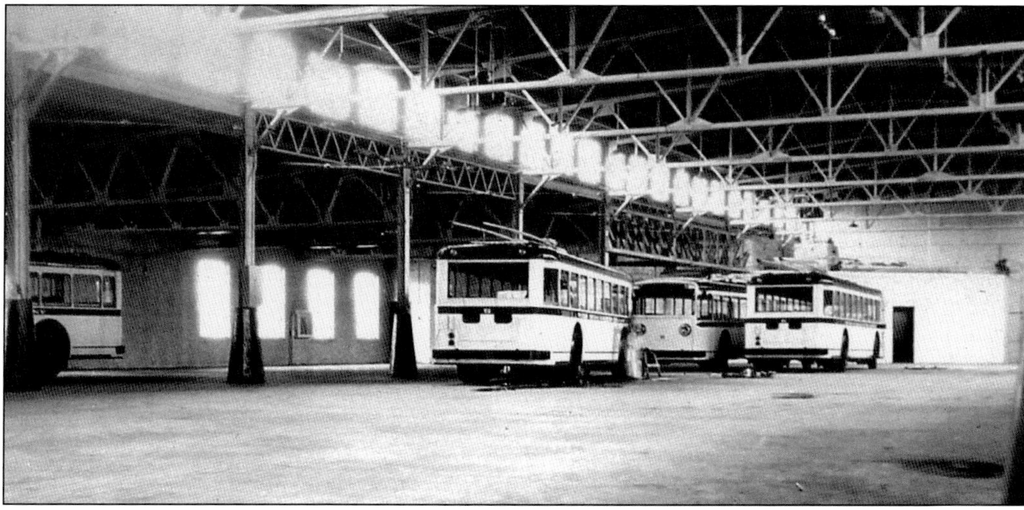

Here is a view of the interior of the remodeled trackless trolley garage at Fifty-second Street and Sheridan Road in February 1932. The garage still stands today as a boathouse. All four trackless trolleys are Yellow Coaches, as the St. Louis Car Company coaches have yet to arrive. Within a short period of time, all streetcar and gas buses would be replaced with trackless trolleys. (Photograph by HMP, courtesy of RES, KPM, HLH.)

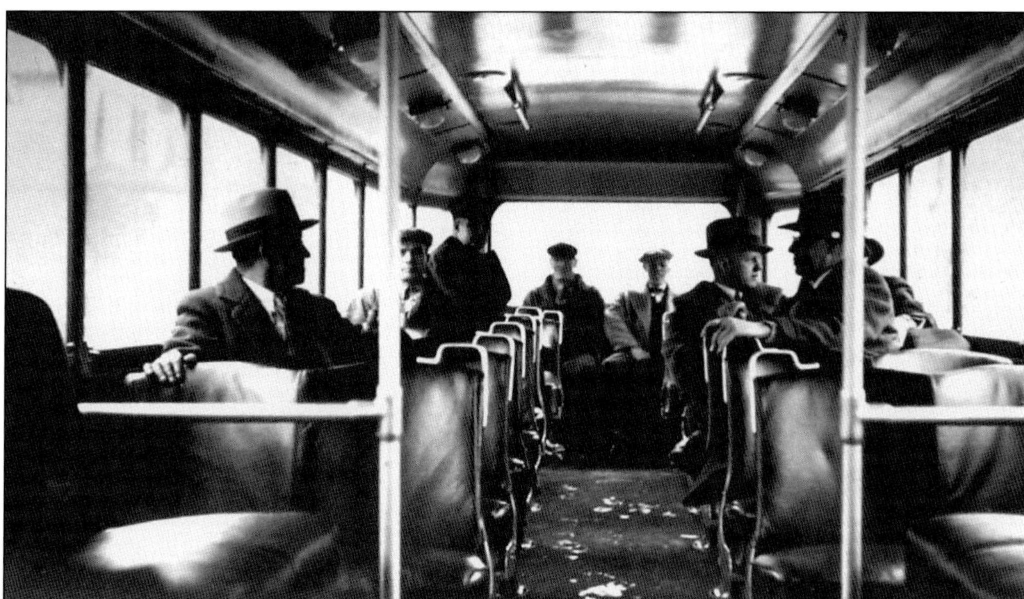

This WG&E Yellow Coach trackless trolley hosts officials on February 14, 1932. This interior photograph was taken while the trackless trolley was on a demonstration run. Note the all-leather bucket seats. (Photograph by HMP, courtesy of RES, KPM, HLH.)

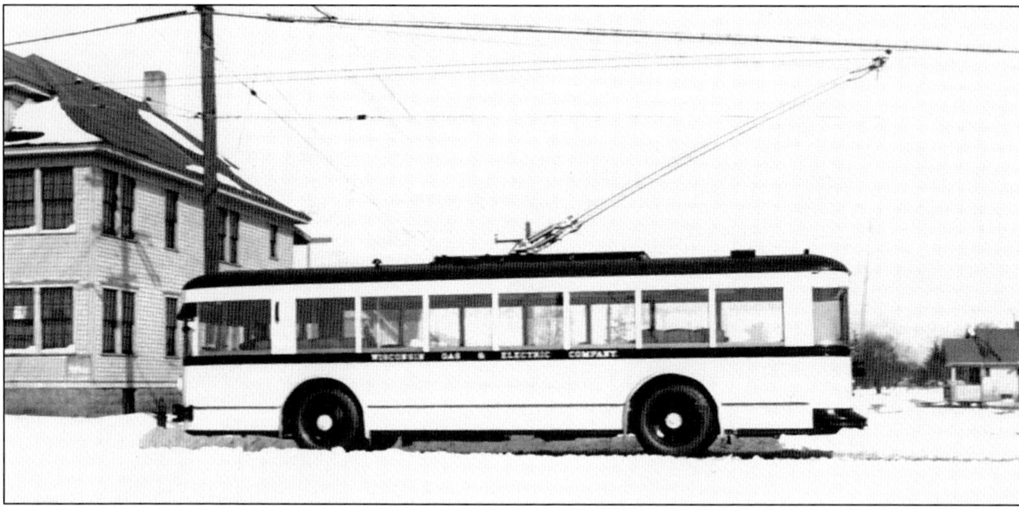

A new Kenosha trackless trolley is splendid in its livery of white and maroon against a snowy Kenosha landscape in February 1932. This trackless trolley was part of a 10-coach order built by the St. Louis Car Company of St. Louis, Missouri, and delivered between February 28 and March 20, 1932. The St. Louis–built trackless trolleys, along with the Yellows Coaches, would bring the fleet up to 22 coaches. (Photograph by HMP.)

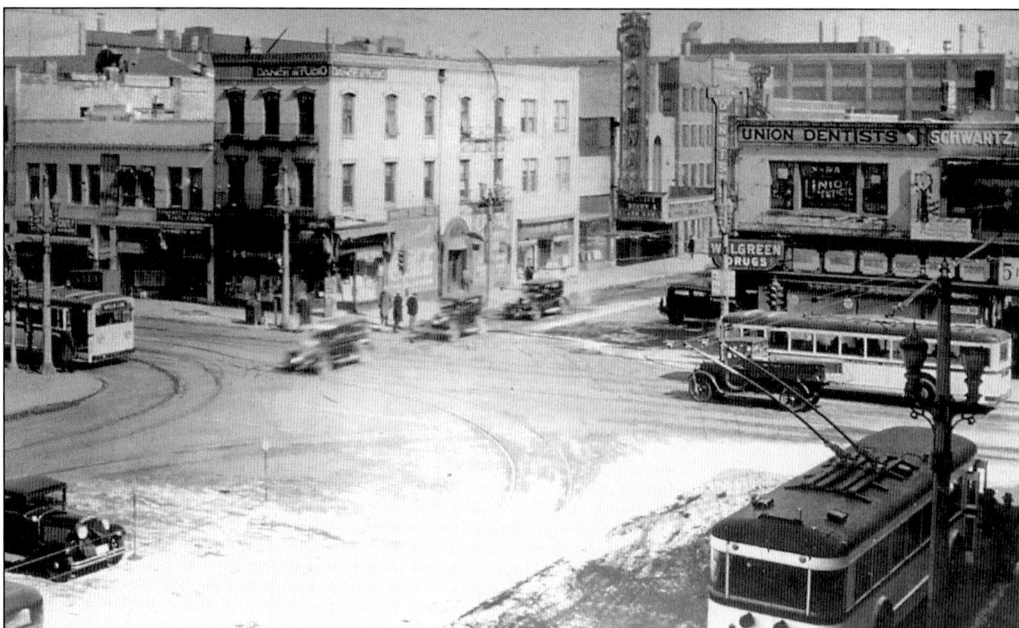

The snow is melting and streetcar tracks are still in use for MRK interurbans at Sixth Avenue and Fifty-sixth Street, looking northeast in early March 1932. St. Louis Car Company trackless trolley No. 13 at the bottom of the photograph after loading will turn south into Sixth Avenue and continue the run over the Red Line to Twenty-sixth Avenue and Eightieth Street. Two Yellow Coach Green Line trackless trolleys, northbound and southbound, await the traffic signal change. The photograph was taken from the Kenosha Public Service Building. (Photograph by OB, courtesy of RES.)

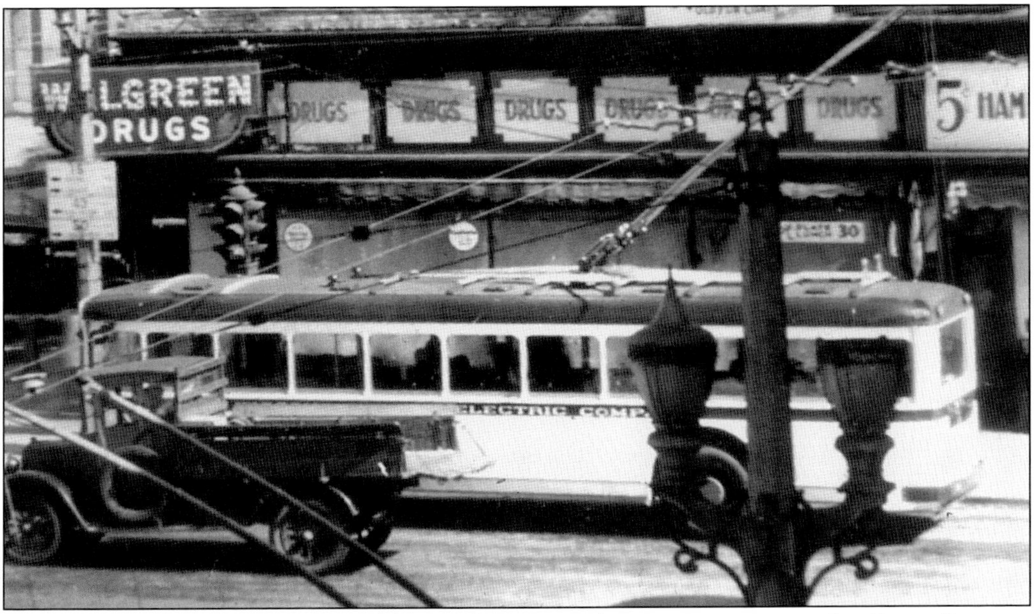

A northbound Yellow Coach trackless trolley is seen here operating over the Green Line on Sixth Avenue at Fifty-sixth Street in 1932. The trackless trolley will run into Seventh Avenue and turn west on Washington Road to Fourteenth Avenue. Running north to Twenty-seventh Street, then turning west, the line will terminate at Eighteenth Avenue. With the new 1932 alignment, there was no longer transit service over Seventh Avenue between Washington Road and Thirty-eighth Street. (Photograph by OB, courtesy of RES.)

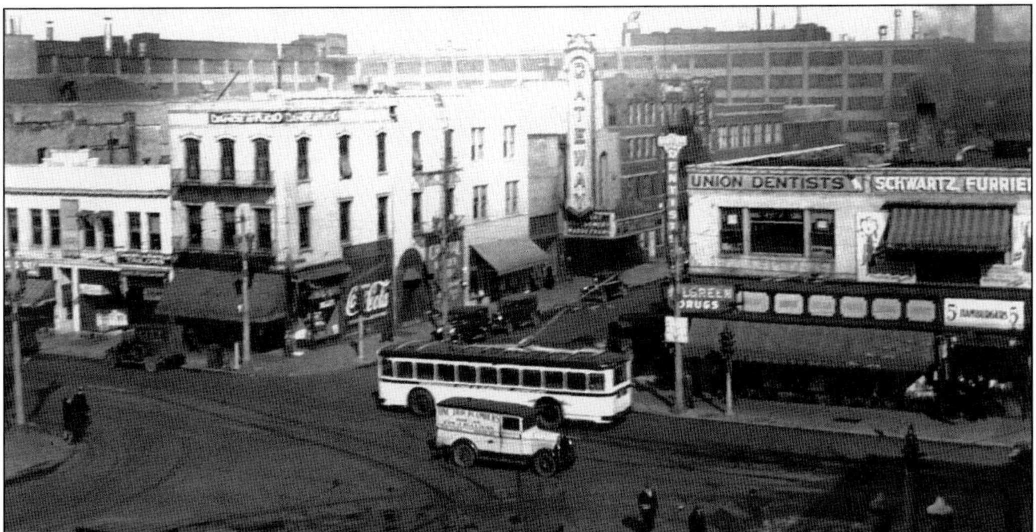

A WG&E Yellow Coach trackless trolley serving the Green Line is northbound on Sixth Avenue crossing Fifty-sixth Street, looking northeast in March 1932. Today the factories are gone; most of the buildings in the left foreground, including the Gateway Theater, have survived. The building to the right is gone due to the widening of Fifty-sixth Street. Today streetcars operate eastbound on neutral ground in the center of Fifty-sixth Street serving the redeveloped HarborPark area. (Photograph by HMP.)

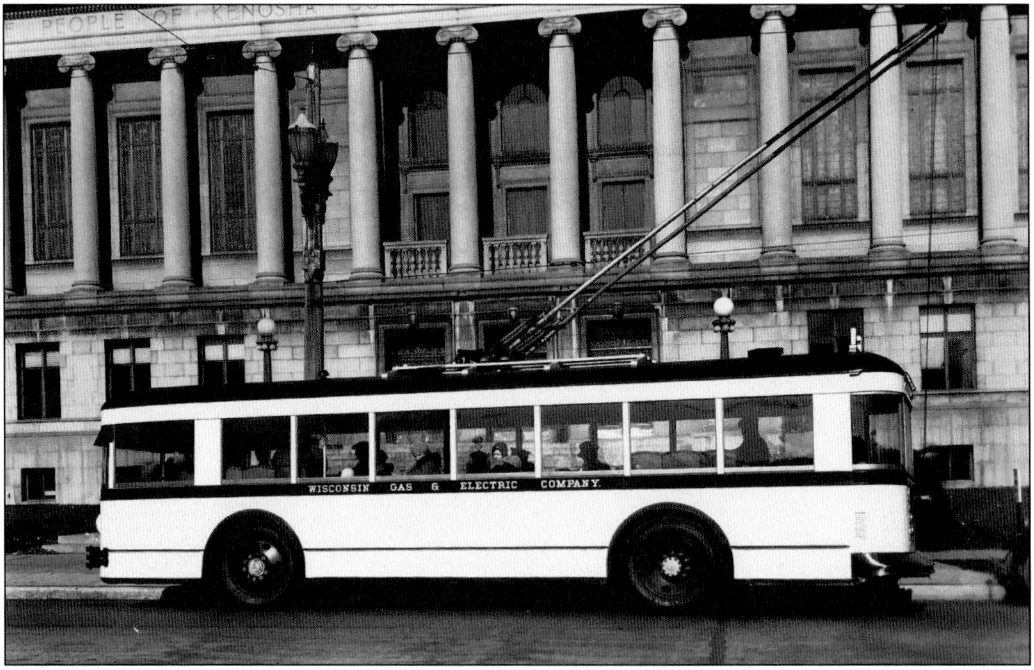

Trackless trolley No. 15 has its photograph taken in front of the Kenosha County Courthouse on Fifty-sixth Street in March 1932. This series of 10 coaches was built by the St. Louis Car Company during 1931. With picture windows and leather seating, this electric vehicle had dynamic braking that would return power to the overhead and could be today's answer to pollution. (Courtesy of JEG.)

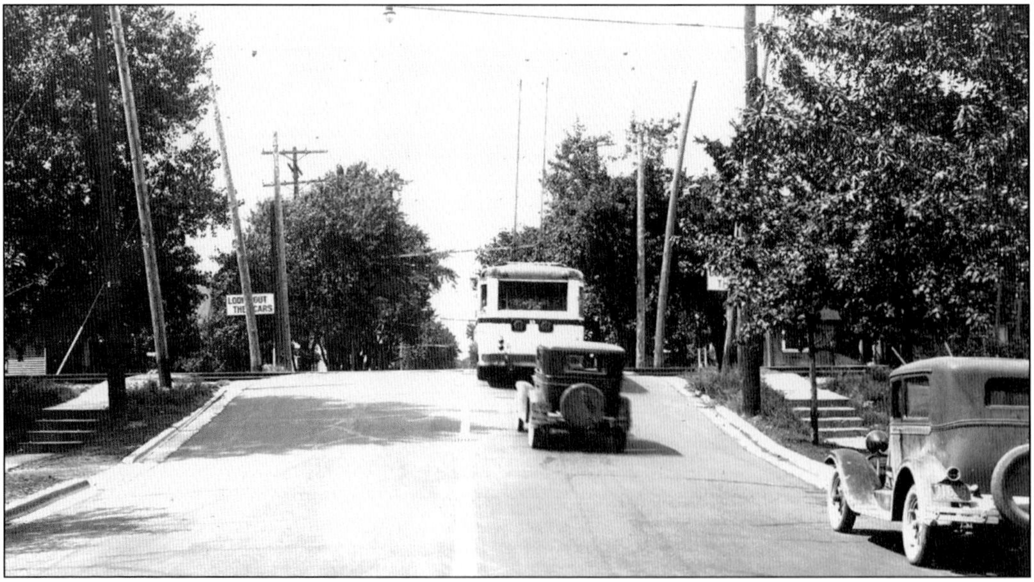

The year is 1932, and a westbound trackless trolley on the Red Line is about to cross the North Western Railroad tracks on Sixty-eighth Street. The photograph was apparently taken by the city in regards to elevating the North Western tracks from Thirty-fifth Street to Eightieth Street. The elevation, which became known as the "Chinese Wall," took place between 1930 and 1939. This section would be the final part to be elevated. (Courtesy of JEG.)

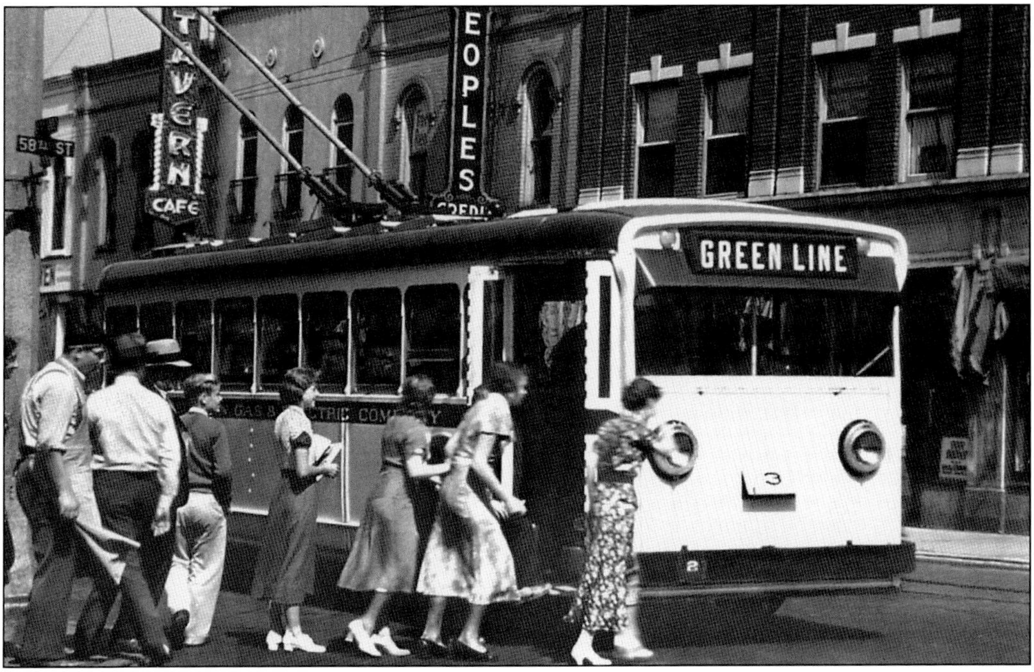

This southbound Yellow Coach trackless trolley No. 3, run No. 2, loads passengers at Fifty-eighth Street and Sixth Avenue in busy downtown Kenosha. This summer 1932 photograph shows the fashions of the day for men, women, girls, and boys. The grocery store clerk to the left has the adding machine of the day (pencil) on his ear. (Photograph by GE, courtesy of RES.)

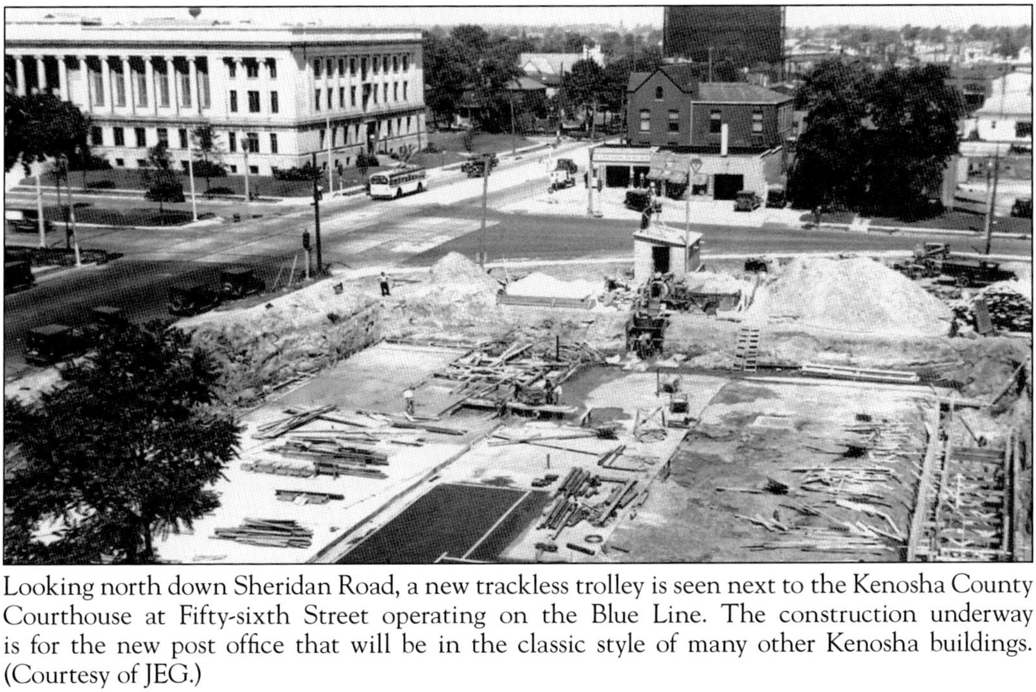

Looking north down Sheridan Road, a new trackless trolley is seen next to the Kenosha County Courthouse at Fifty-sixth Street operating on the Blue Line. The construction underway is for the new post office that will be in the classic style of many other Kenosha buildings. (Courtesy of JEG.)

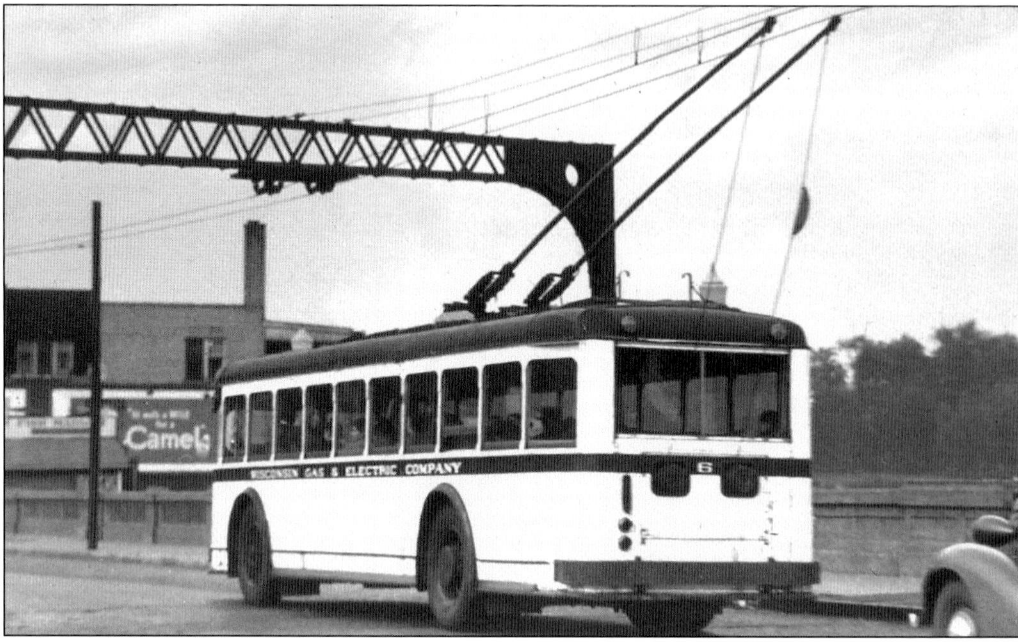

WG&E Yellow Coach trackless trolley No. 6 is seen here northbound on the Green Line, crossing Pike Creek on the Sixth Avenue bridge (looking northeast) in 1934. The Green Line would run through downtown from the north at Twenty-seventh Street and Eighteenth Avenue, and then turn west serving Sixty-third Street and Sixtieth Street. It would terminate at Sixtieth Street and Thirty-ninth Avenue. (Photograph by OB, courtesy of RES.)

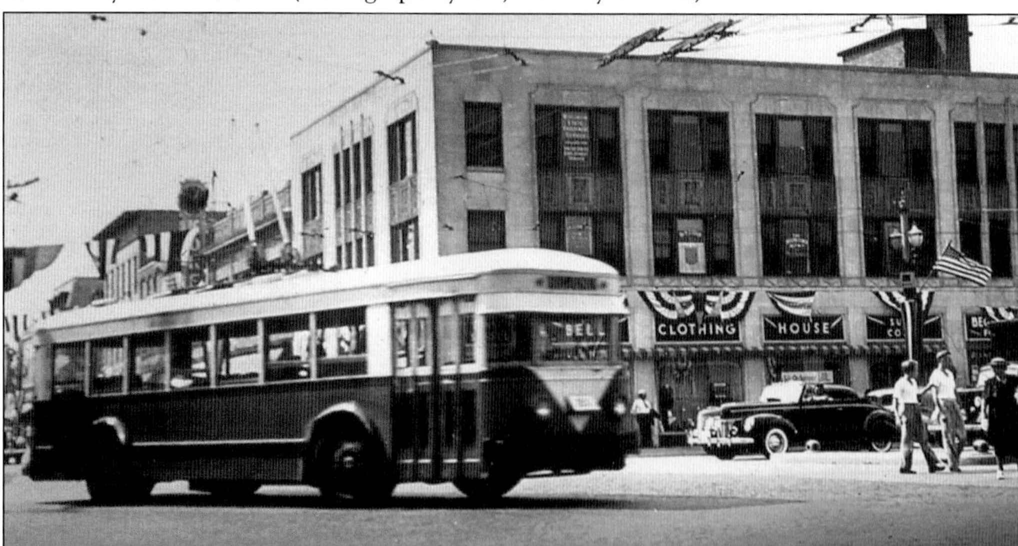

WG&E trackless trolley coach No. 20 built by the St. Louis Car Company is at Market Square turning off of Sixth Avenue west into Fifty-sixth Street around 1942. The coach will run north on Sheridan Road and west on Fifty-second Street to Thirty-second Avenue where it will loop south around the block and start the return trip at Thirty-third Avenue. The coach is painted in the Milwaukee Transport Company's city livery of orange and cream with a maroon belt rail. (Courtesy of KCHM, RES.)

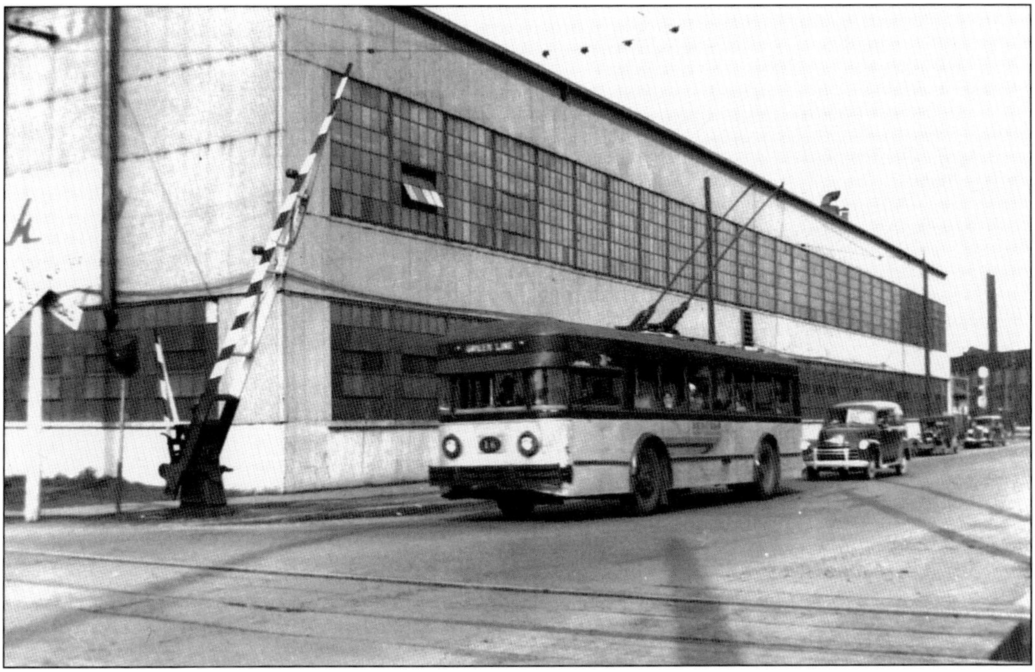

Kenosha Motor Coach Lines (KMCL) trackless trolley No. 16 built by the St. Louis Car Company makes a safety stop at the Chicago, North Shore and Milwaukee Railway (called the North Shore) crossing on Sixtieth Street on April 11, 1949. The trackless trolley is operating westbound on the Green Line and will terminate at Sixtieth Place and Thirty-ninth Avenue. The building to the left is the Nash Motors assembly plant. (Photograph by JEG.)

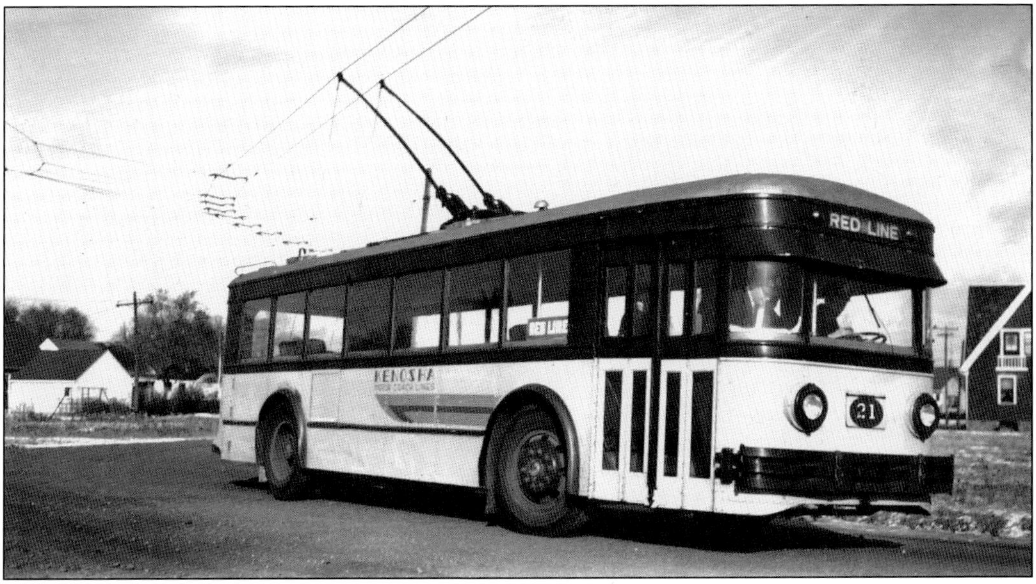

KMCL trackless trolley No. 21 sits at the south end of the Red Line at Twenty-sixth Avenue and Eightieth Street looking northwest on November 24, 1950. The livery at this time was maroon and deep cream with a silver roof and a silver and orange wing logo with Broadway font. The designer was Brooks Stevens of Milwaukee, who also designed the Hiawatha livery for the Milwaukee Road. (Photograph by RED.)

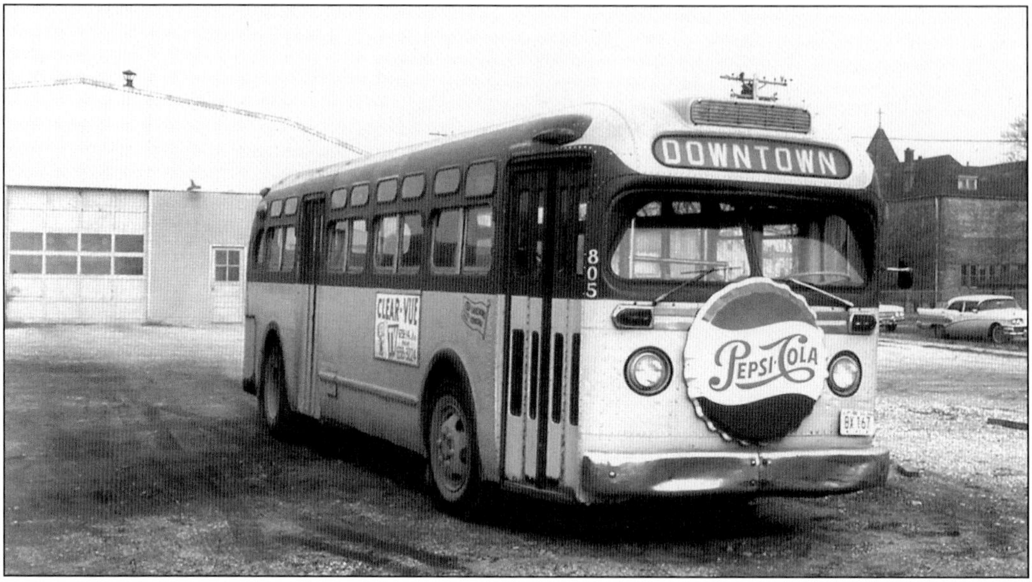

Now under the ownership of Lake Shore Transit, this General Motors 32-passenger transit diesel bus was part of an eight-bus order delivered new to Kenosha Motor Coach Company, formerly KMCL, in 1952. The bus is still painted in its original livery of deep cream and maroon with a silver roof. This picture was taken at the Lake Shore Transit garage, at Fifty-first Place and Eighth Avenue, looking northeast from the south side of the garage that still stands today as the Holsum (formerly Kappus Bread) Bakery thrift store and bread route depot, November 1966. (Photograph by RK, courtesy of DS.)

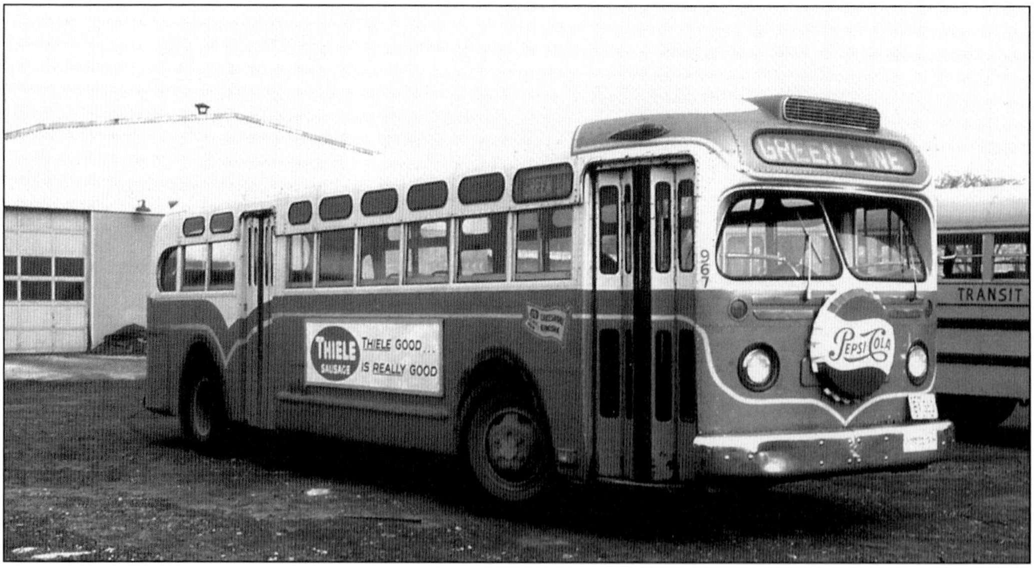

Lake Shore Transit bus No. 967, a General Motors transit diesel is parked at the Kenosha bus garage in November 1966. This bus was part of an order of 15 diesels delivered to Kenosha Motor Coach Company from General Motors on February 14, 1949. The bus is painted two-tone aqua with bright yellow striping in the livery of another Lake Shore Transit holding, the Madison Bus Company of Madison, Wisconsin. (Photograph by RK, courtesy of DS.)

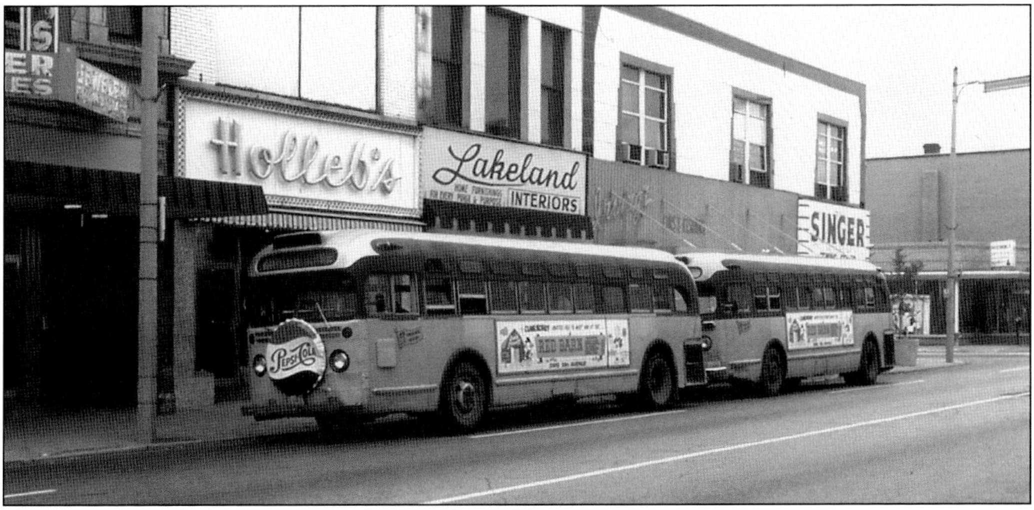

Lake Shore Transit diesel buses await riders on Sixth Avenue facing north between Fifty-sixth and Fifty-seventh Streets in November 1966. The two buses are part of a 1949 and 1952 delivery from General Motors to Kenosha Motor Coach Company and are still painted in the livery of KMCL, minus the Brooks Stevens art deco logo behind the front wheels. Note the Lake Shore Transit logo under the operator's window. (Photograph by RK, courtesy of DS.)

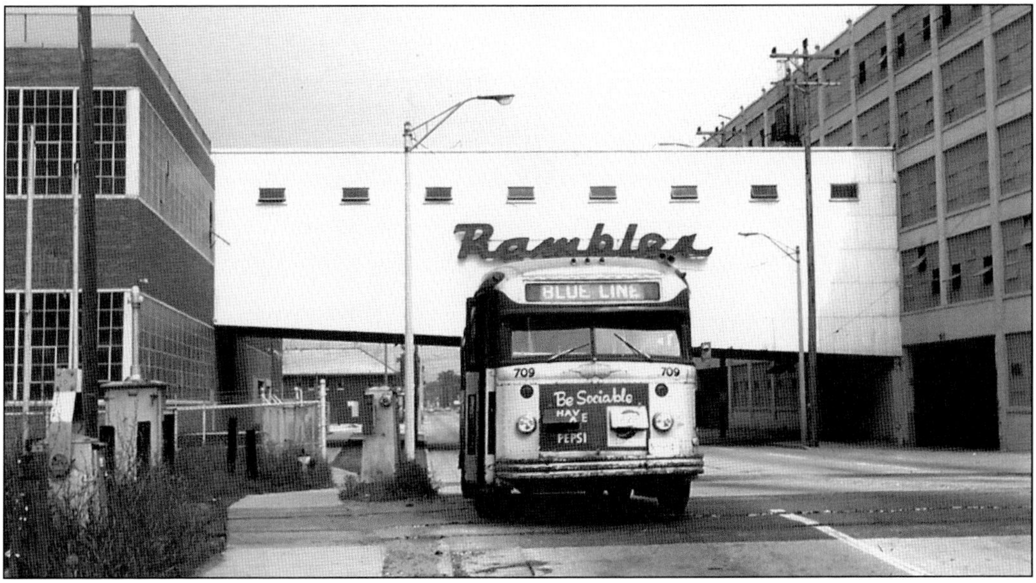

Signed for the Blue Line, Lake Shore Transit White bus No. 709 pauses on Fifty-second Street at the abandoned North Shore Line crossing with the Rambler plant in the background just east of Twenty-eighth Avenue, looking east, on July 9, 1967. By February 1969, the system would be abandoned due to an employee strike. (Photograph by RK, courtesy of DS.)

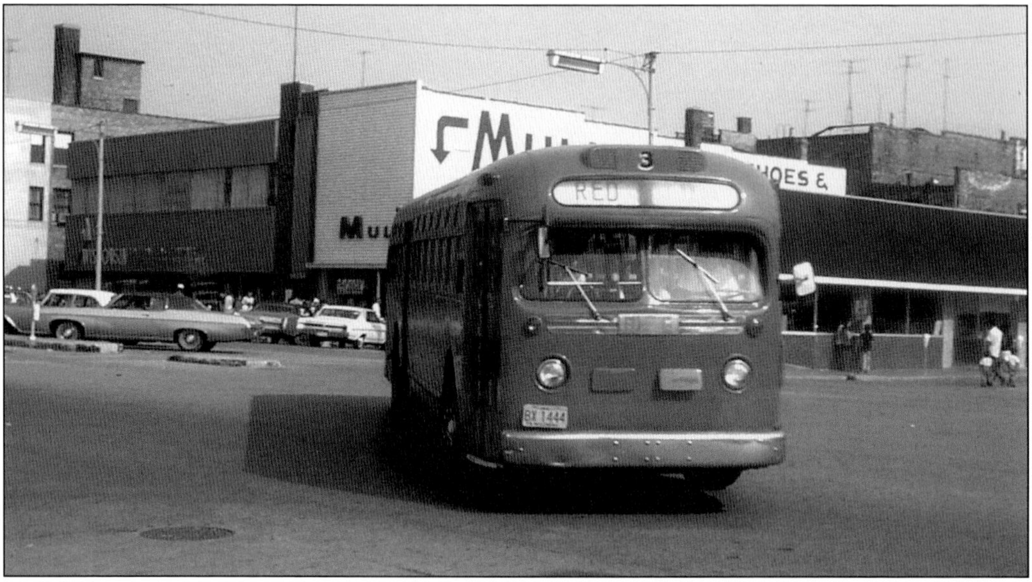

Pathfinder City Transit Lines, operating under subsidy from the City of Kenosha, resumed bus service on August 4, 1969. Seen here, a General Motors transit diesel hydraulic bus is turning north into Eighth Avenue from Fifty-sixth Street, looking southeast in August 1970. The bus is painted brilliant red for service on the Red Line. (Photograph by RK, courtesy of DS.)

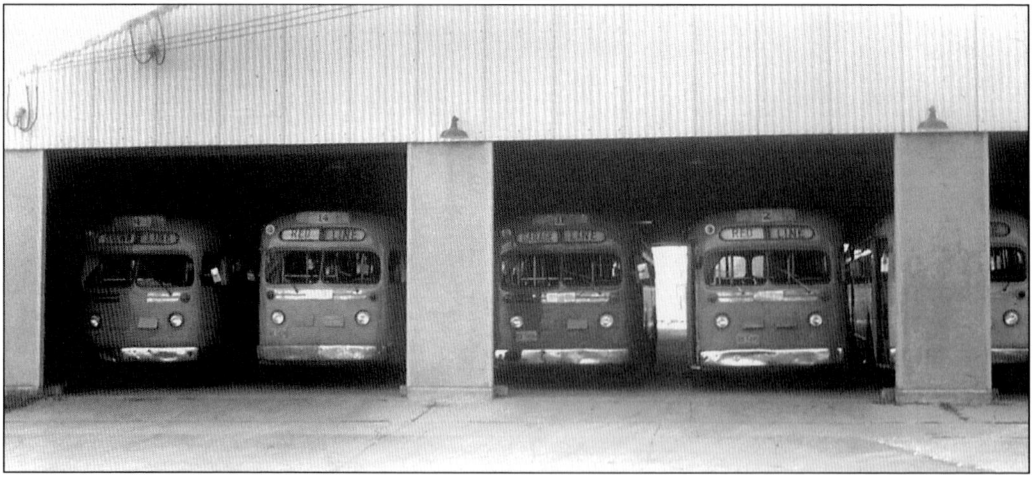

Pathfinder City Transit buses line up at the Kenosha garage looking east just before rush hour in August 1970. Sheridan Road is behind the photographer, and Eighth Avenue is directly behind the open doors at the rear of the garage. The first two buses (from left to right) are painted pastel brown, the second two are red, and the last bus is pastel blue. These former Indianapolis Railways buses are painted for their respective Kenosha routes. (Photograph by RK, courtesy of DS.)

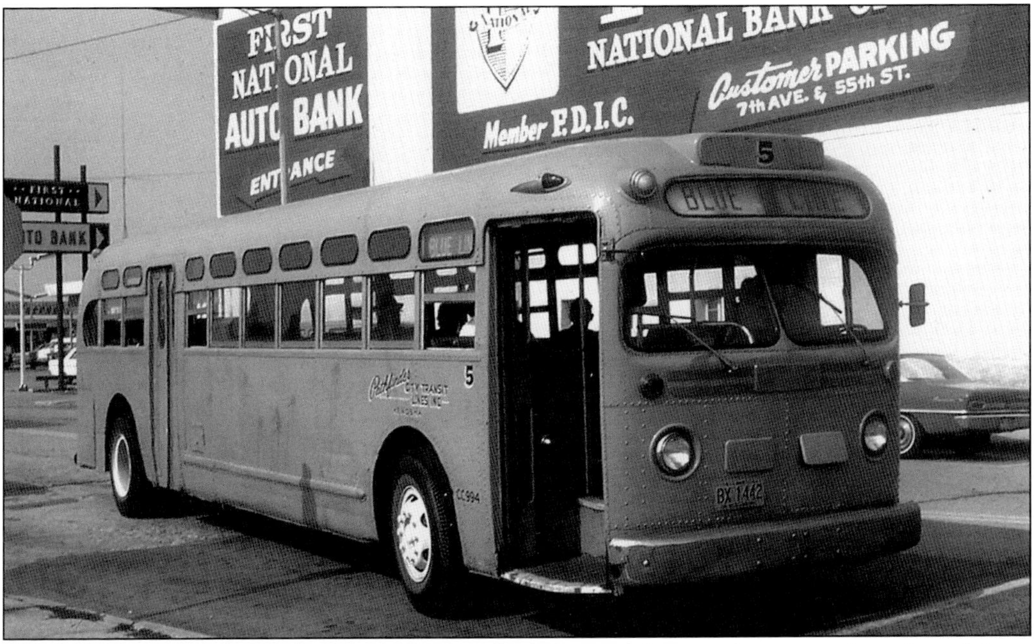

Pathfinder City Transit bus No. 5 is one of 16 General Motors buses purchased used from Indianapolis Railways. Painted pastel blue for the Blue Line, this view is looking northeast on Seventh Avenue to Fifty-sixth Street, August 1970. Owner Gordon McAleer also ran an automobile and truck paint shop known as Roosevelt Body Shop at 2907 Sixty-third Street. This probably accounted for his exotic paint liveries. (Photograph by RK, courtesy of DS.)

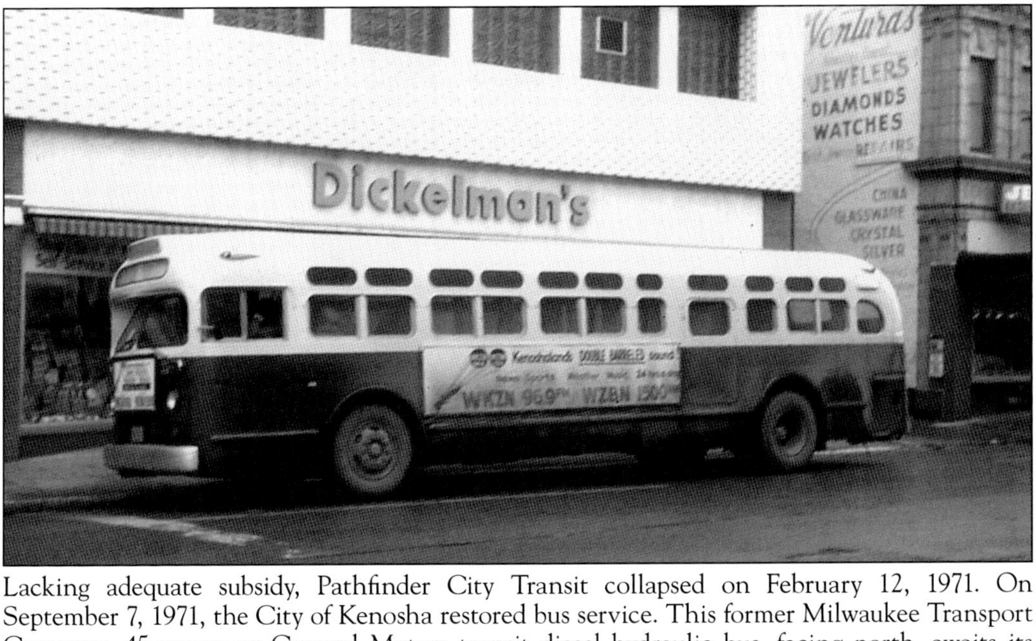

Lacking adequate subsidy, Pathfinder City Transit collapsed on February 12, 1971. On September 7, 1971, the City of Kenosha restored bus service. This former Milwaukee Transport Company, 45-passenger General Motors transit diesel hydraulic bus, facing north, awaits its running time at Sixth Avenue and Fifty-sixth Street in January 1972. The bus has been repainted in dark green and light cream and is without destination readings or fleet numbers. (Photograph by RK, courtesy of DS.)

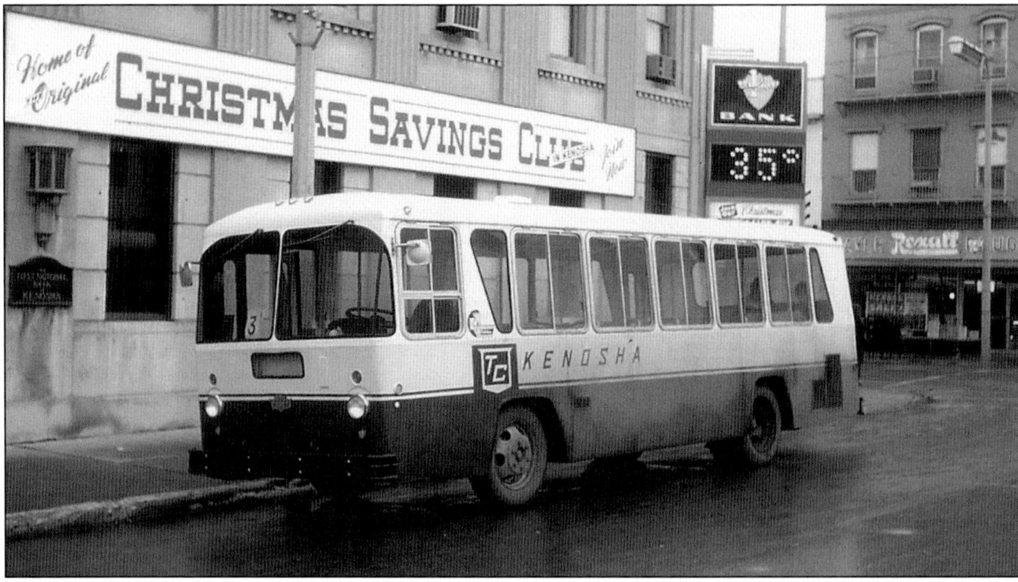

This 29-passenger bus was an attempt by Highway Products of Kent, Ohio, to develop a transit bus for smaller cities, similar to a Birney Safety Car streetcar. These buses were troublesome and, with competition from other manufacturers, were withdrawn from the market after a few years of production. The bus is shown facing west on Fifty-sixth Street with Sixth Avenue in the background in January 1972. Note the cardboard sign in the window designates route by number, not color. (Photograph by RK, courtesy of DS.)

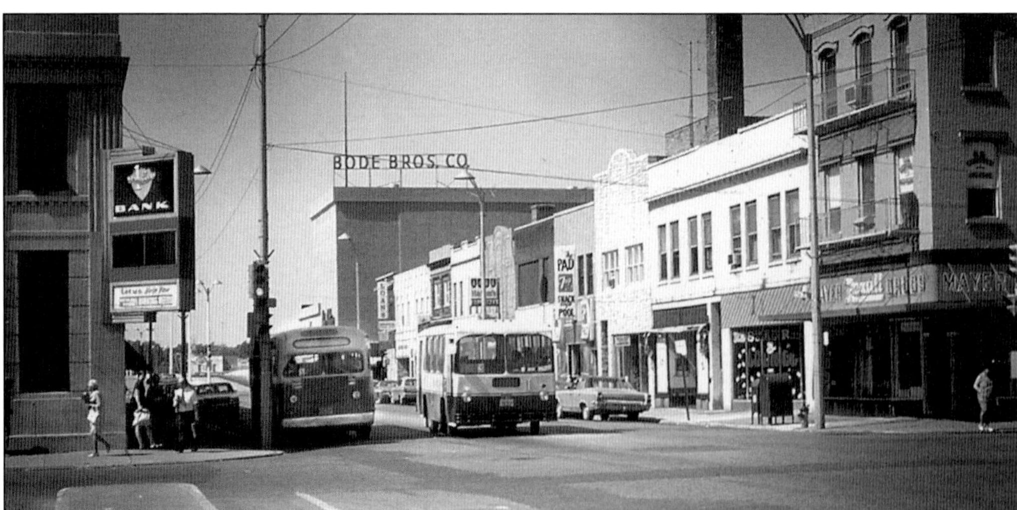

A former Milwaukee Transport Company, 45-passenger General Motors diesel transit bus is to the left while a Twin Coach, 25-passenger gas bus is to the right. The scene is looking north down Sixth Avenue at Fifty-sixth Street in July 1973. Streetcars would return to this scene 27 years later, operating eastbound on Fifty-sixth Street to the current location of the HarborPark redevelopment area. (Photograph by RK, courtesy of DS.)

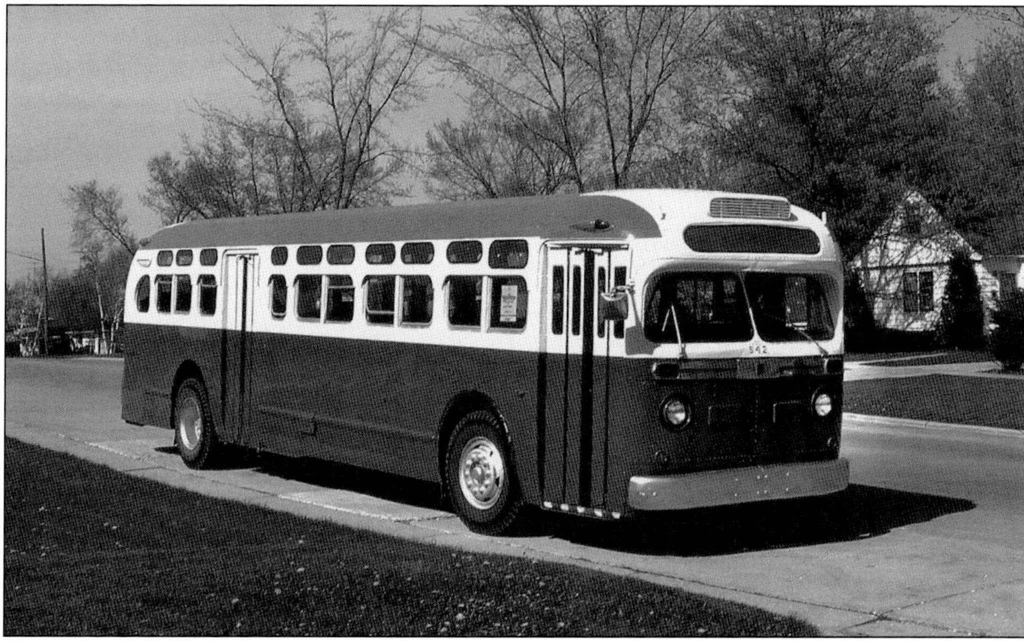

Kenosha Transit Commission bus No. 542 was purchased from the Milwaukee Transport Company in 1971. Originally numbered 1306, this bus was built by General Motors in 1951. Seen here operating on Roosevelt Road on April 29, 1976, the bus is painted in a brilliant livery of red, white, and blue for the nation's bicentennial celebration. (Photograph by RES.)

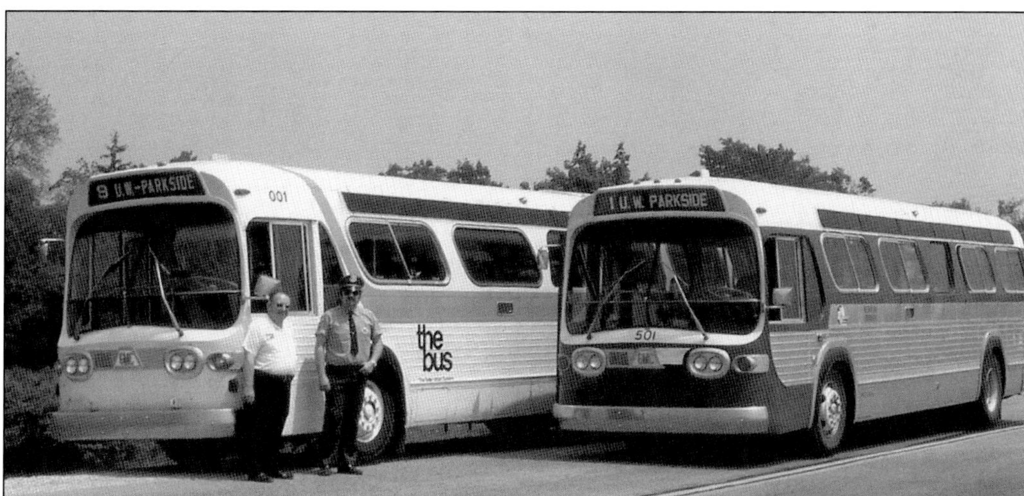

Kenosha bus operator Louis Rugani, to the right, and an unidentified Racine bus operator pose during the Fred J. Beamish special bus fans charter with their diesel buses at University of Wisconsin at Parkside on May 21, 1977. Today Rugani serves on the Kenosha Transit Commission Board and the Kenosha Streetcar Society Board and hosts a local Kenosha radio show *Music of the Stars*. (Photograph by RK, courtesy of DS.)

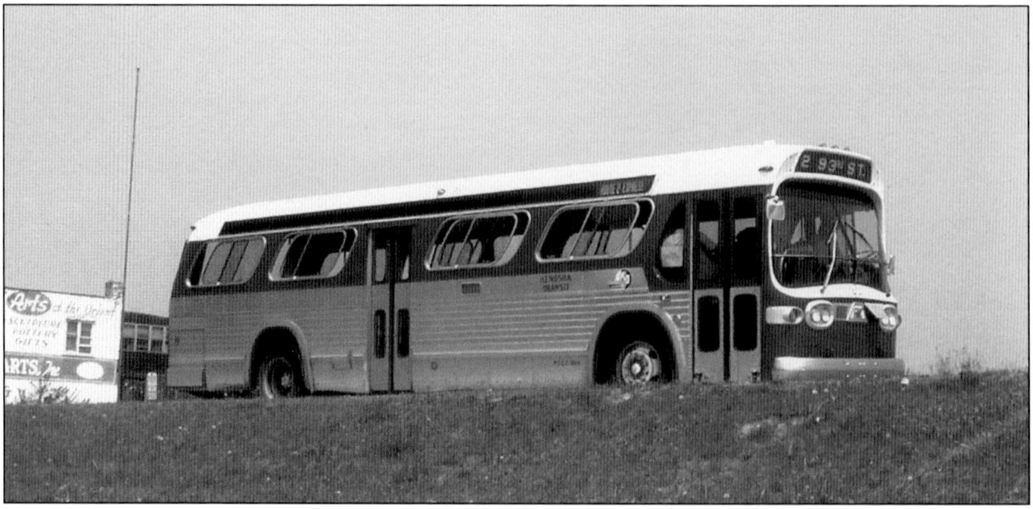

Seen here is Kenosha Transit Commission bus No. 501. A 45-passenger General Motors transit diesel bus on the Fred J. Beamish charter is about to cross the bridge into downtown Kenosha. The bus is southbound on Sixth Avenue and Fifty-fourth Street on Saturday, May 21, 1977. (Photograph by RK, courtesy of DS.)

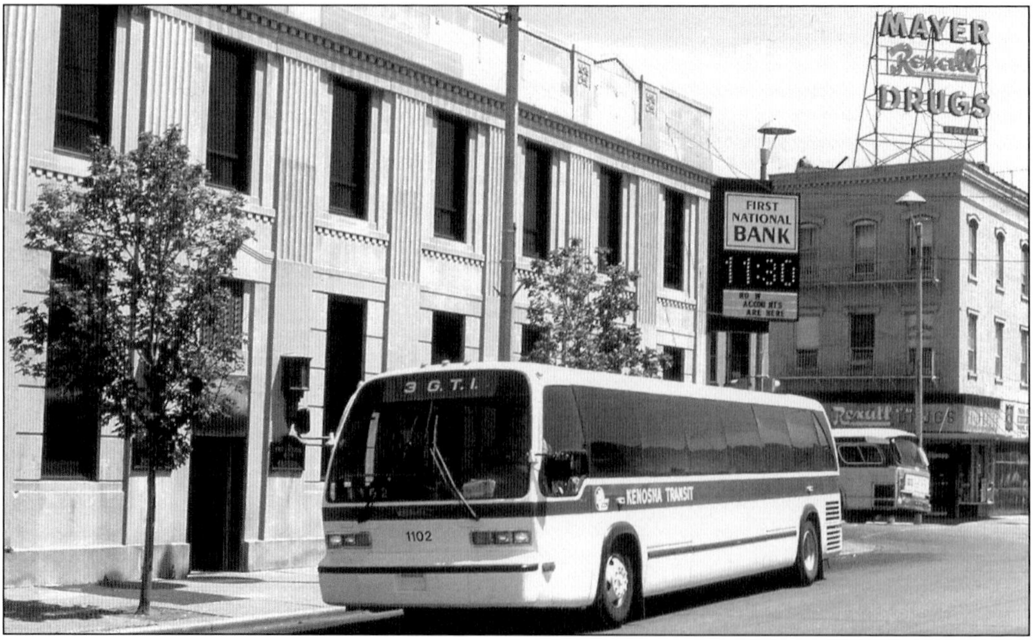

General Motors RTS (Rapid Transit Series) diesel bus No. 1102 was relatively new in this photograph; it awaits passengers at Fifty-sixth Street and Sixth Avenue in June 1981. Air conditioning on this bus was a welcomed feature to Kenosha's riders. Looking east to Sixth Avenue, this view shows the rear of an older General Motors transit diesel bus in front of the drugstore. (Photograph by DOE.)

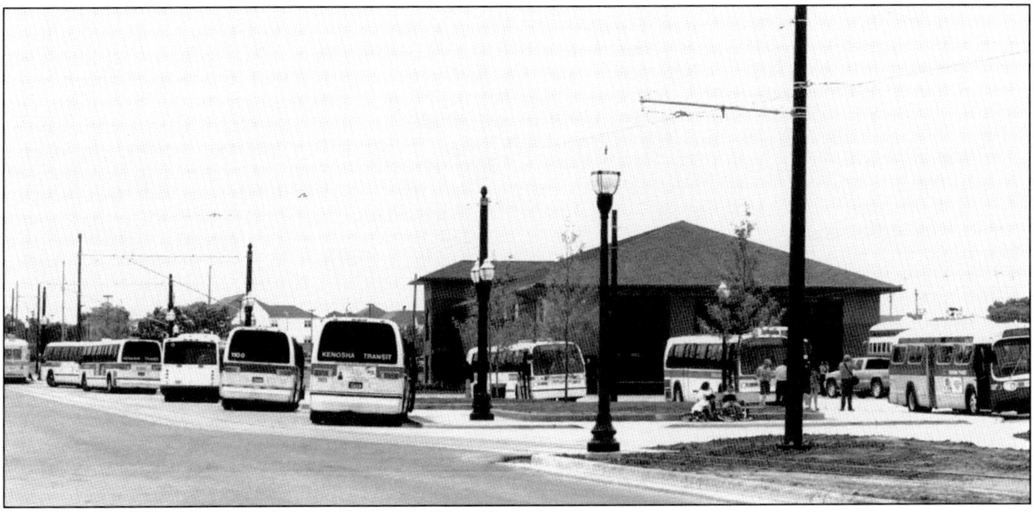

Looking west from Fifty-fourth Street and Seventh Avenue, this view shows buses of Kenosha Transit waiting for their running time at the new terminal in 2000. The terminal would later become known as the Joseph McCarthy Transit Center. (Photograph by EF.)

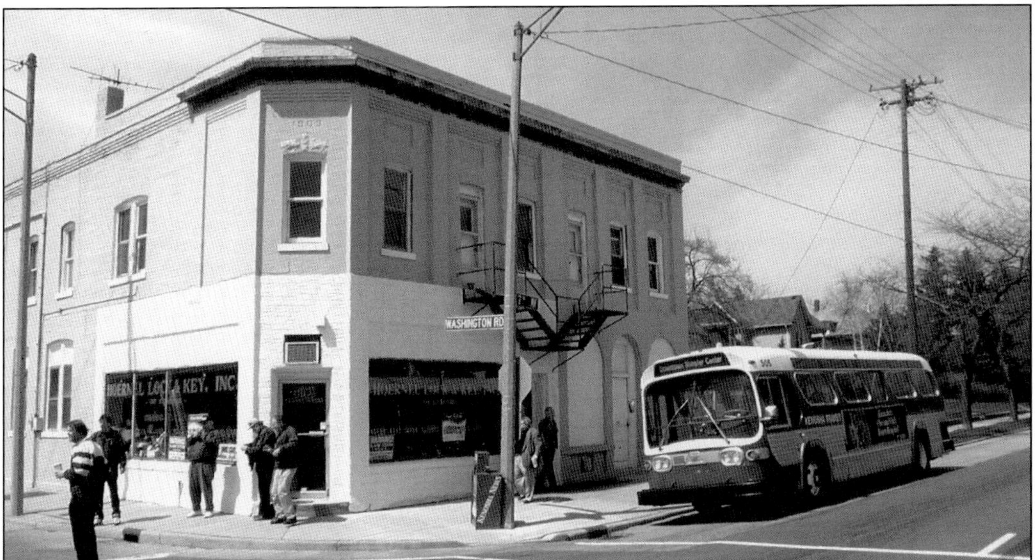

The Kenosha Streetcar Society is sponsoring a four-hour excursion on Saturday, April 17, 2001, using one of Kenosha's 500 series "fishbowl" General Motors transit buses and two streetcars later in the day. The group's first photograph stop is at Seventh Avenue and Washington Road, looking northwest. Until 1932, the old building saw many interurban and city streetcars pass by on Seventh Avenue. In that same year, the new trackless trolleys would turn west onto Washington Road serving the Green Line. (Photograph by DOE.)

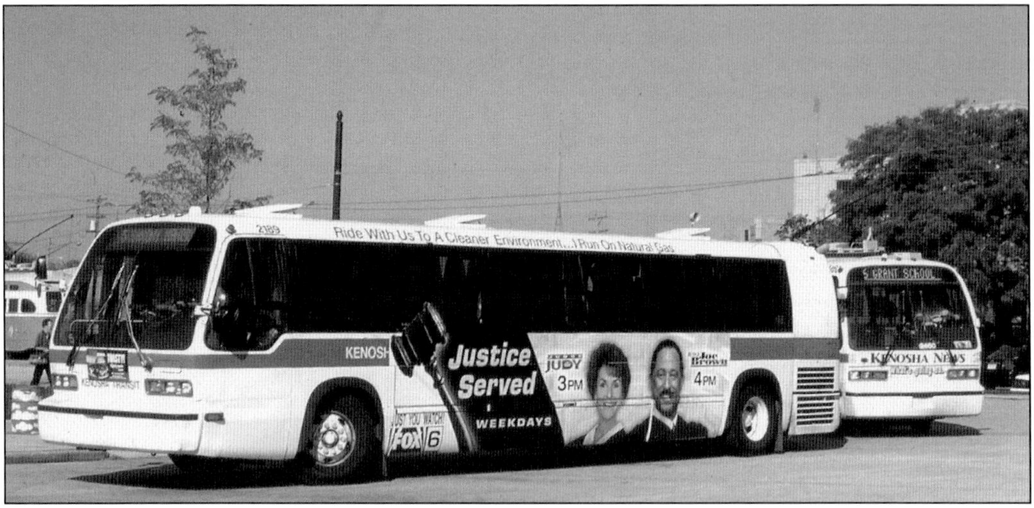

Kenosha Transit Commission director Joseph McCarthy obtained clean air funds from the federal government in order to purchase compressed natural gas buses. RTS bus No. 2189, one of those coaches, is seen here in late October 2002 signed for Route 5 Saxony Manor at the Joseph McCarthy Transit Center. The scene is looking northwest. (Photograph by DOE.)

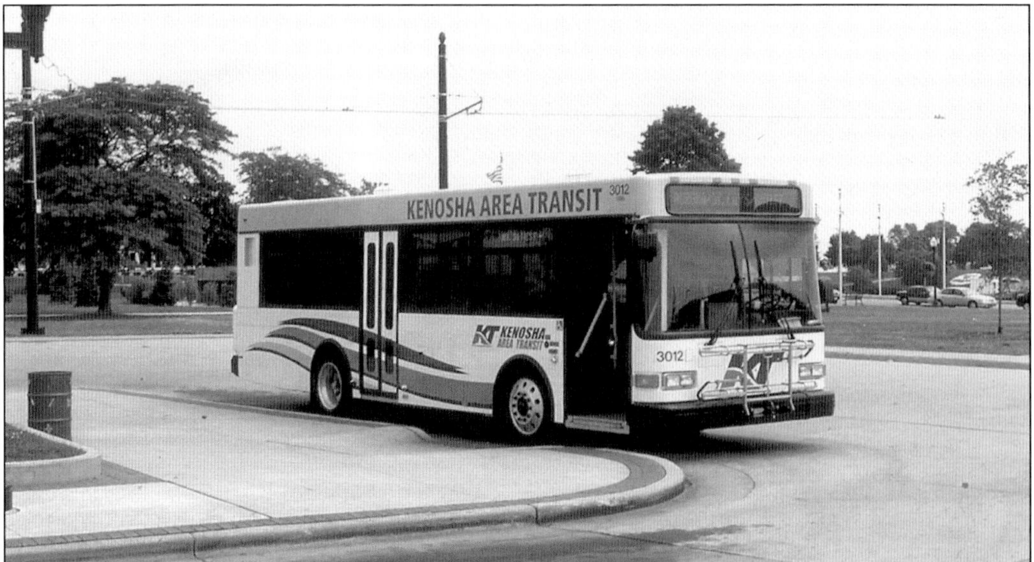

Kenosha Area Transit bus No. 3012, a new Gillig 26-passenger diesel bus, awaits its running time behind the Joseph McCarthy Transit Center looking northeast on Saturday, July 17, 2004. Note the streetcar wire in the background. The colors, two shades of blue, yellow, and white, provide an impressive paint livery. (Photograph by DS.)

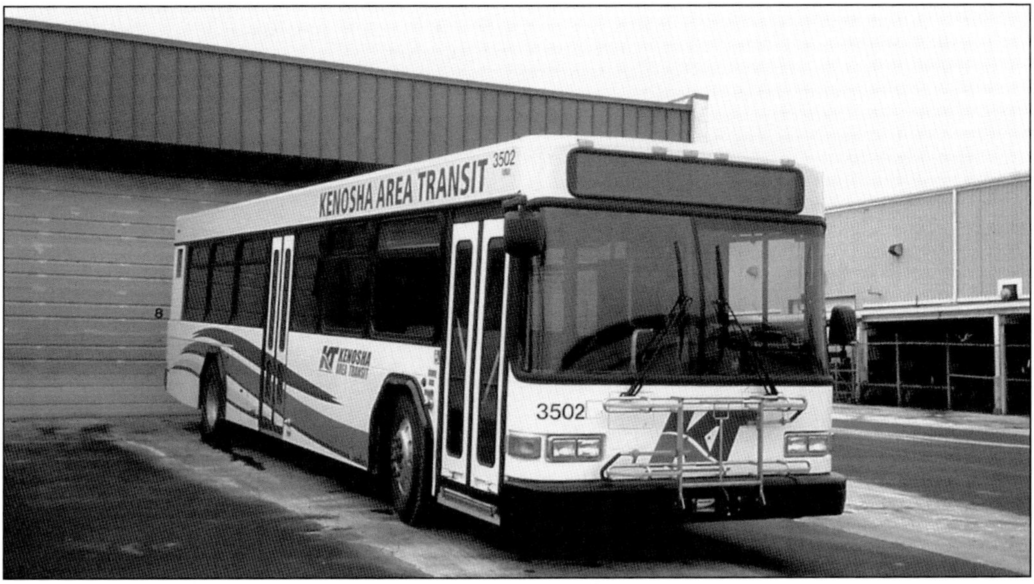

Kenosha Area Transit bus No. 3502, a Gillig diesel bus, is seen at the Kenosha City Garage at Sixty-fifth Street and Thirty-eighth Avenue on December 27, 2004. This new state-of-the-art transit bus was part of a 21–new bus order with 12 buses delivered in 2004 and 9 more in 2005. Of the new buses, 8 would hold 26 passengers and 13 would hold 32 passengers. (Photograph by EMO.)

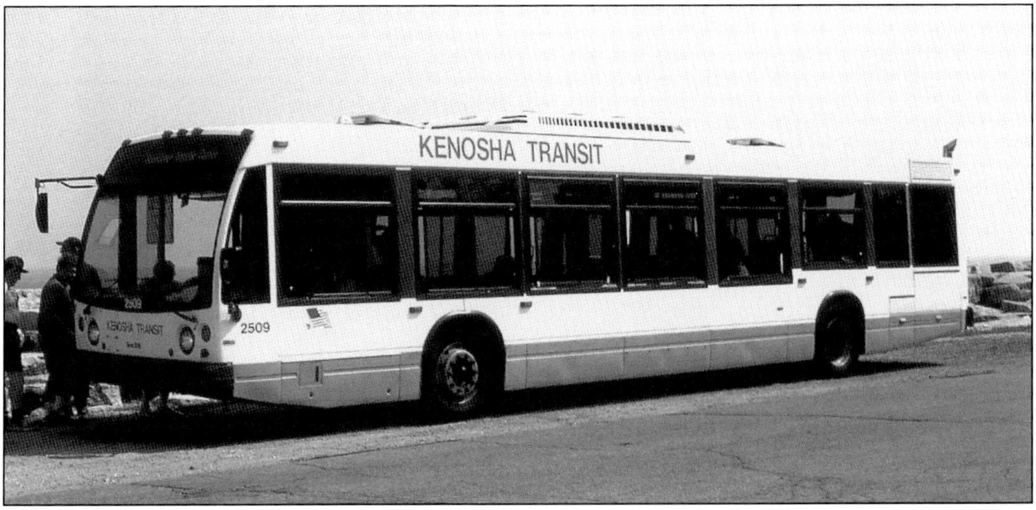

Kenosha Area Transit bus No. 2509, still lettered for Kenosha Transit, is seen at Kenosha's lakefront on September 10, 2005. This Nova 37-passenger diesel bus was part of a 1999 order for three low-floor buses purchased from Nova Bus of Quebec, Canada. (Photograph by DS.)

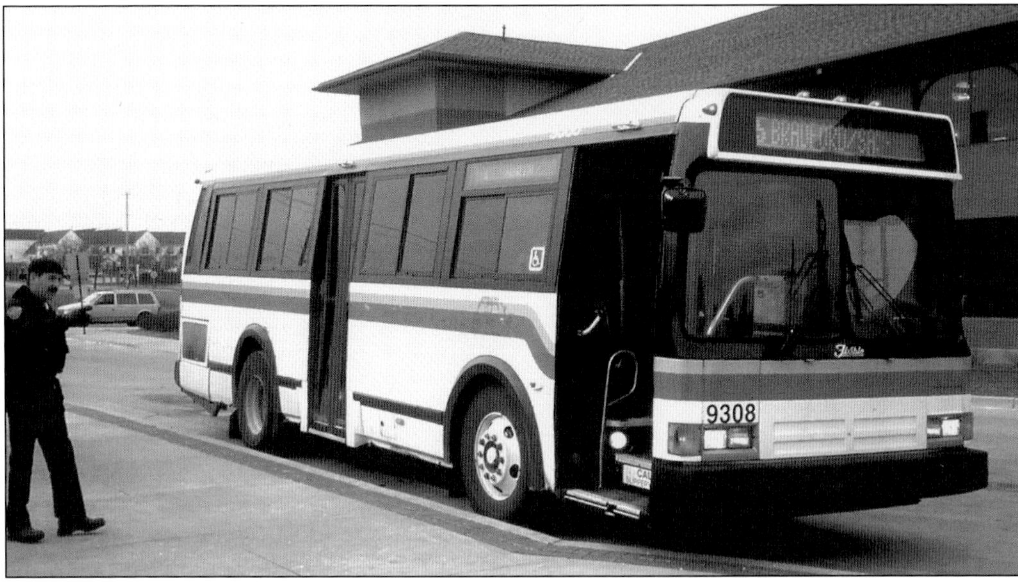

Secondhand Kenosha Area Transit diesel, Flexible Bus No. 9308, is parked at the Joseph McCarthy Transit Center, Fifty-fourth Street and Eighth Avenue, looking west on December 27, 2004. As Kenosha's bus fleet was aging, secondhand equipment was put into service until new equipment was delivered. As of September 4, 2004, the name Kenosha Transit was changed to Kenosha Area Transit. (Photograph by EMO.)

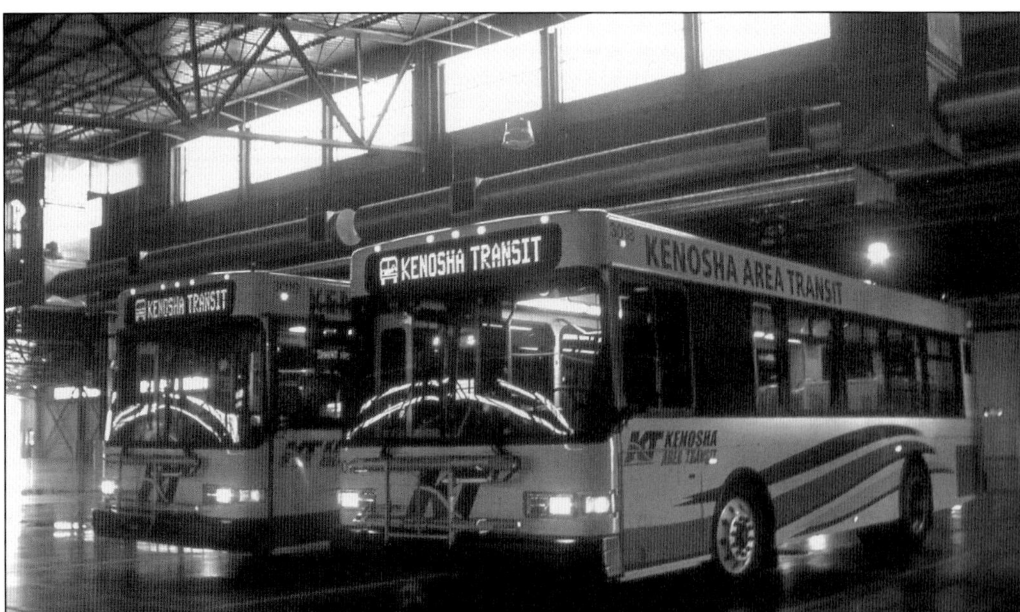

To meet the needs of a growing population, Kenosha Area Transit opened a new state-of-the-art bus garage at 4303 Thirty-ninth Avenue on November 2, 2006. Shown here are two of the new Gillig low-floor transit diesel buses on July 5, 2007. The Kenosha bus system provides excellent service for a $1 fare. (Photograph by DOE.)

Two

The MRK Line

From its humble beginnings in 1897, the MRK interurban line would change from a typical side-of-the-road operation to a first-rate rapid transit line. The MRK line's original rolling stock consisted of smaller suburban-type electric streetcars, and by 1903, new larger interurbans would start to replace the older equipment. The 600-volt DC MRK line was part of a large interurban electric railway system radiating out of downtown Milwaukee in all directions. That system was owned and operated by the the Milwaukee Electric Railway and Light Company (TMER&L).

In 1924, TMER&L started to rebuild older interurbans at its Cold Spring shops at Thirty-eighth and McKinley Streets in Milwaukee. Kenosha would now be served by these modernized interurbans, known as the "Green Specials." The large cars would be a mainstay on the MRK until the end of service in 1947.

In 1929, TMER&L purchased eight secondhand interurbans built in 1923 by the St. Louis Car Company from the Indianapolis and Cincinnati Traction Company. These long interurbans were spliced in the middle, lengthened, and articulated at the Cold Spring shops. The cars, known as duplexes, would also become standard equipment on the MRK.

The running time on the MRK from Kenosha to Milwaukee in 1927 was two hours and two minutes. TMER&L decided to build a new rapid transit line on the MRK. The new line, built in six segments, had limited stops and would bypass streets running in St. Francis, Cudahy, and the city of South Milwaukee. The first segment, from south Howell Avenue in Milwaukee to South Junction (Ryan Road), was completed on July 15, 1928. The last section, from Lakeview siding just north of Kenosha to the new rapid transit terminal in downtown Kenosha, was completed on April 17, 1932 (see the map on page 23). Running time between Kenosha and the interurban depot located in the Milwaukee Public Service Building at Third and Michigan Streets in downtown Milwaukee would now be 1 hour and 10 minutes.

Between 1943 and 1944, the MRK line was sold to its last owner, Henry P. Bruner and renamed Kenosha Motor Coach Lines (KMCL). In 1947, only 15 years after completion, the new MRK line was abandoned and sold for scrap.

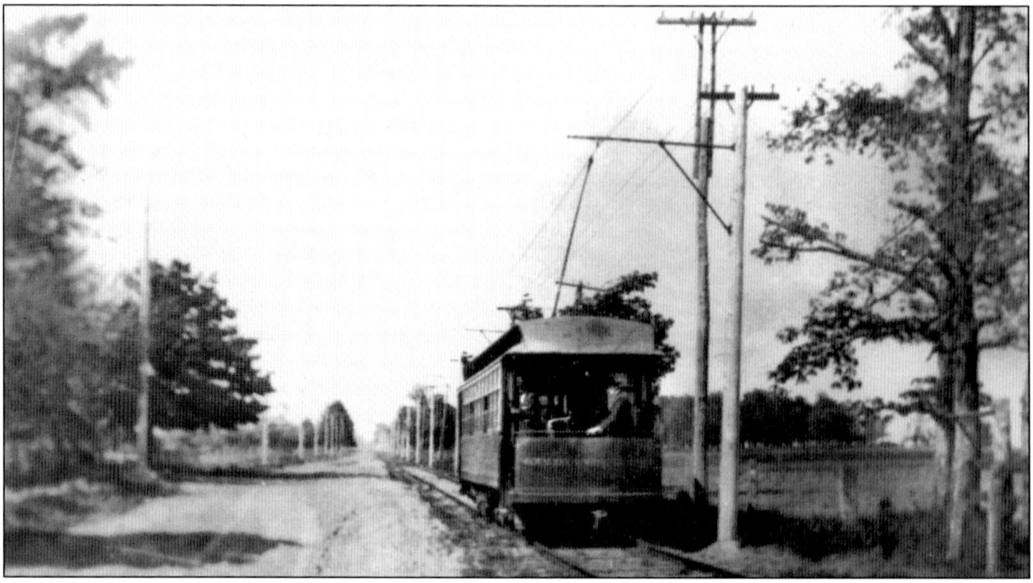

An open-ended MRK northbound interurban is seen here north of Kenosha operating to the side of Chicago Road (Sheridan Road) around 1900. By March 1899, the MRK was under the operating control of the Milwaukee Light Heat and Traction Company, a subsidiary of TMER&L. This clean, silent, electric car must have seemed like a space ship compared to road travel at the time. (Courtesy of KCHM.)

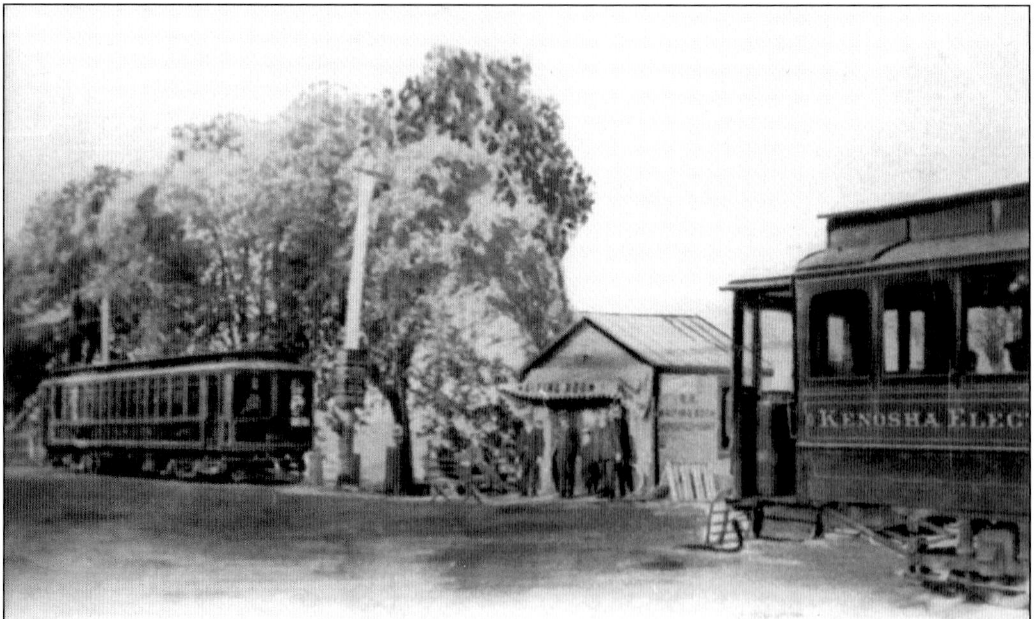

This postcard view depicts a KER streetcar at city limits on Milwaukee Avenue. Across the street are the transfer depot and an MRK 1000 class interurban of TMER&L. By 1912, both companies would be under the same ownership, and the interurbans would run over city streetcar tracks to downtown Kenosha. (Courtesy of RES.)

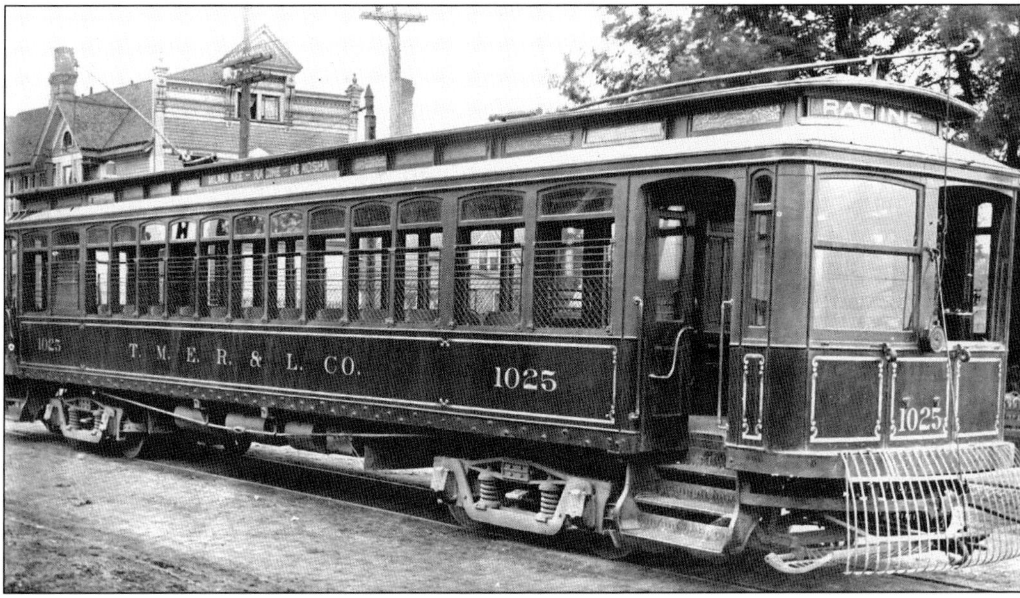

This handsome interurban was part of a 25-car order built by the St. Louis Car Company in 1903. Splendid in its olive green and yellow livery with a terra-cotta red roof, these 30-ton cars were standard operating equipment on the MRK. By the mid-1920s, the cars would gradually be replaced by the Green Specials, similar interurbans that were completely rebuilt and modernized at the Cold Spring shops in Milwaukee. (Courtesy of RF.)

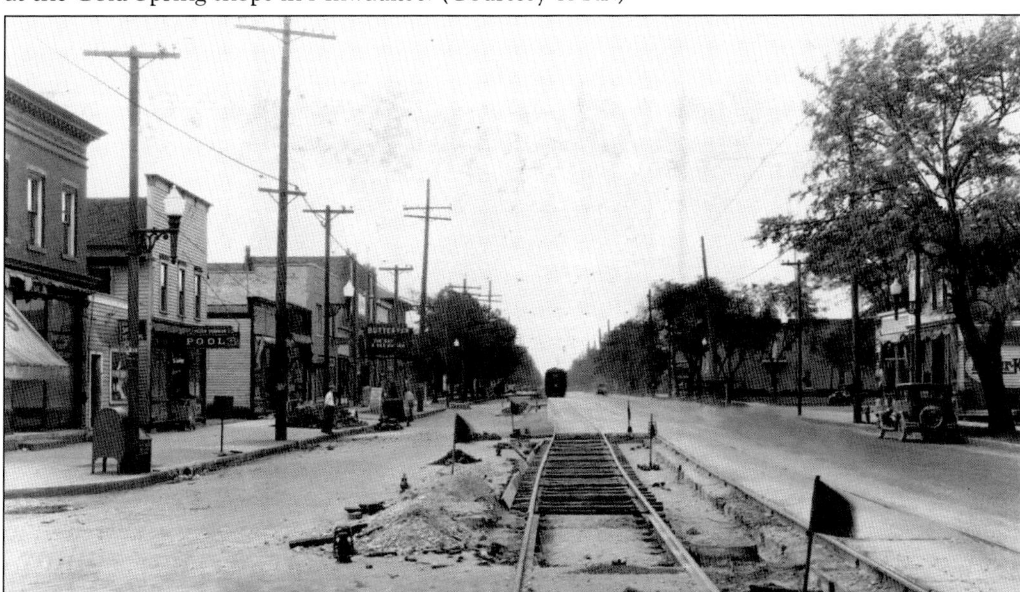

New track was installed in three segments on Seventh Avenue between 1924 and 1929. In this company photograph, track renewal is seen here on May 25, 1927, looking north on Seventh Avenue from Fiftieth Street. The new track gave the city streetcars, along with the rebuilt Green Special interurban (far background), the best ride they ever had. Within three years, the tracks would never be used again. With street renewal in August 2007, the tracks were finally removed along with their cement roadbed. (Courtesy of BWR, KBR.)

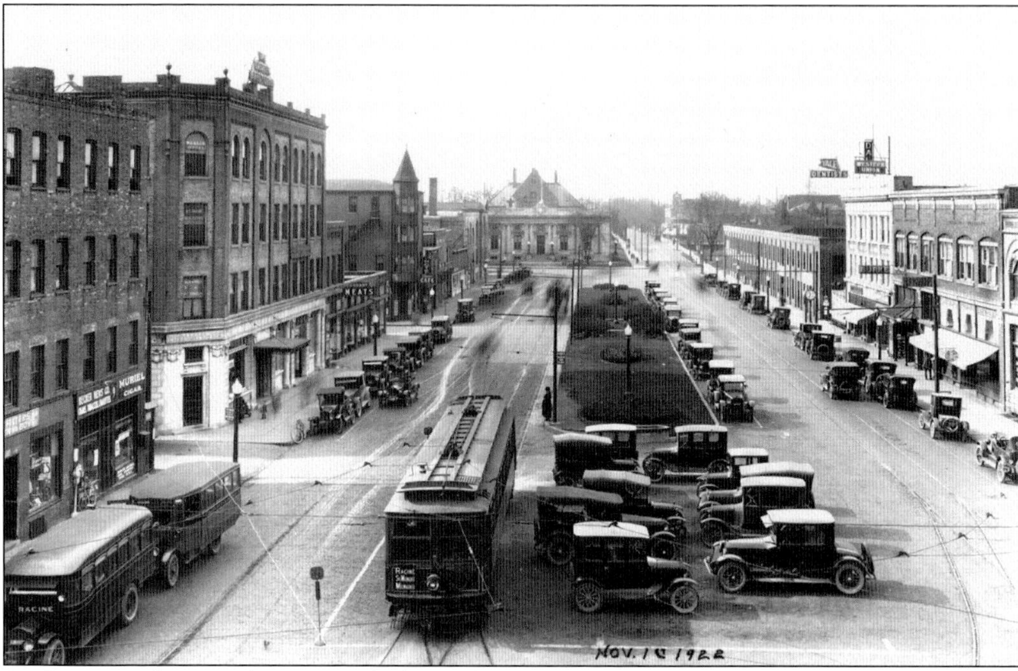

Looking west from Market Square (Fifty-sixth Street), a 1000 class MRK interurban of TMER&L can be seen about to turn north into Main Street (Sixth Avenue) on November 14, 1922. To the left is a bus operating on the local Racine/Kenosha bus line with another gas bus behind it. (Courtesy of KCHM.)

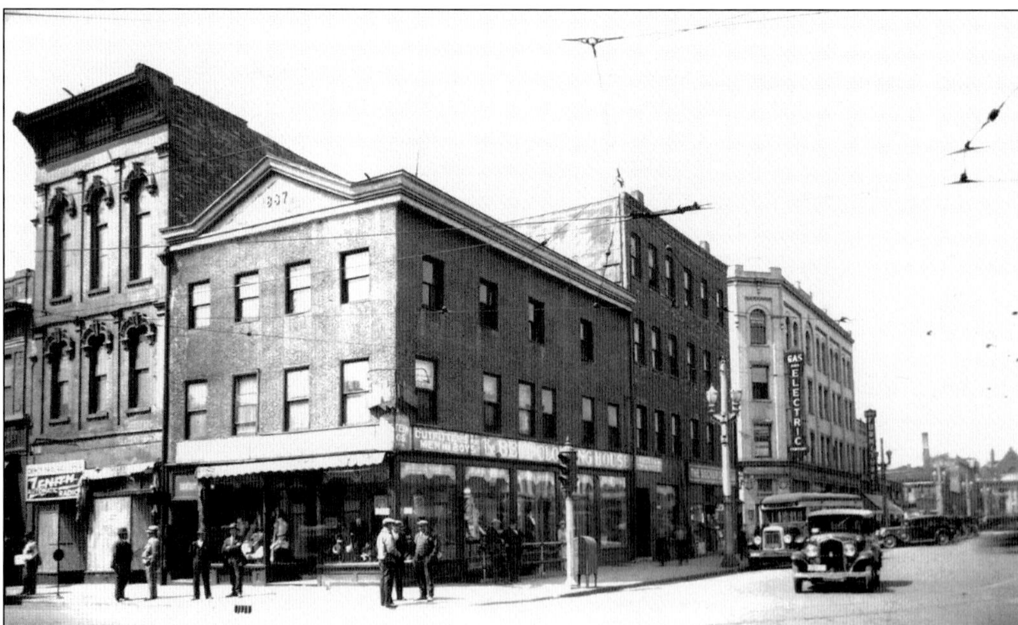

Looking west down Market Street from Main Street (Fifty-sixth Street and Sixth Avenue), a Yellow Coach type Z bus of TMER&L can be seen, awaiting its departure time just east of the Kenosha Public Service Building. This gas motor coach is operating on the local Racine–Kenosha bus line. (Courtesy of KCHM, JEG.)

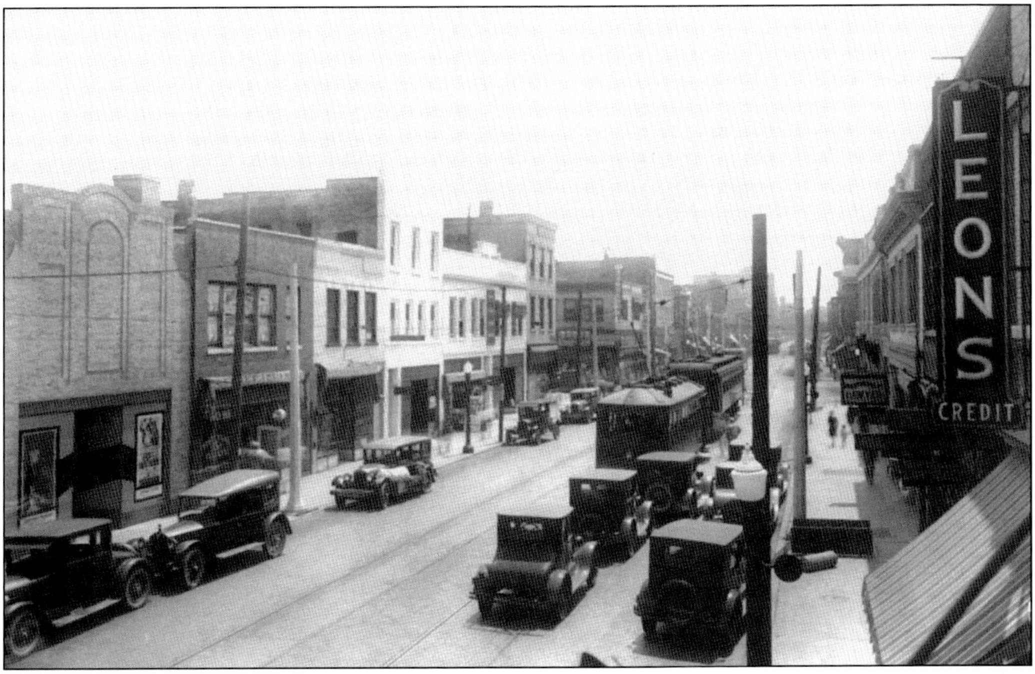

Looking south on Sixth Avenue to Market Square (Fifty-sixth Street) in downtown Kenosha, an interurban exchanges passengers with a 990 series city streetcar in 1928. The Green Special interurban is about to turn west on Fifty-sixth Street, then north on Sheridan Road, where it will loop behind the city streetcar barn at Fifty-fourth Street and Sheridan Road. By 1932, this single-ended car would enter Kenosha on a new rapid transit right-of-way, eliminating street running. (Courtesy of KCHM, ICS.)

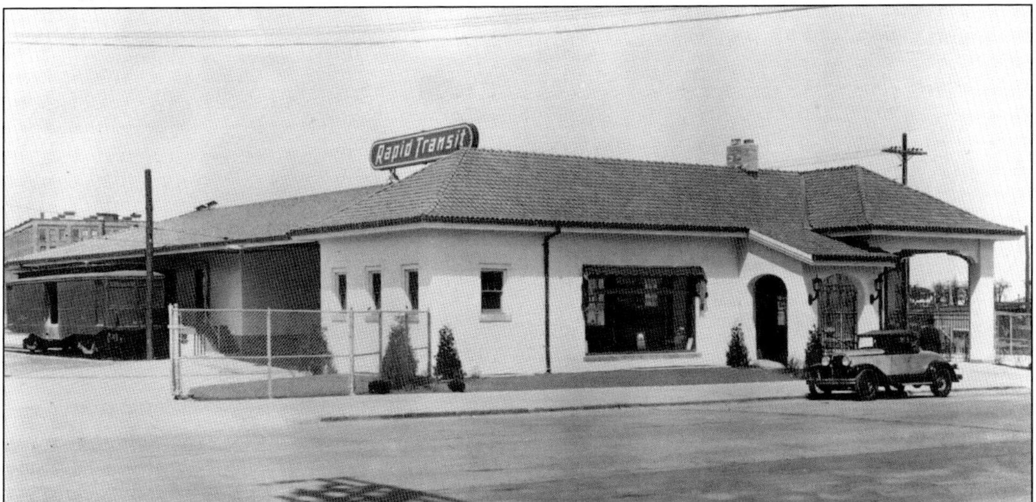

It is grand opening day, April 18, 1932, for this handsome Spanish Colonial passenger and express terminal. Built for the new MRK rapid transit line, the building will provide all the conveniences that passengers need, including a lunch counter. The scene is looking northeast from Fifty-fifth Street with Eighth Avenue behind the structure. The canopy to the far right is for the local Racine and Kenosha bus line. Note the freight trailer M-5 to the left was rebuilt from a 1200 series interurban passenger trailer. (Courtesy of RG.)

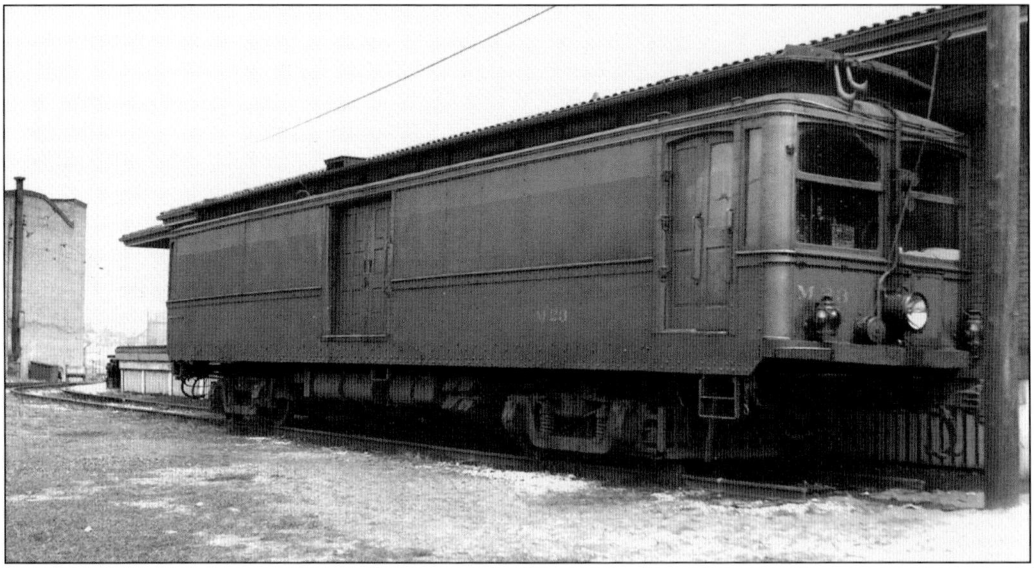

TMER&L car No. M-23, built as a passenger car by St. Louis Car Company in 1903 and rebuilt in 1924 as a freight motorcar, sits at the loading dock of the Kenosha MRK terminal in this late-1930s scene. Freight service initiated in 1915 proved to be very successful even during the Depression. The car painted in olive green with a yellow letter board is facing south. (Photograph by AC, courtesy of WRK.)

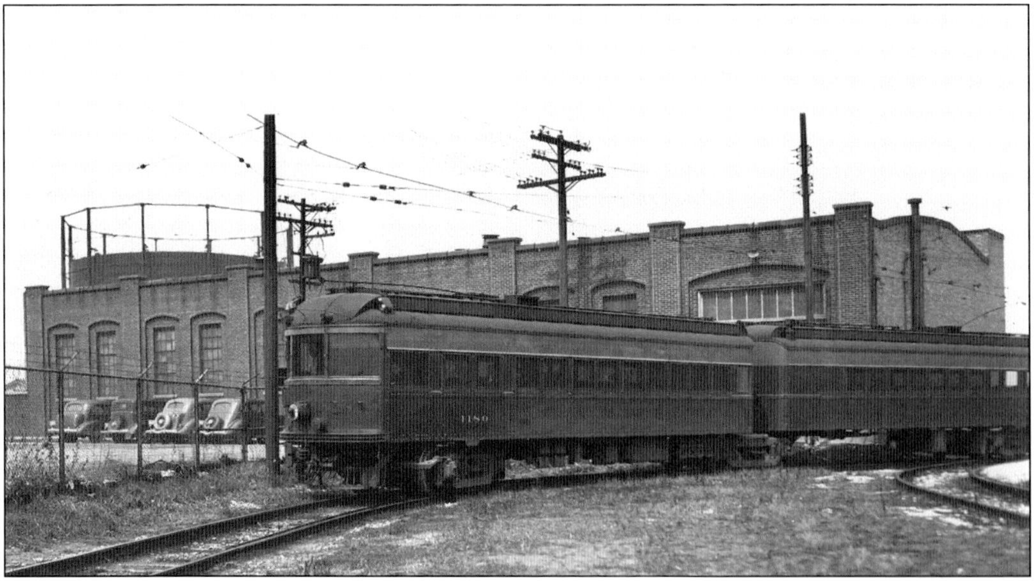

TMER&L duplex car Nos. 1180 and 1181, facing south, is about to enter the Kenosha depot. Looking northwest in the background is the former WG&E gasoline bus garage. In the far background, the giant gas tank that sat between Fifty-second and Fifty-third Streets at Sheridan Road is the site of a Wendy's restaurant today. The duplex units, with a seating capacity of 84 (compared to 60 for regular cars), were a cost-cutting effort on the part of the company. (Photograph by AC, courtesy of WRK.)

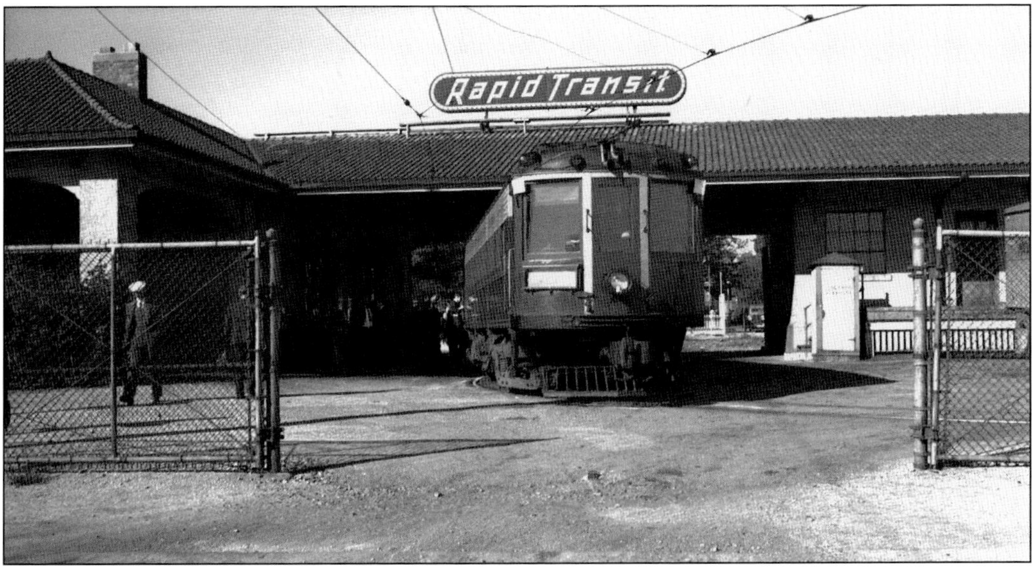

Central Electric Railfans Association (CERA) members are boarding cars No. 1143 and No. 1142 of the Milwaukee Electric Railway and Transport Company on CERA trip No. 16 at the Kenosha MRK depot on September 17, 1939. At Milwaukee, the riders will switch to a North Shore train. In those days, traveling possibilities on interurbans and transit systems were unlimited. (Photograph by JFH, courtesy of RH.)

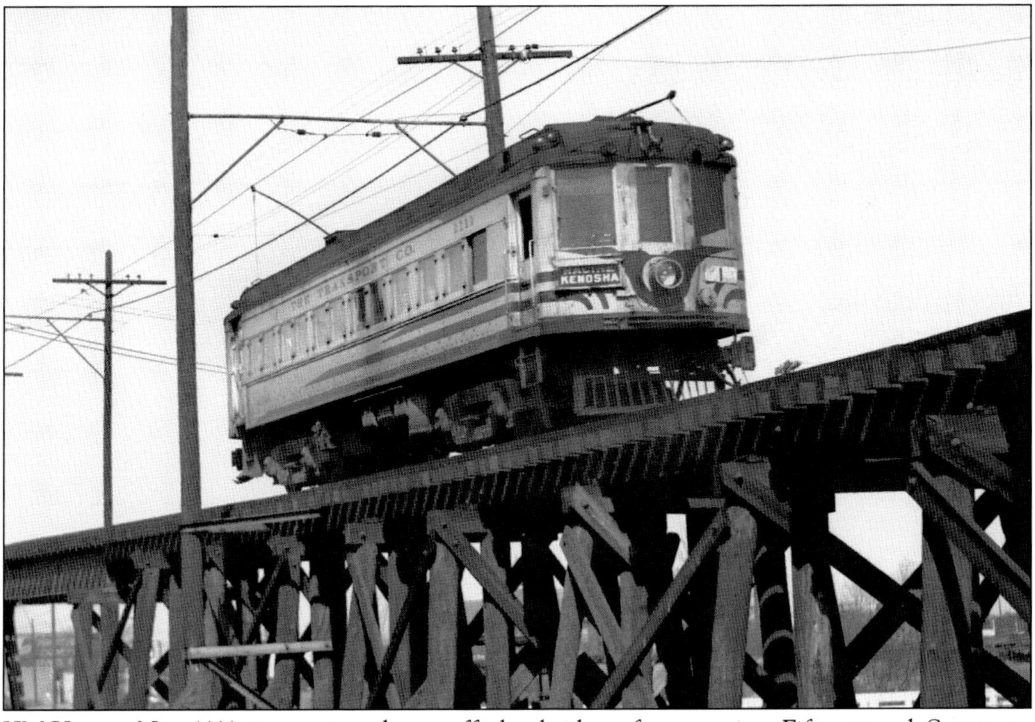

KMCL car No. 1111 is coming down off the bridge after crossing Fifty-second Street on March 3, 1945. Note the children looking out the window at the photographer as the interurban is about to end its run at Kenosha's rapid transit depot, Fifty-fifth Street and Eighth Avenue. (Photograph by RWG, courtesy of JFD, GEK.)

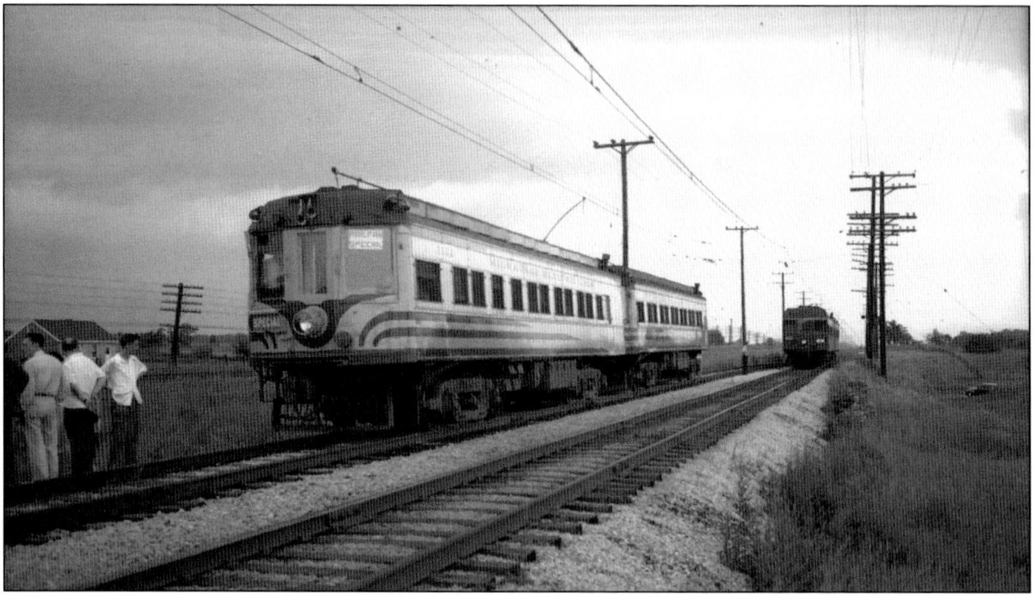

While the conductor watches from the rear end of his special rail fan chartered train, in-service duplex car Nos. 1186 and 1187 is about to pass the siding at Caladonia Junction on July 30, 1946. At this point, the MRK line is 18 miles from Milwaukee and 16 miles from Kenosha. (Photograph by JFH, courtesy of RH.)

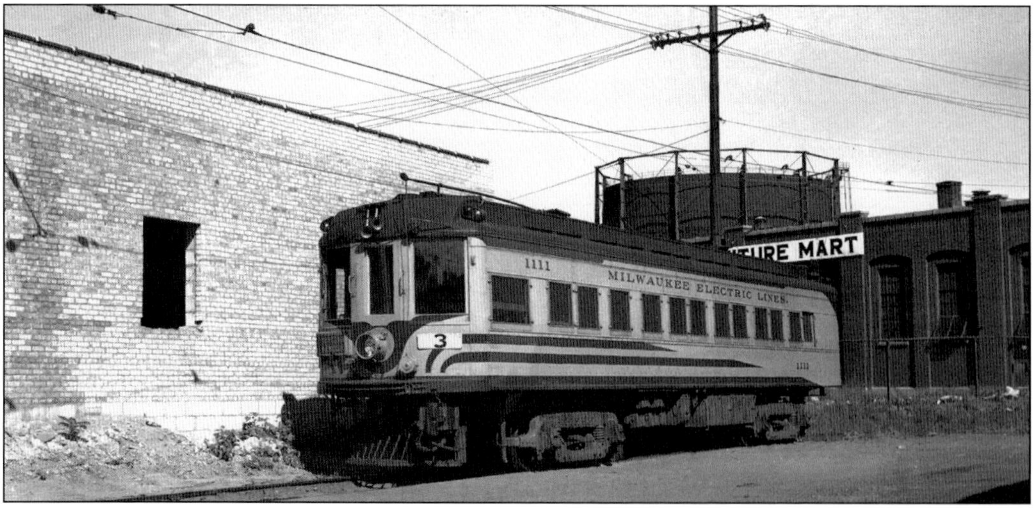

The big gas tank in the background had an ill-reputed saloon adjacent to it called Gas House Annie's. If one had too much to drink at Annie's, there was no need to drive since there was ample transportation to get one home. The interurban pictured behind the Kenosha MRK depot on September 2, 1946, could get one to downtown Milwaukee in 1 hour and 10 minutes. (Photograph by RWG, courtesy of JFD, GEK.)

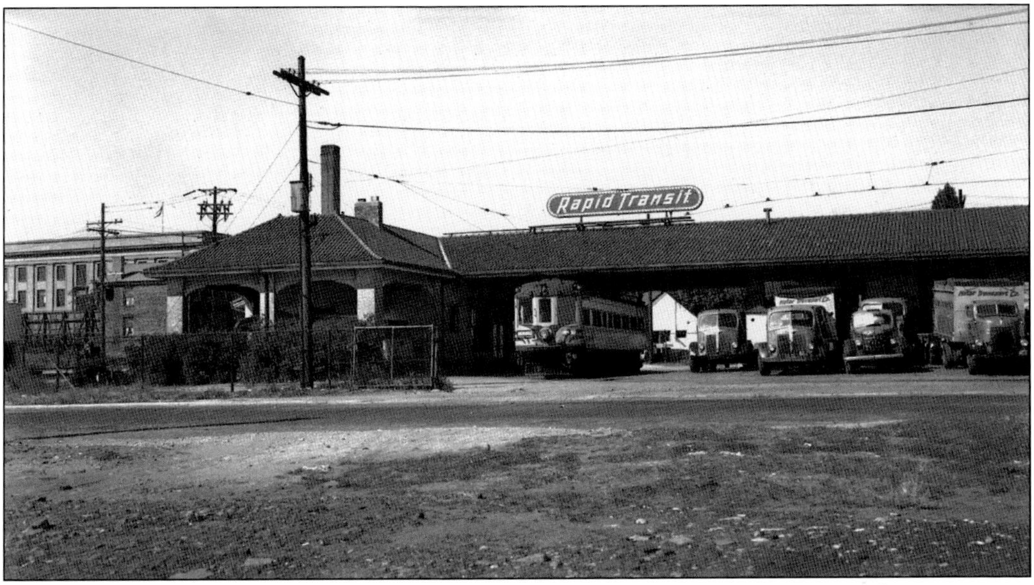

Looking west across Eighth Avenue on Sunday, September 2, 1946, an interurban awaits its departure time while trucks of the Motor Transport Company are parked for the next day's loading. A Ford transit bus, operating on the local Kenosha to Racine route, can barely be seen sitting under the canopy. To the far left is the Kenosha County Courthouse. (Photograph by RWG, courtesy of JFD, GEK.)

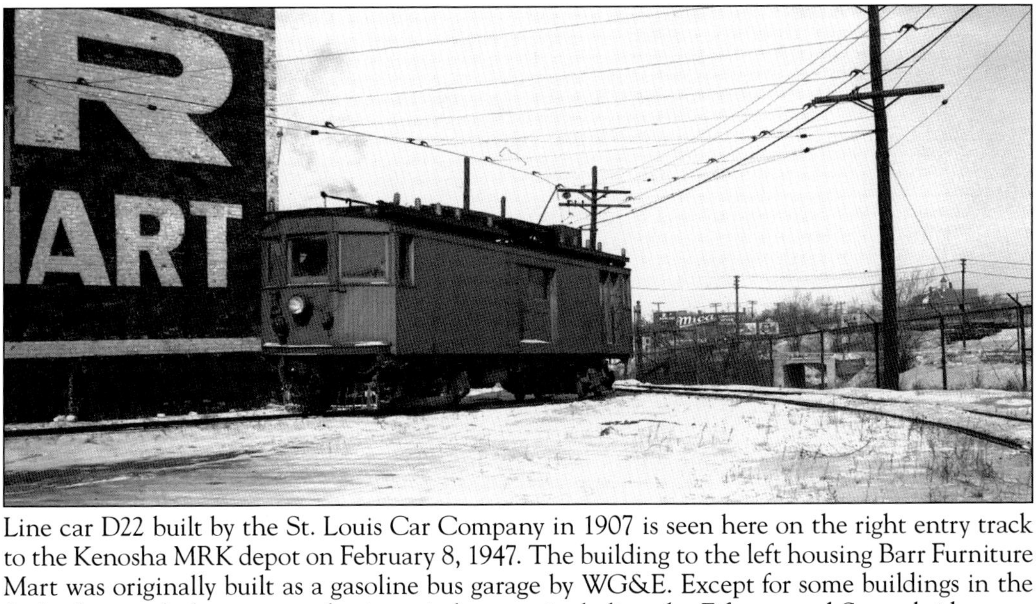

Line car D22 built by the St. Louis Car Company in 1907 is seen here on the right entry track to the Kenosha MRK depot on February 8, 1947. The building to the left housing Barr Furniture Mart was originally built as a gasoline bus garage by WG&E. Except for some buildings in the far background, this scene today is entirely gone, including the Fifty-second Street bridge over Pike Creek. The scene is looking northwest toward Fifty-second Street. (Photograph by JFH, courtesy of RH.)

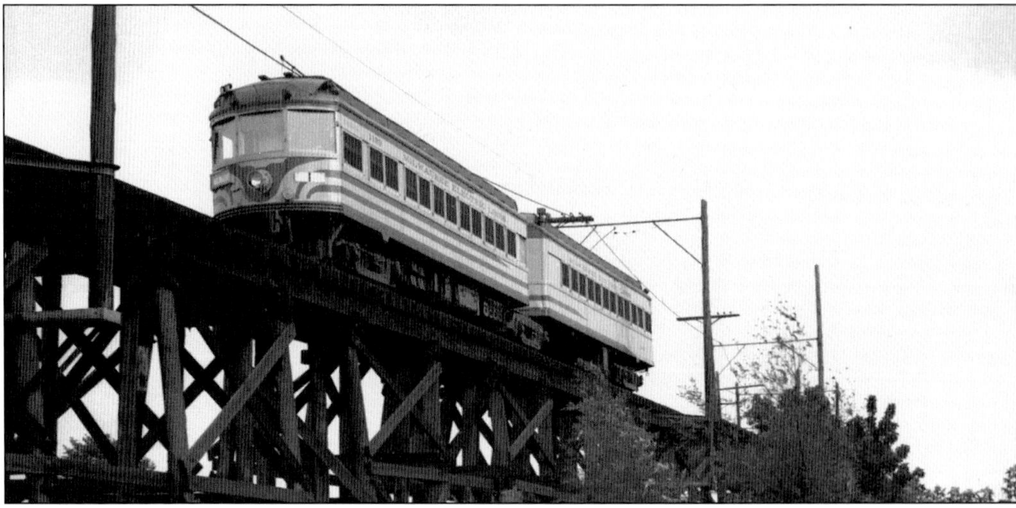

Signed for Milwaukee, duplex car Nos. 1190 and 1191 crosses the wood piling structure looking southeast from Forty-eighth Street on August 24, 1947. This articulated interurban will follow the elevated private way to Thirty-fifth Street with a second Kenosha stop (a flag stop) at Washington Road. (Photograph by JFH, courtesy of RH.)

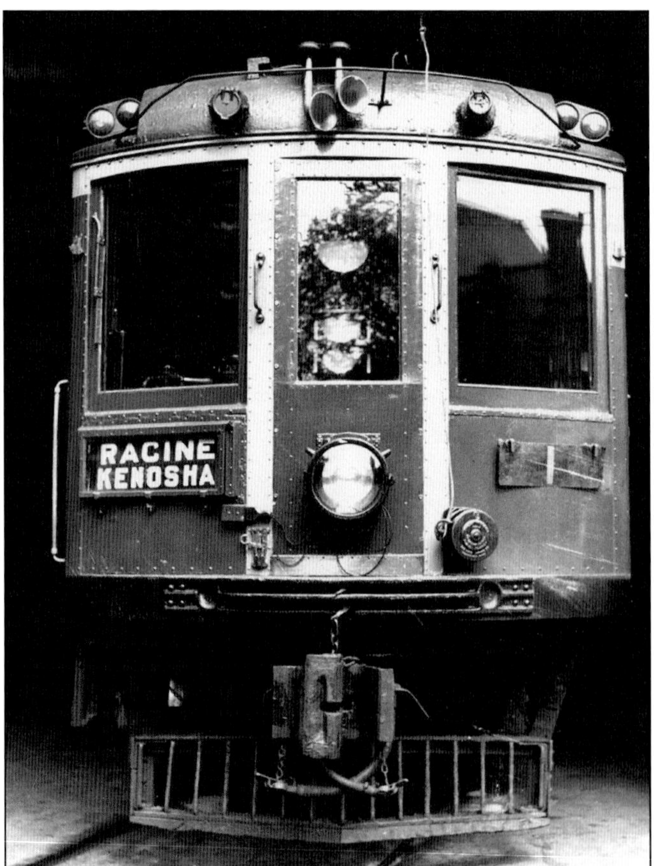

The next 18 photographs are a pictorial ride across the MRK from Milwaukee to Kenosha. Seen here, Milwaukee Electric Railway and Transport Company car No. 1143 awaits its running time at the west end of the Milwaukee Public Service Building on Third Street, a few yards south of Michigan Street in downtown Milwaukee. (Courtesy of KPA.)

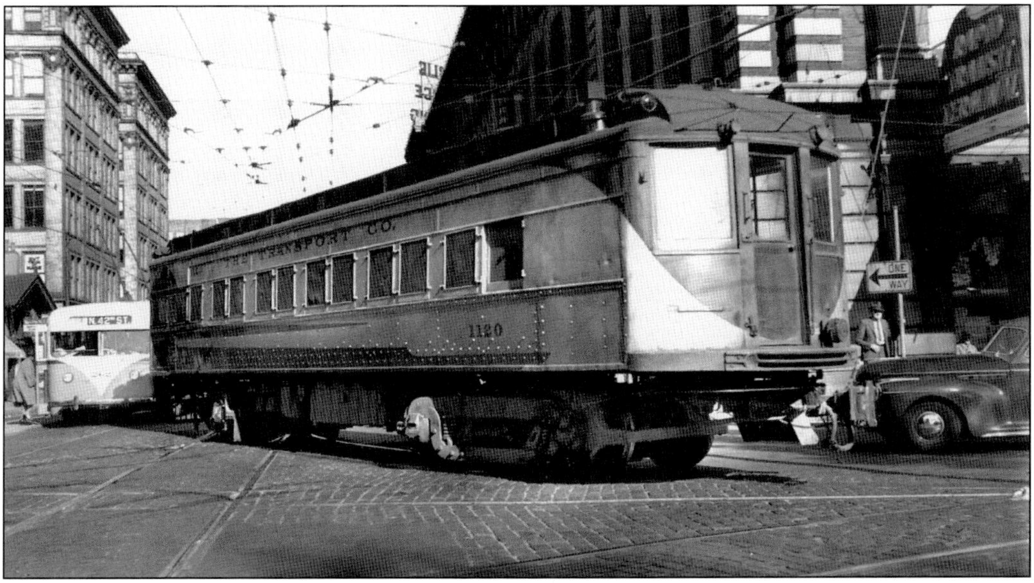

KMCL car No. 1120 is turning east into Michigan Street from Third Street and has just departed the Milwaukee Public Service Building for Kenosha and Racine on March 14, 1945. To the left is Milwaukee Transport Company trackless trolley No. 262 built by the St. Louis Car Company in 1941 and painted orange and cream with maroon trim. (Photograph by RWG, courtesy of JFD, GEK.)

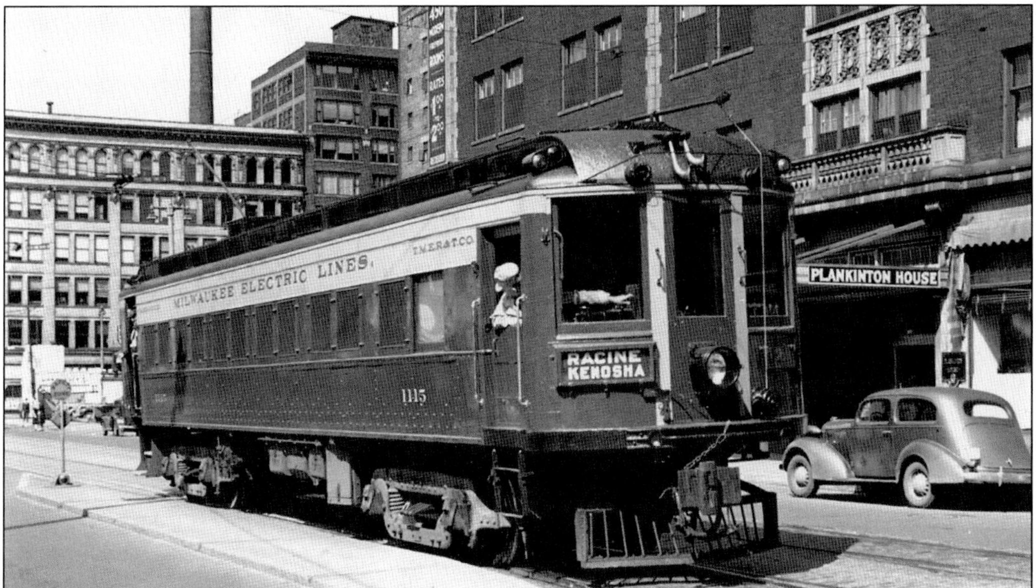

The motorman of Milwaukee Electric Railway and Transport Company car No. 1115 checks traffic before turning the Kenosha-bound interurban south into Plankinton Avenue from Michigan Street in downtown Milwaukee (looking west) in the early 1940s. The interurban in olive green and yellow livery will navigate city streetcar tracks to Howell Avenue and Burdick Streets, where it will then turn east into private right-of-way on the rapid transit MRK line. (Photograph by GK, courtesy of KPA.)

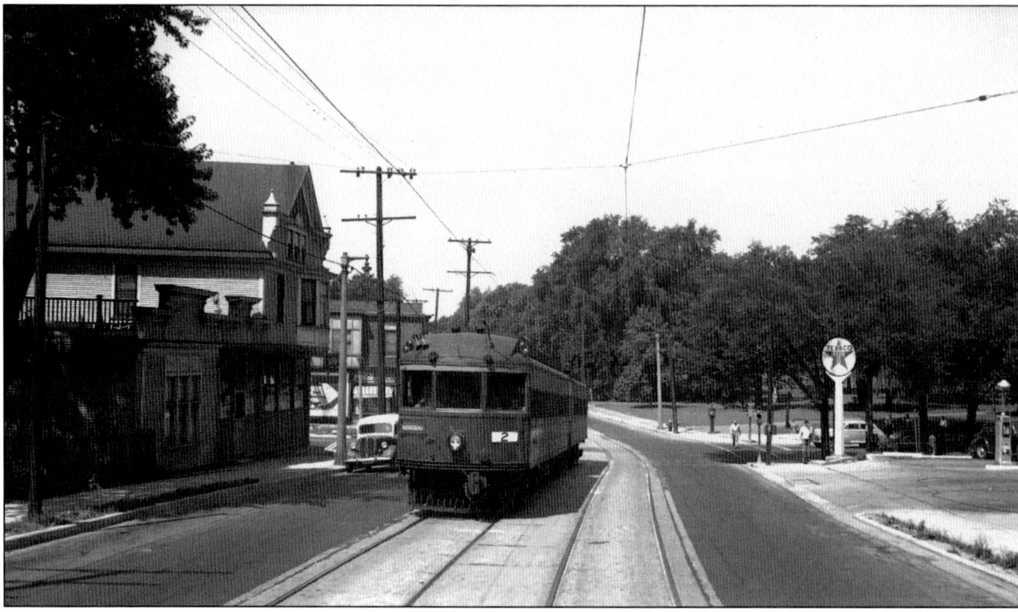

KMCL duplex car Nos. 1194 and 1195 is seen here in Milwaukee operating southbound on Howell Avenue at Oklahoma Avenue on August 9, 1947. Humbolt Park is to the right of the picture across the street from the Texaco gas station. Notice the run number sign on the front right side of the interurban. (Photograph by JFH, courtesy of RH.)

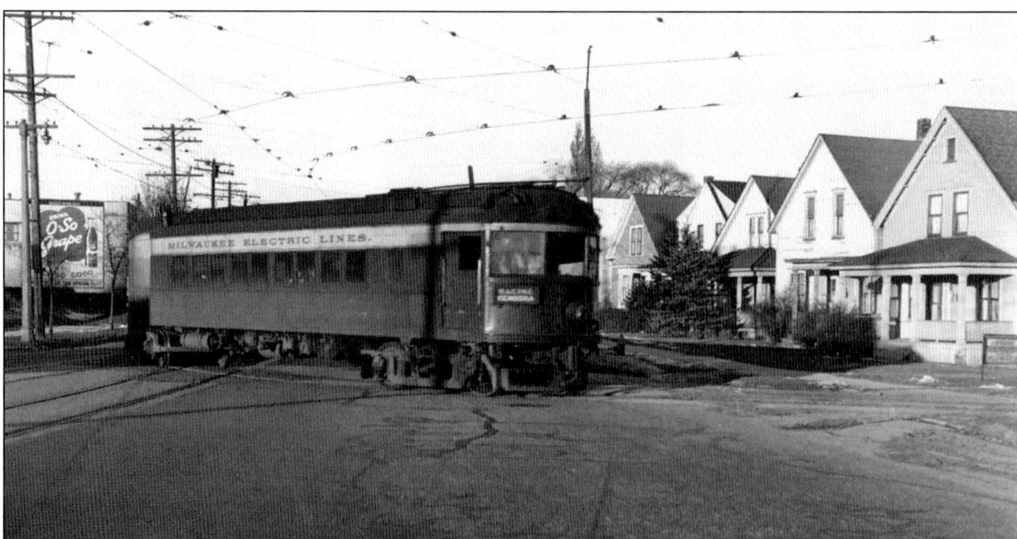

KMCL (formerly the Milwaukee Electric Railway and Transport Company) duplex car Nos. 1188 and 1189 is turning east off of Howell Avenue at Burdick Street into private right-of-way on the south side of Milwaukee on October 28, 1947. The Kenosha-to-Racine portion of the line was abandoned 35 days earlier, and the Racine-to-Milwaukee segment would be abandoned on December 31, 1947, ending 50 years of interurban service on the MRK line. (Courtesy of AH.)

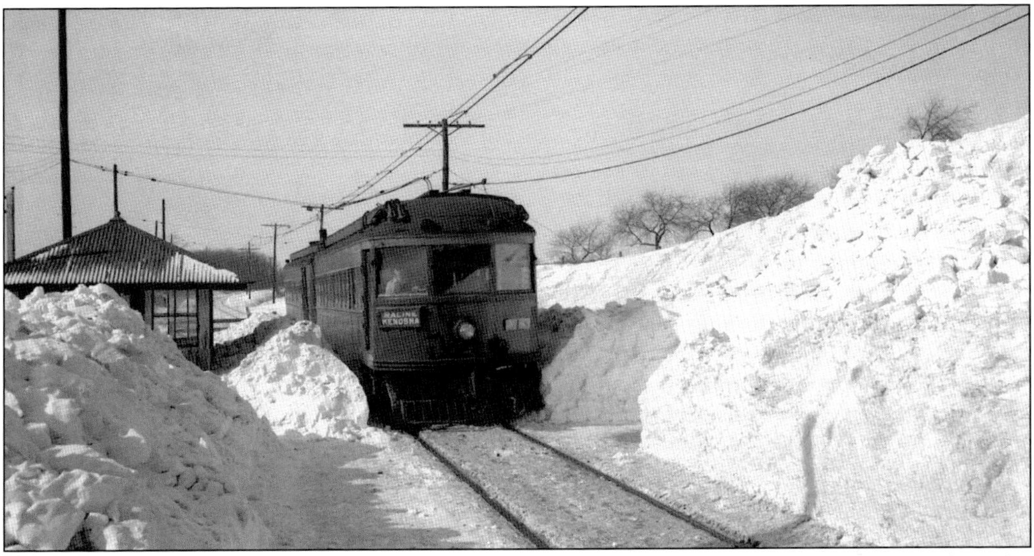

On January 29 and 30, 1947, 18 inches of snow had fallen in the immediate area crippling the MRK line—but not for long. Seen here on February 8, 1947, duplex car Nos. 1196 and 1197, rebuilt from second-hand interurbans by TMER&L in 1929, has a clear road ahead on what appears to be a beautiful day in spite of the snow. Notice the passenger path from the waiting shed at South Junction. (Photograph by JFH, courtesy of RH.)

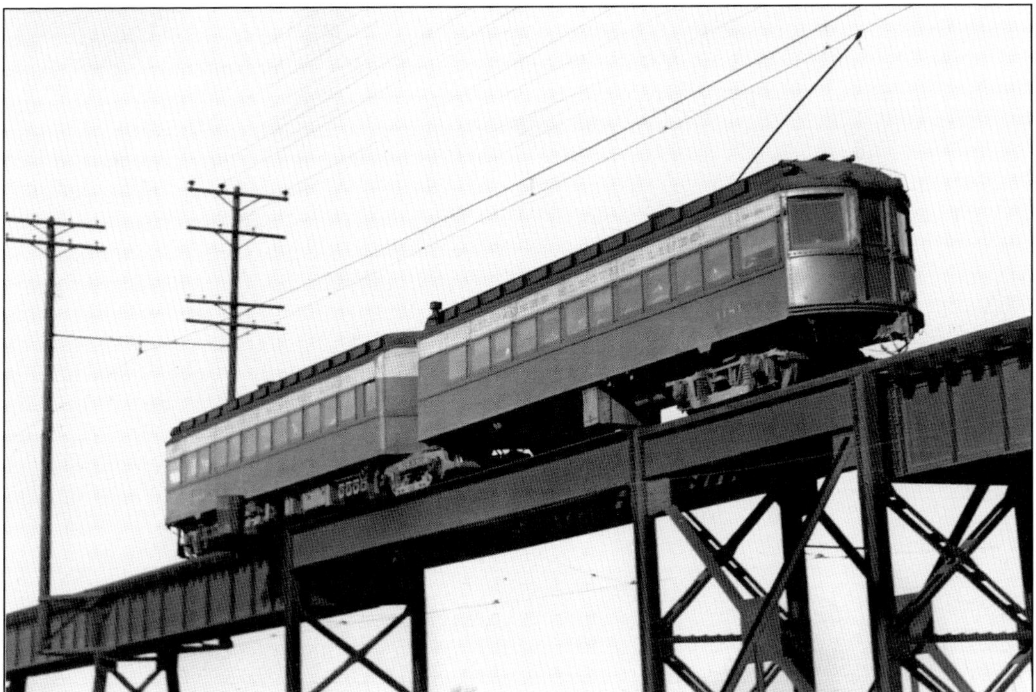

KMCL duplex car Nos. 1180 and 1181 is northbound crossing Three Mile Road on the steel trestle bridge at Ives just north of Racine on March 14, 1945. (Photograph by RWG, courtesy of JFD, GEK.)

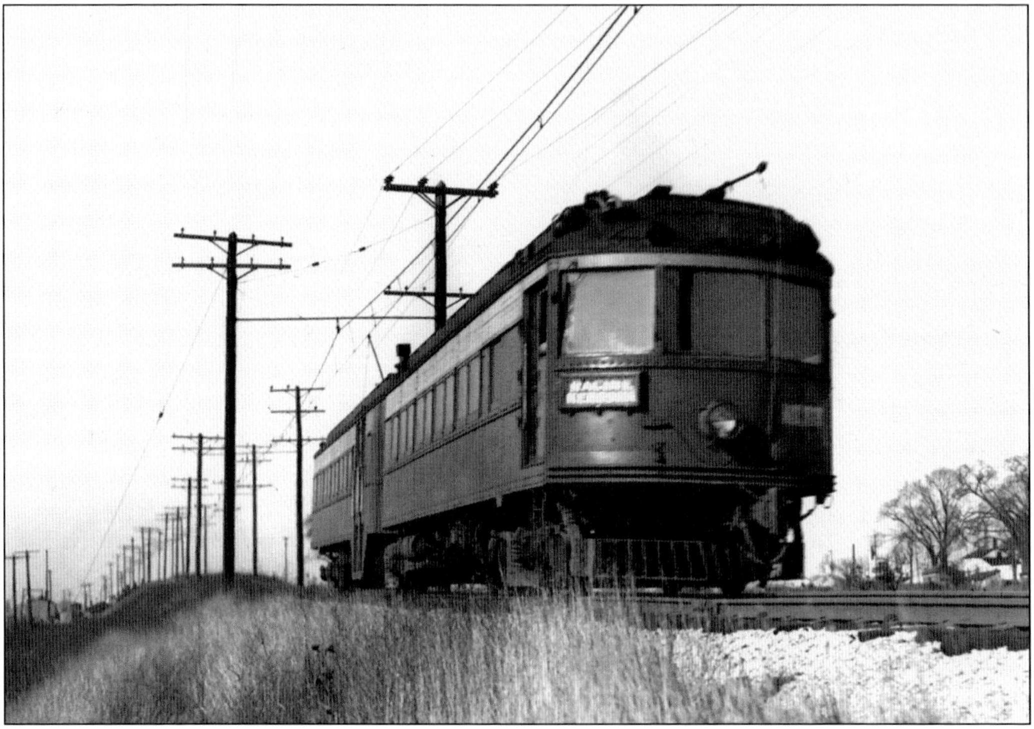

Racing past the tall grass, southbound KMCL duplex car Nos. 1184 and 1185 has just crossed the trestle over the Chicago and North Western Railroad Ives Quarry spur and Three Mile Road in Caledonia on March 14, 1945. The train is only minutes away from the Goold Street stop on the north side of Racine. (Photograph by RWG, courtesy of JFD, GEK.)

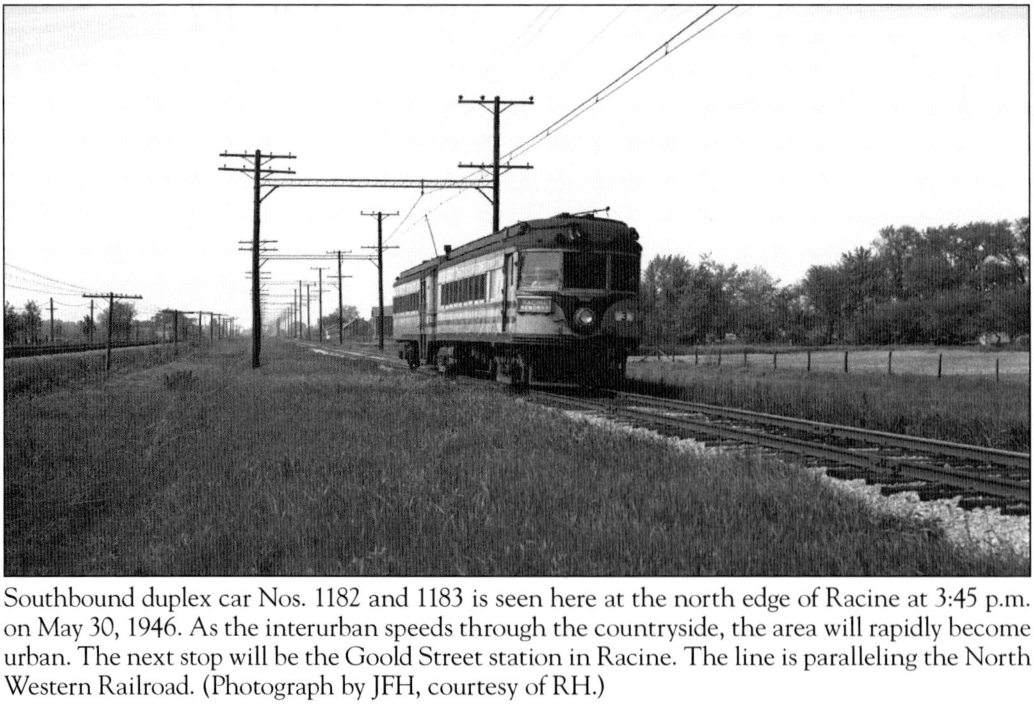

Southbound duplex car Nos. 1182 and 1183 is seen here at the north edge of Racine at 3:45 p.m. on May 30, 1946. As the interurban speeds through the countryside, the area will rapidly become urban. The next stop will be the Goold Street station in Racine. The line is paralleling the North Western Railroad. (Photograph by JFH, courtesy of RH.)

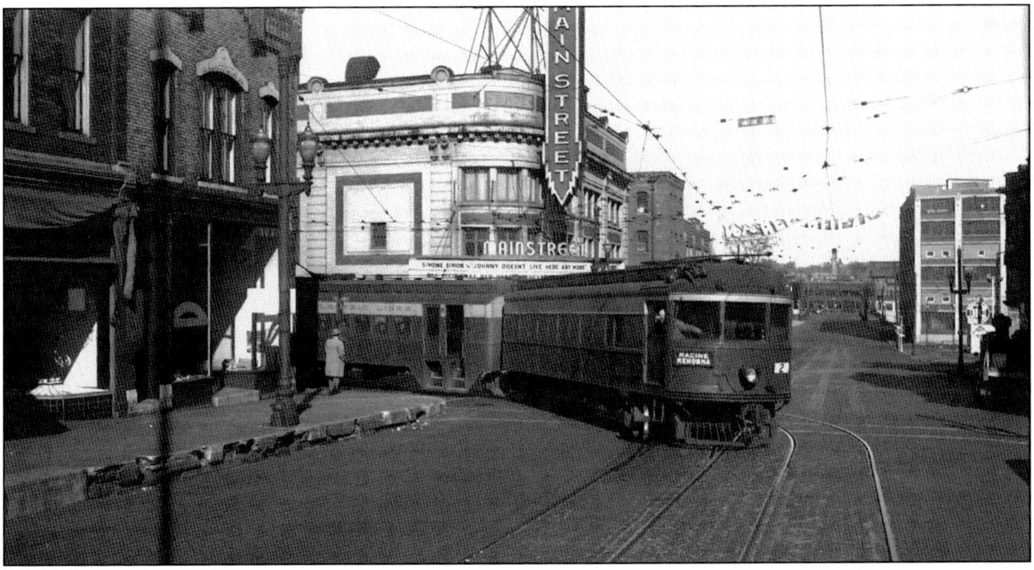

There was no shortage of movie theaters in Racine on October 22, 1944, as duplex car Nos. 1184 and 1185 turns onto Main Street from State Street. Looking north, evidence of city streetcar tracks can still be seen in the background. The motorman looks back to assure the curve is clear of other traffic. (Photograph by JFH, courtesy of RH.)

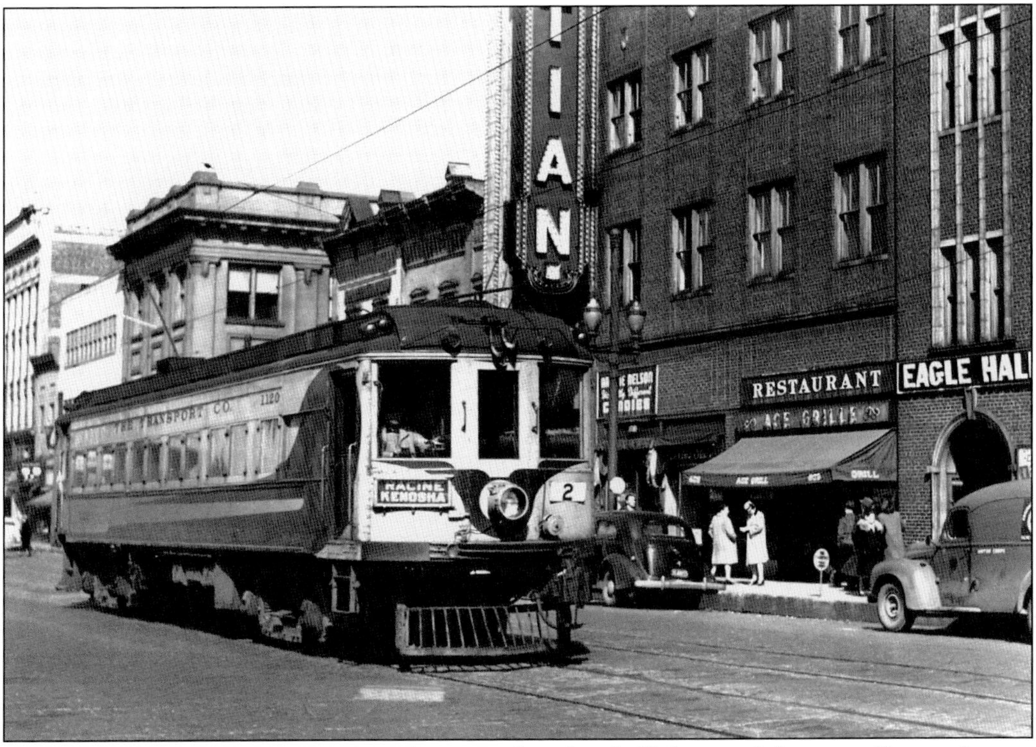

Southbound KMCL car No. 1120 in the streamline "spitball" livery of chrome yellow and green passes Monument Square at Fifth and Main Streets in downtown Racine, just a few blocks north of the terminal on Wisconsin Avenue on March 14, 1945. (Photograph by RWG, courtesy of JFD, GEK.)

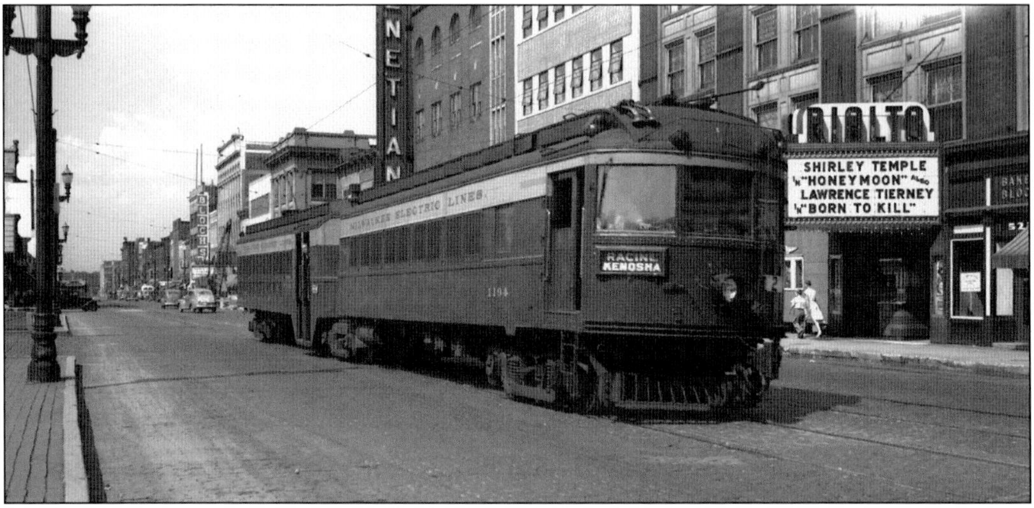

Shirley Temple and Lawrence Tierney are the stars of the week in this double feature playing at the Rialto Theater across from Racine's Monument Square on August 24, 1947. Looking north, duplex car Nos. 1194 and 1195 can be seen traveling south on Main Street between Sixth and Fifth Streets, still painted in their original colors of dark olive green (coach green) and a bright yellow letterboard. (Photograph by JFH, courtesy of RH.)

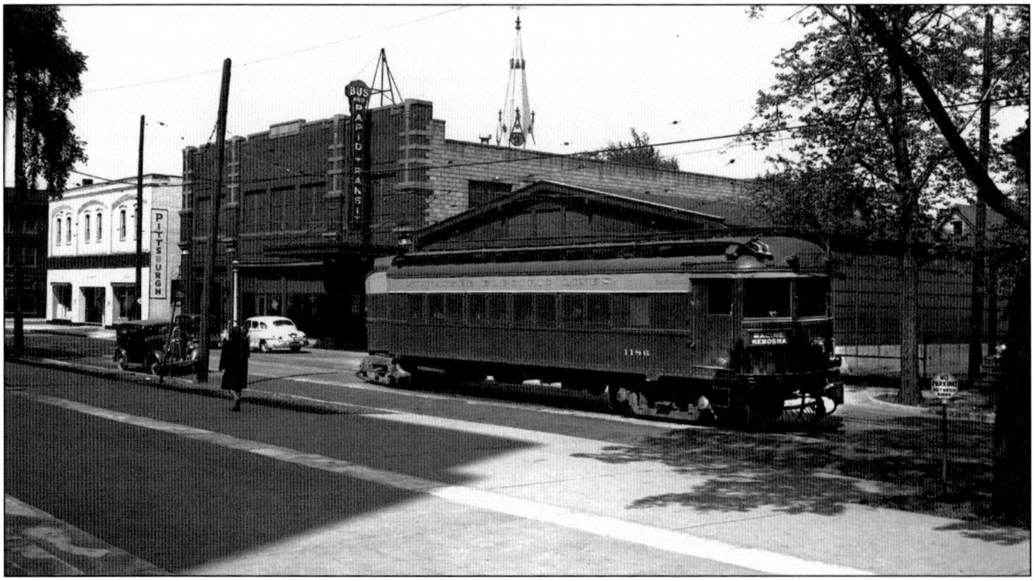

KMCL duplex car Nos. 1186 and 1187 is seen here turning south into Wisconsin Avenue just south of Seventh Street on May 30, 1946, from the Racine bus and rapid transit Union Station. Interurban cars would enter the train shed from Main Street behind the depot and exit into Wisconsin Avenue. (Photograph by JFH, courtesy of RH.)

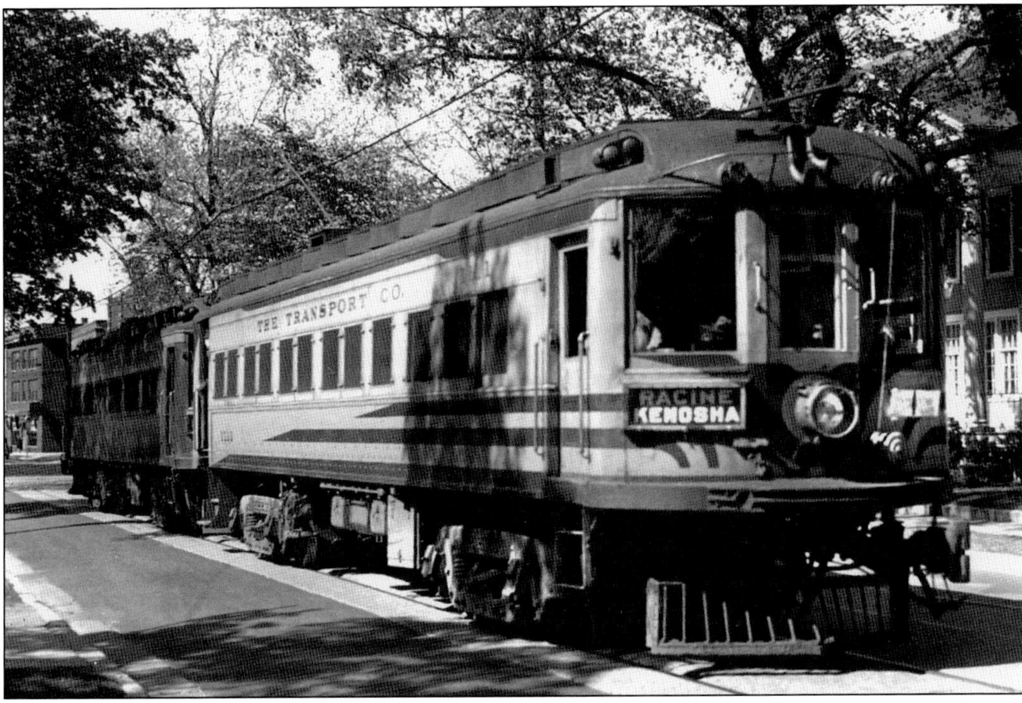

KMCL car No. 1115 leading a two-car train, glides down a shady Wisconsin Avenue in Racine on the third segment of its run to Kenosha in June 1945. The streamline livery is chrome yellow and dark green with a black roof. (Photograph by GK, courtesy of KPA.)

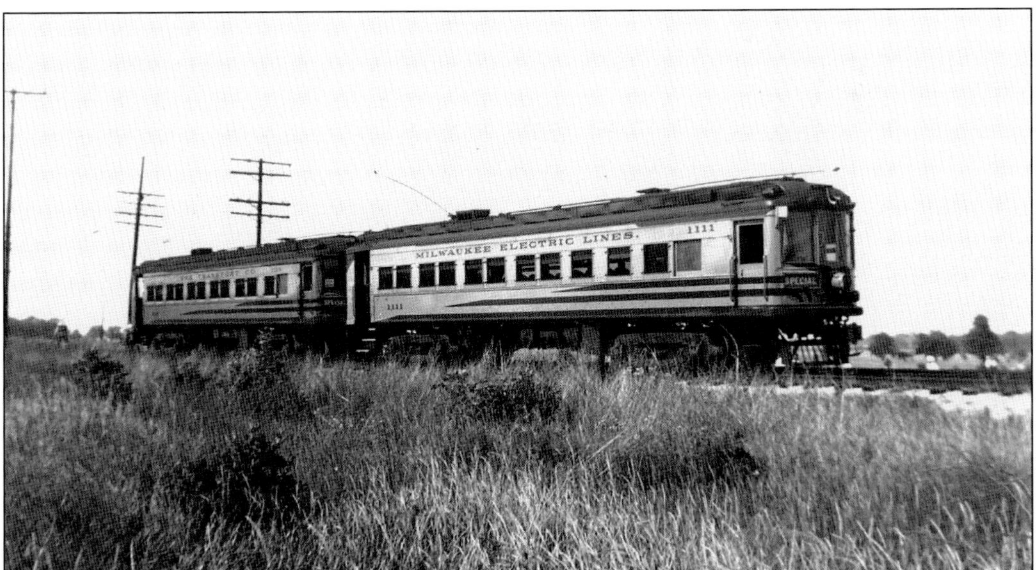

KMCL cars Nos. 1111 and 1118 are on a special rail fan outing stop for the cameras north of Kenosha on the MRK line. This excellent high-speed transit right-of-way with its bridges, trestles, and embankments was completely rebuilt to high-speed standards between 1928 and 1932. Unfortunately by December 31, 1947, the entire line would be abandoned. (Photograph by FK, courtesy of WRK.)

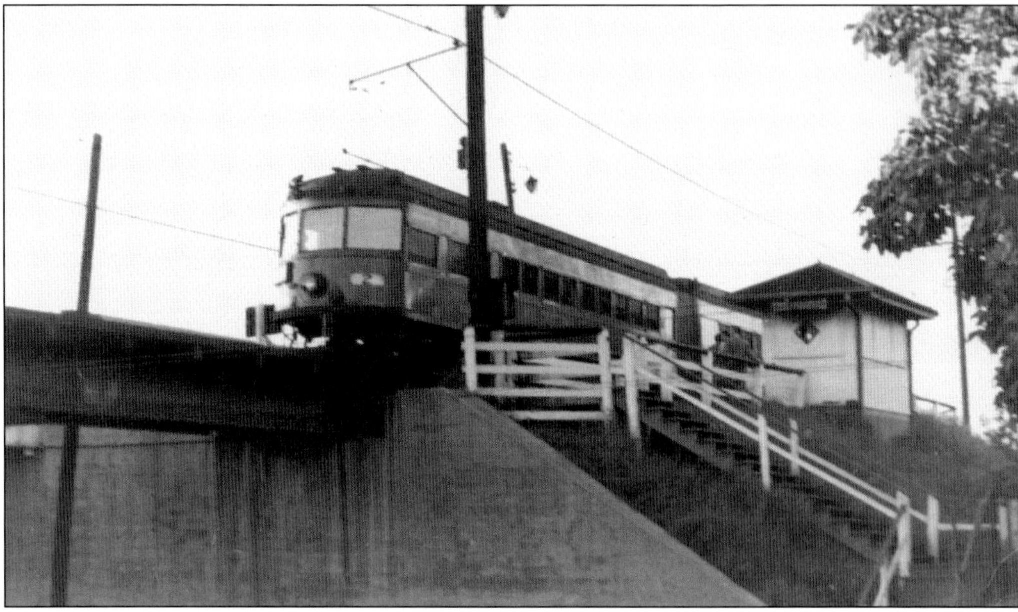

On the last day of interurban service to Kenosha, a southbound MRK train stops at Washington Road, Kenosha, on September 13, 1947. The MRK would share the elevated structure with the North Western from Thirty-fifth Street before veering away southeast at Forty-fifth Street. (Photograph by JEG.)

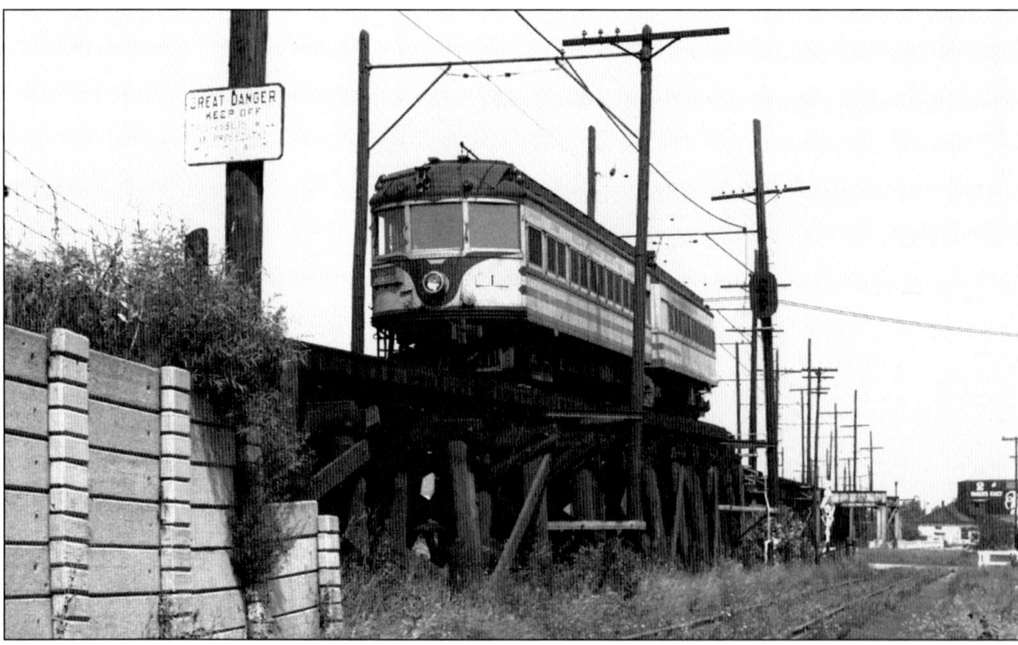

This pictorial ride over the MRK is about to end as KMCL duplex car Nos. 1182 and 1183 is coming down the wood piling section of right-of-way to the Kenosha downtown MRK terminal. The interurban has just crossed the North Western spur track, Pike Creek, Sheridan Road, and Fifty-second Street on the combination bridge and trestle. (Photograph by JFH, courtesy of RH.)

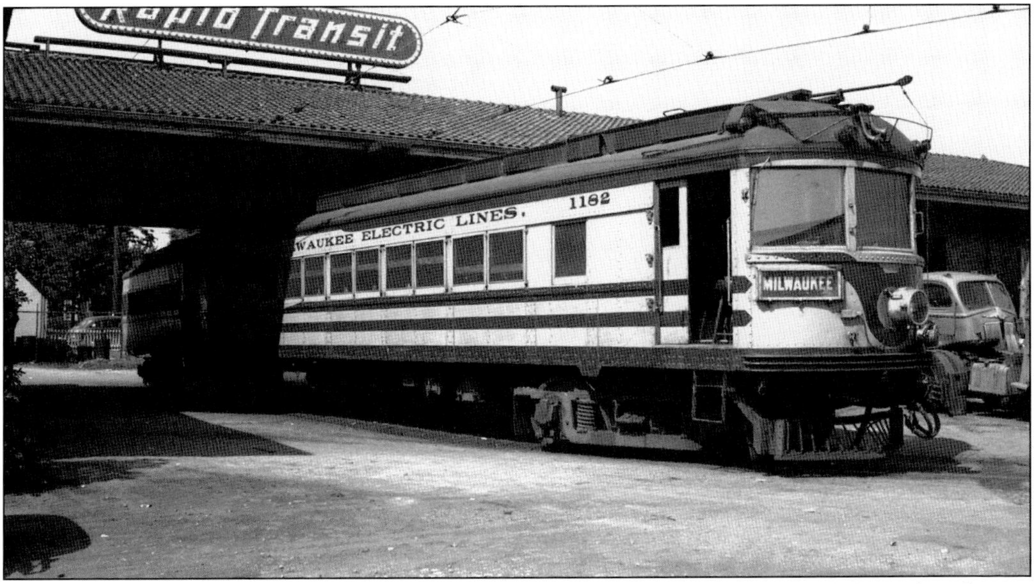

The pictorial ride has ended as KMCL duplex car Nos. 1182 and 1183, signed for Milwaukee, is waiting departure time at the Kenosha MRK depot on August 24, 1947. In less than three weeks, September 13, 1947, the line between Kenosha and Racine would be abandoned. (Photograph by JFH, courtesy of RH.)

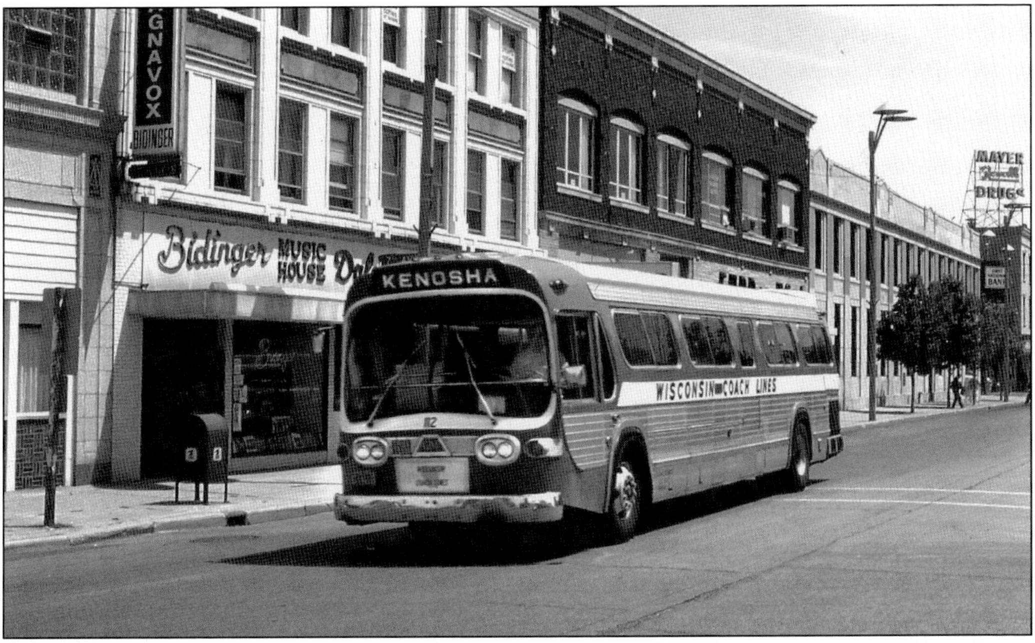

Waukesha Transit Lines started branching out in interurban bus service in 1951 and was reorganized as Wisconsin Coach Lines in the 1960s. In this June 1981 scene, General Motors suburban diesel bus No. 115, fitted with larger seats and overhead luggage racks, is seen on Fifty-sixth Street looking east. Painted in a livery of lime green, cream, and white, the bus will operate between Kenosha, Racine, and Milwaukee. (Photograph by DOE.)

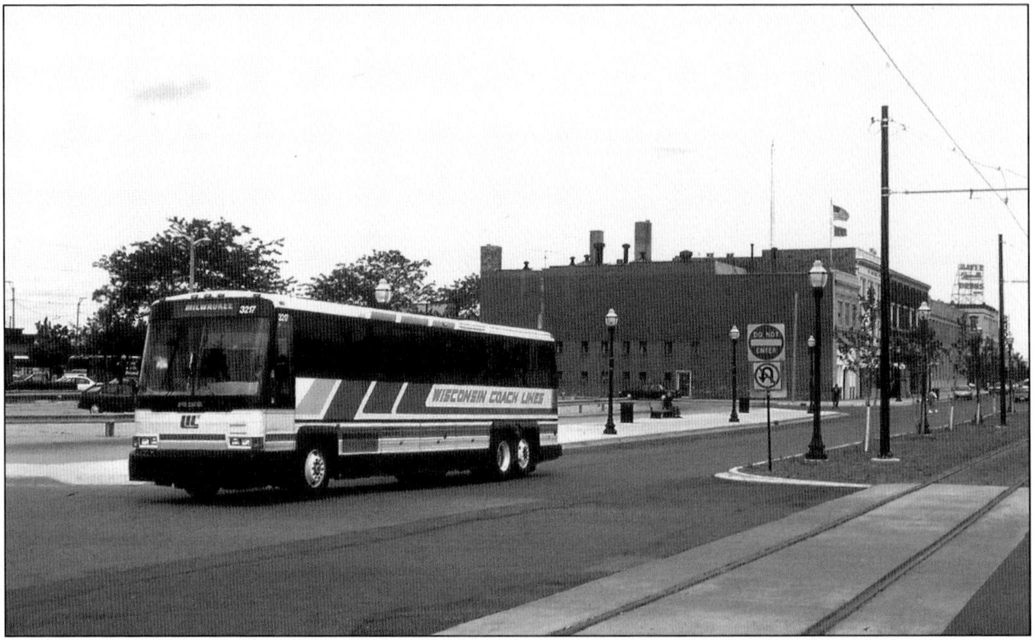

In June 2000, Wisconsin Coach Lines No. 3217 is using this inter-city coach to provide service between downtown Milwaukee, Mitchell Field, Racine, and Kenosha, following some of the old MRK interurban route. Seen here westbound on Fifty-sixth Street, the bus is painted lime green, chrome yellow, and light cream. (Photograph by DOE.)

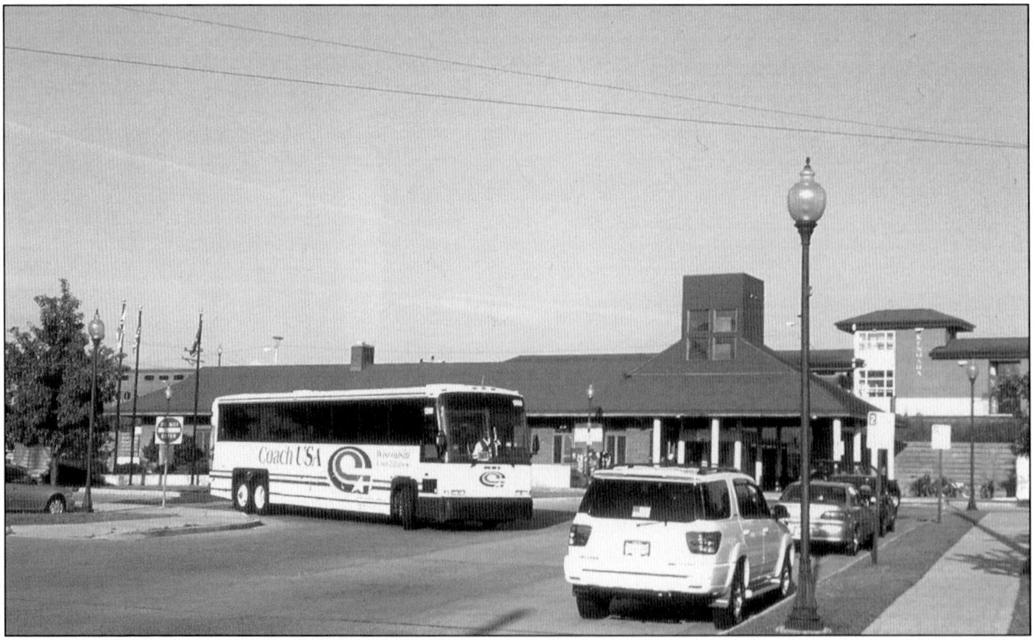

On a midsummer morning in June 2006, Coach USA No. 1208 is seen here leaving the Kenosha Metra Station at Thirteenth Avenue, turning east into Fifty-fourth Street. The bus painted, white with red and blue trim, is beginning its northward journey to Milwaukee making local stops along the way. By this time, Wisconsin Coach Lines was part of Coach USA. (Photograph by DOE.)

Three

The North Shore Line

The North Shore interurban to Chicago and Milwaukee provided convenience for the citizens of Kenosha. The North Shore interurban also provided freight service along the route and pioneered piggyback operations in 1927. The North Shore Line would bring its riders into the heart of Chicago via the elevated rapid transit tracks. North of Kenosha, the North Shore interurban stopped at Racine, and then entered city-street running on the south side of Milwaukee to its downtown terminal at Sixth and Michigan Streets.

Imagine the year 1950; a mother is waiting at the Kenosha North Shore station for the Saturday, 11:40 a.m. southbound Electroliner to Chicago with her two small sons. As they look north into the distance, the bright headlight becomes apparent. The Electroliner running through the middle of the Nash plant begins to slow for the Kenosha stop. The mother instinctively pulls the boys back so they are far from the tip of the platform. The Electroliner stops, and the conductor and collector quickly gather their passengers. With a signal from the conductor to the motorman, the Electroliner accelerates away from Kenosha. Making three more stops at Zion, Waukegan, and North Chicago, the train will soon be running nonstop across the Skokie Valley route. Ordering lunch from the menu in the club car, the selections are the Electroburger with chips, homemade pie, coffee for mother, and milk for the boys.

At Howard Street, the Electroliner makes its first Chicago stop and enters the elevated express tracks of the Chicago Transit Authority (CTA) for its journey across the "L" into the Chicago Loop. Arriving at Randolph and Wells Streets, the Kenosha riders walk to the Oriental Theater for a movie and a stage show. Afterwards dinner is chicken pot pie, served at Stouffer's next to the Trailways bus depot at Randolph and State Streets. After dessert, it is a short walk to the stairway leading to the Wabash and Randolph Streets "L" station just in time to catch the 7:00 p.m. Limited North Shore train to Kenosha. Arriving at 8:22 p.m. in Kenosha, is there anything left after a day like this?

Yes, let's go to Jack Andrea's Confectionery for ice cream.

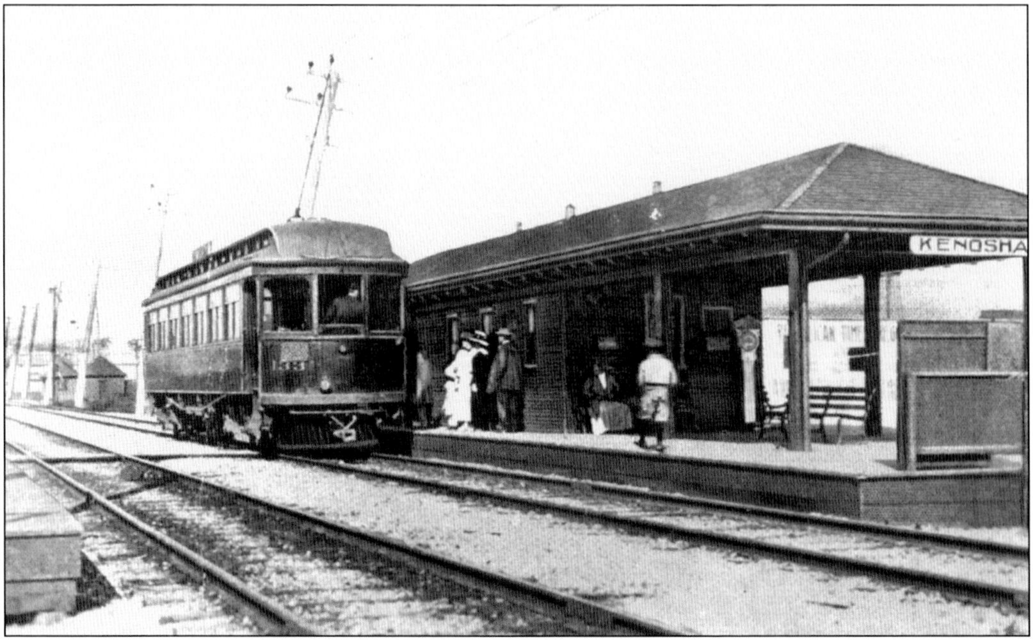

In this postcard view, a northbound interurban can be seen at the original Chicago and Milwaukee Electric Railroad's Kenosha train station at Elizabeth and Erie Streets (Sixty-third Street and Twenty-seventh Avenue). Train doors on the ends would be added later so conductors could move freely between cars. Built by the Jewett Car Company in 1907, this wooden car had an interesting career ending 45 years later on the Chicago, Aurora and Elgin Railway. (Courtesy of JH.)

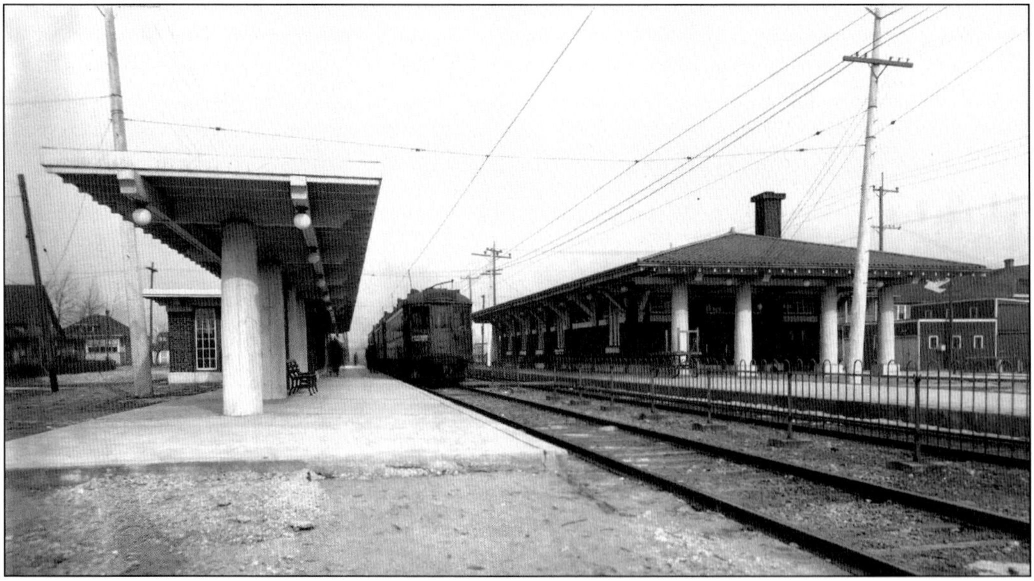

The new Kenosha North Shore station was influenced by the prairie-style architecture of Frank Lloyd Wright and is seen here shortly after completion in 1922. The plans for these buildings were drawn by the North Shore Line's architect Arthur V. Gerber. Looking north to Elizabeth Street (Sixty-third Street), the building to the right still stands today. (Photograph by AFS, courtesy of TJJ.)

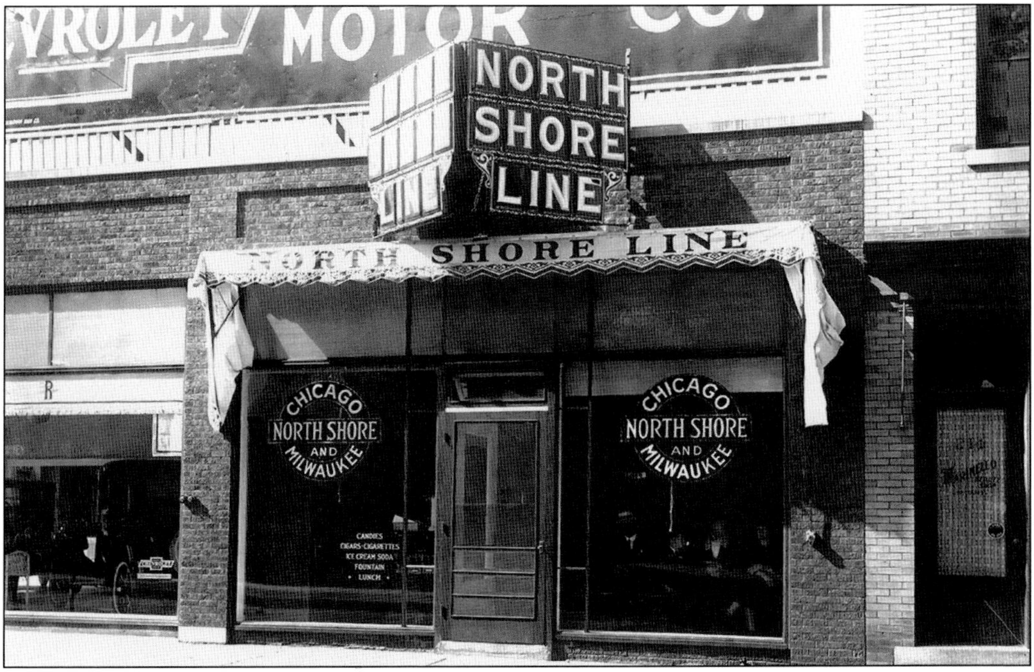

In the 1920s, the North Shore was quick to take advantage of using buses. Bus service would be provided to Lake Geneva, a favorite resort area 35 miles west of Kenosha, and to Waukegan. Seen here in downtown Kenosha on August 17, 1923, is the North Shore bus station located in the Downey Recht Motor Company building at 216 South Street. Although hardly recognizable, the building still stands. Today the doorway on Fifty-ninth Street (to right in the photograph) is numbered 614½ and is just west of Sixth Avenue. (Photograph by AFS, courtesy of TJJ.)

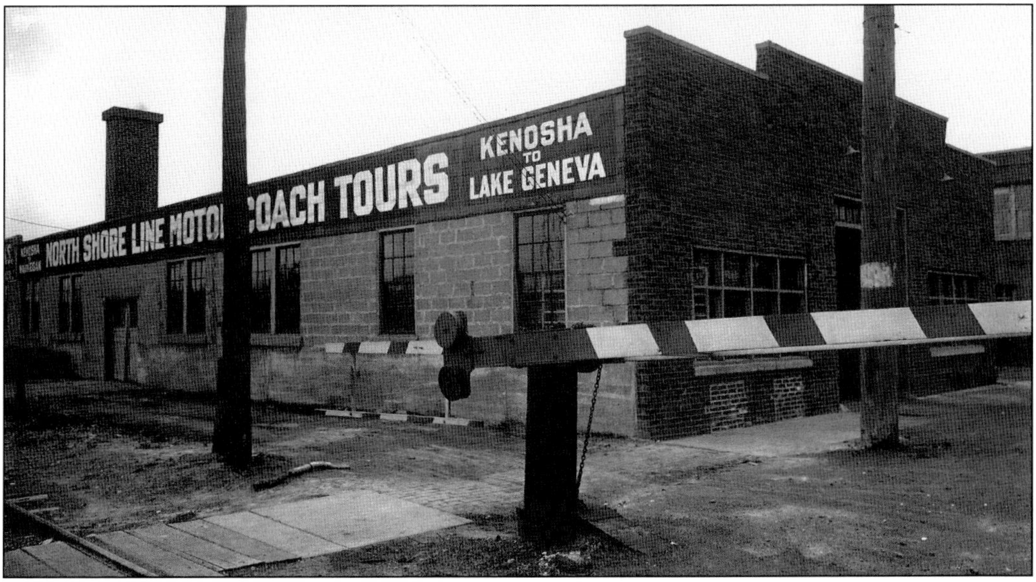

The North Shore bus garage is seen here next to the Kenosha team track on October 25, 1923. This picture is taken from Sixty-fourth Street between Twenty-seventh and Twenty-eighth Avenues looking southwest. The building still stands today with its distinctive chimney and is part of a roofing company's complex. (Photograph by AFS, courtesy of TJJ.)

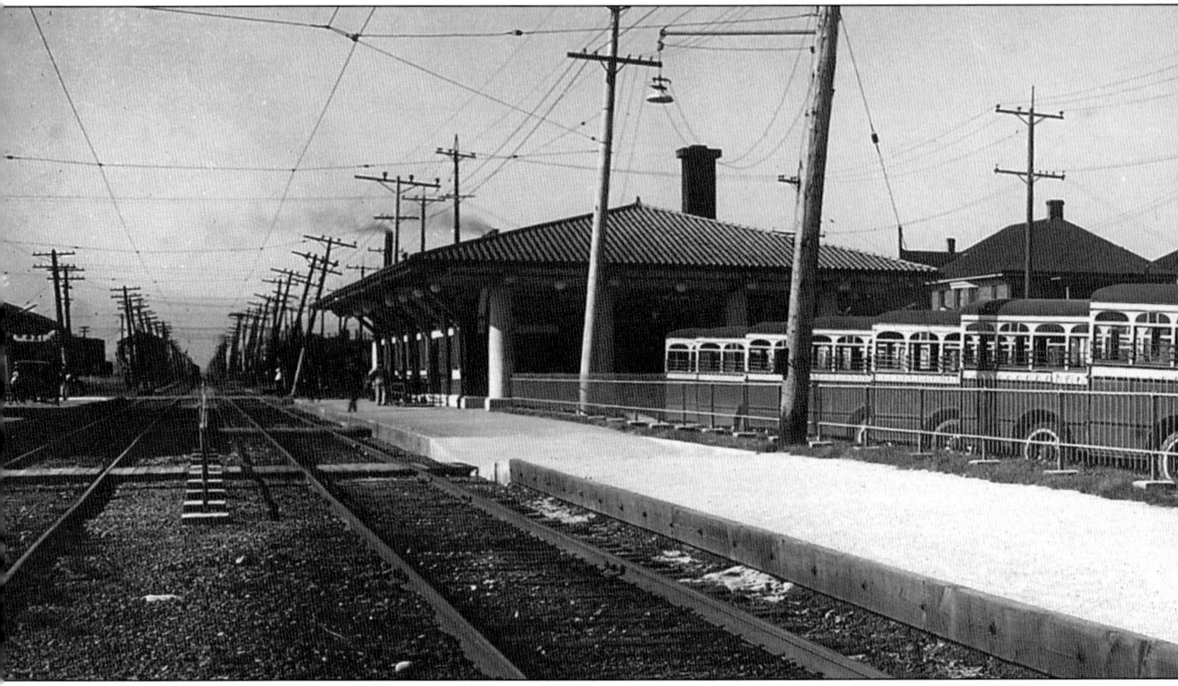

The Chicago, North Shore and Milwaukee Railroad inaugurated bus service from Kenosha to the resort area of Lake Geneva on August 12, 1922. The trip would take 1 hour and 15 minutes, which was a great convenience at the time. The North Shore also ran a parallel local bus

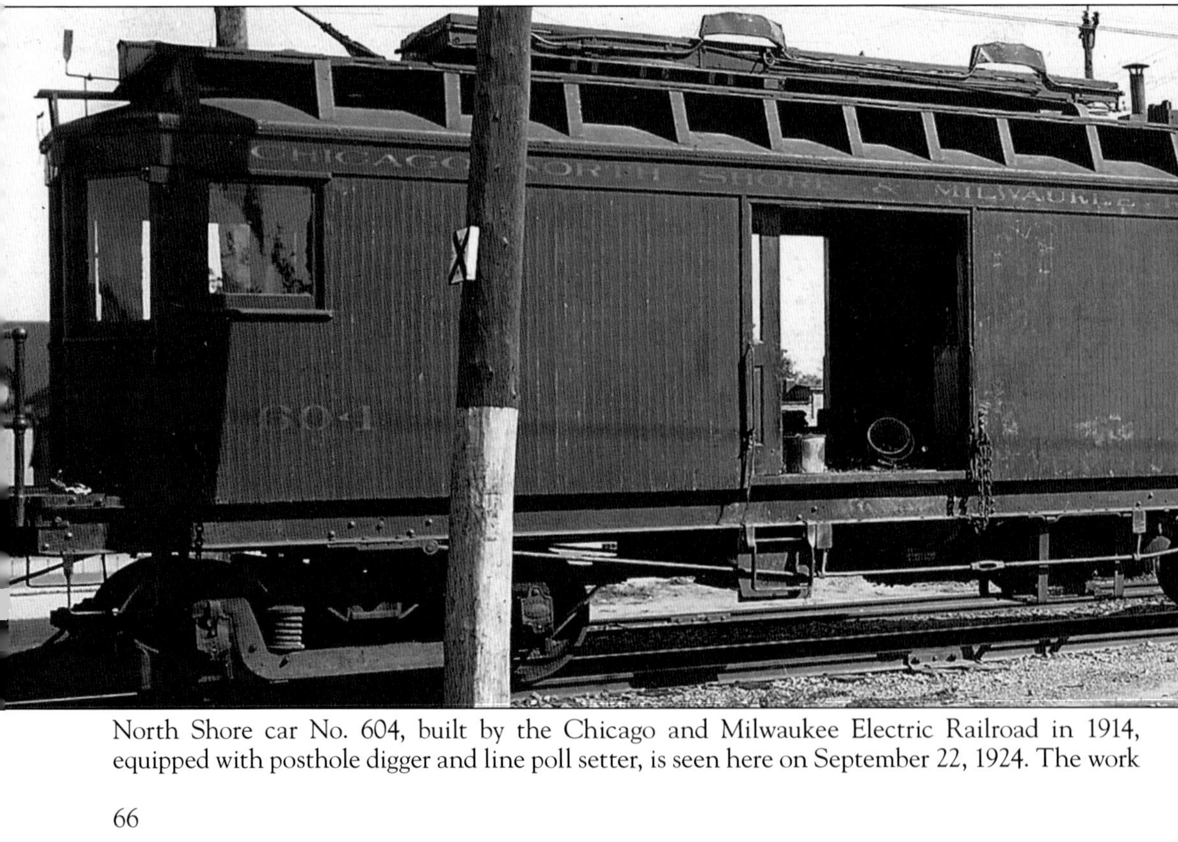

North Shore car No. 604, built by the Chicago and Milwaukee Electric Railroad in 1914, equipped with posthole digger and line poll setter, is seen here on September 22, 1924. The work

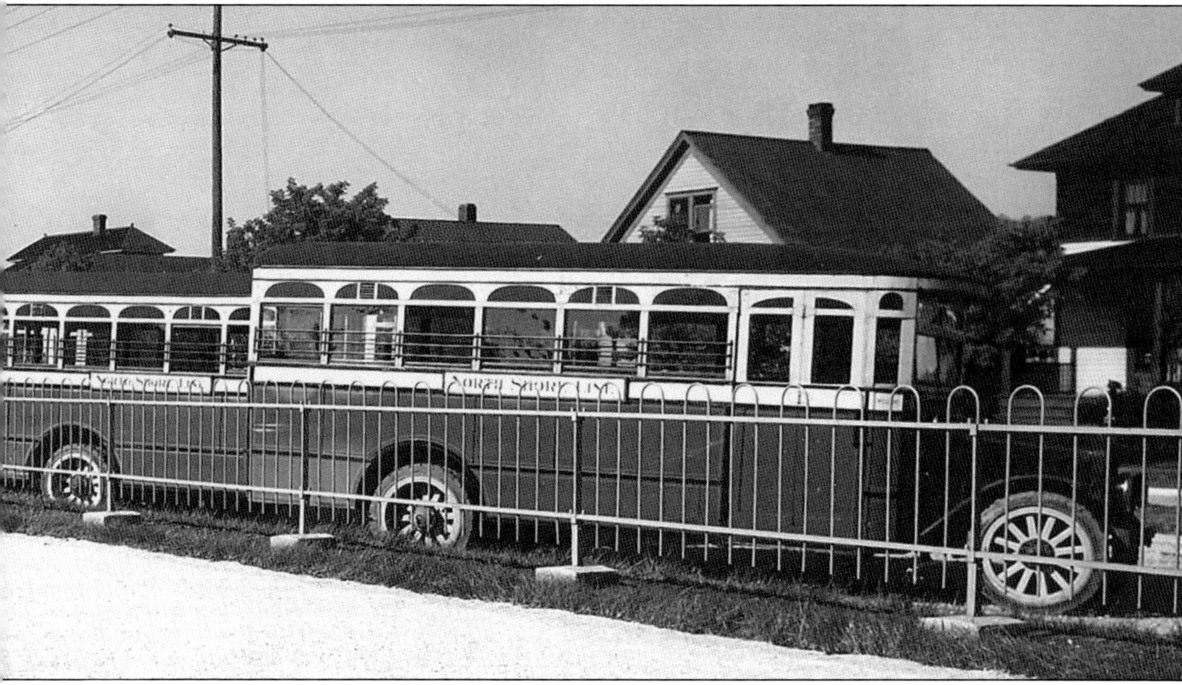

line between Kenosha and Waukegan. On July 1, 1928, the North Shore sold the bus lines to Metropolitan Motor Coach. The buses seen here are lined up at the Kenosha North Shore depot (looking north) on July 12, 1923. (Photograph by AFS, courtesy of KPA.)

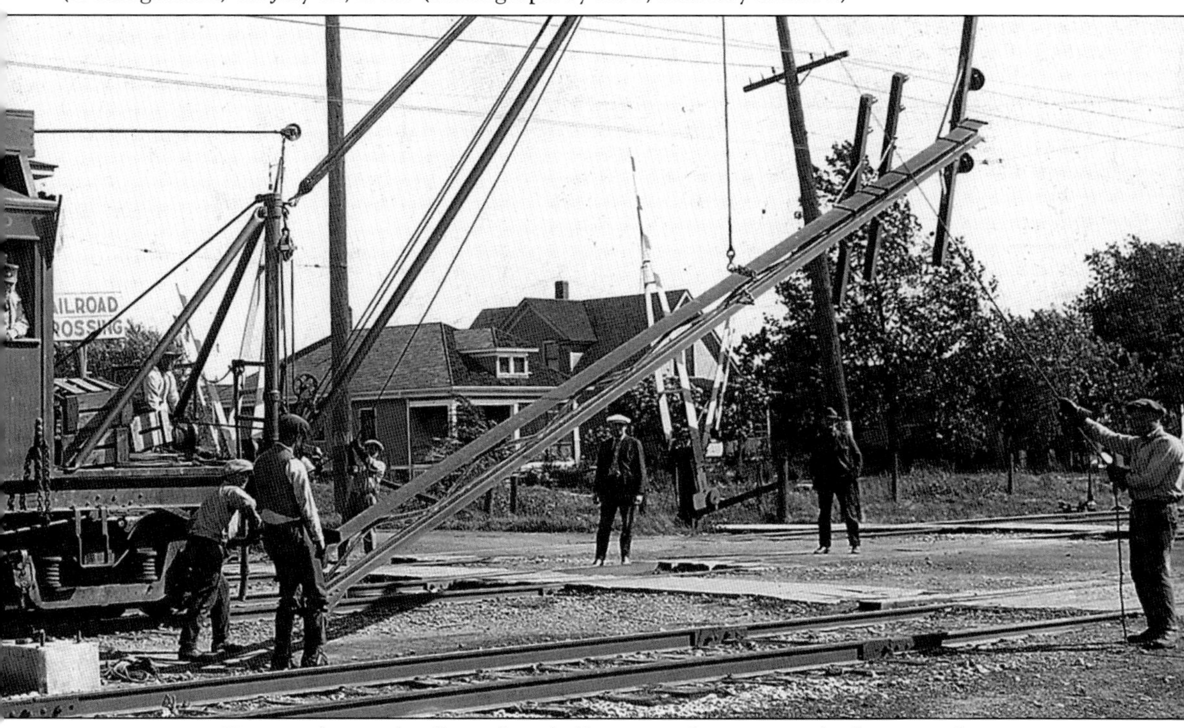

crew is setting Bates poles at the Sixty-fourth Street grade crossing, looking southeast across Twenty-seventh Avenue (Erie Street until 1926). (Photograph by AFS, courtesy of KPA.)

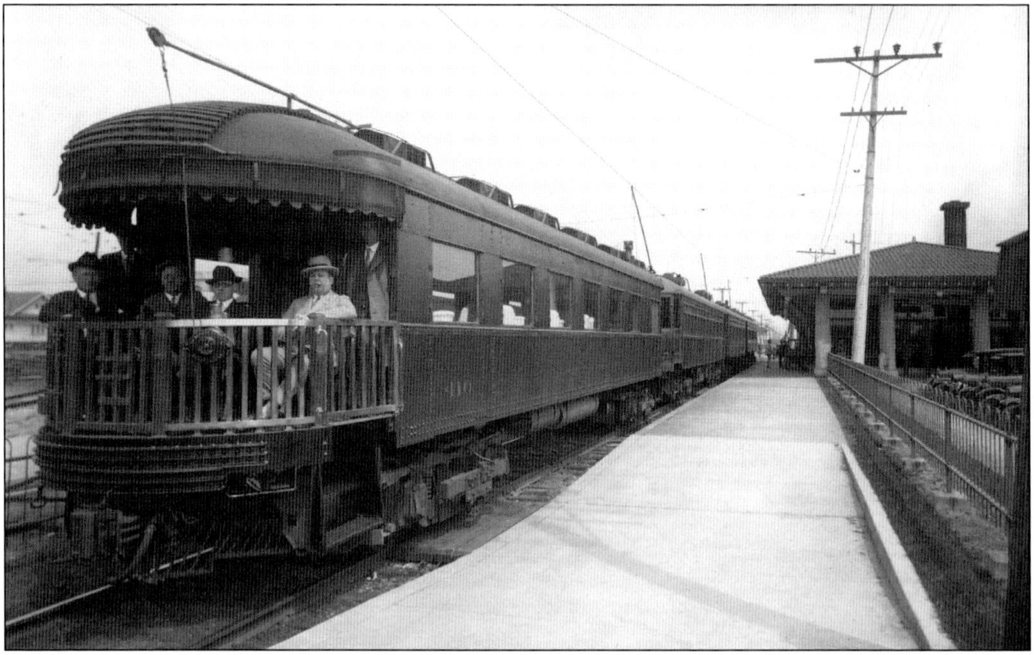

A five-car North Shore train with dignitaries is northbound at the Kenosha station in 1924. The livery on the cars is dark olive green, orange trim, and a terra-cotta red roof. Car No. 410 was one of four parlor observation cars built by the Cincinnati Car Company and entered service on July 11, 1923. The cars were rebuilt in 1942 as full-passenger coaches. (Photograph by AFS, courtesy of KPA.)

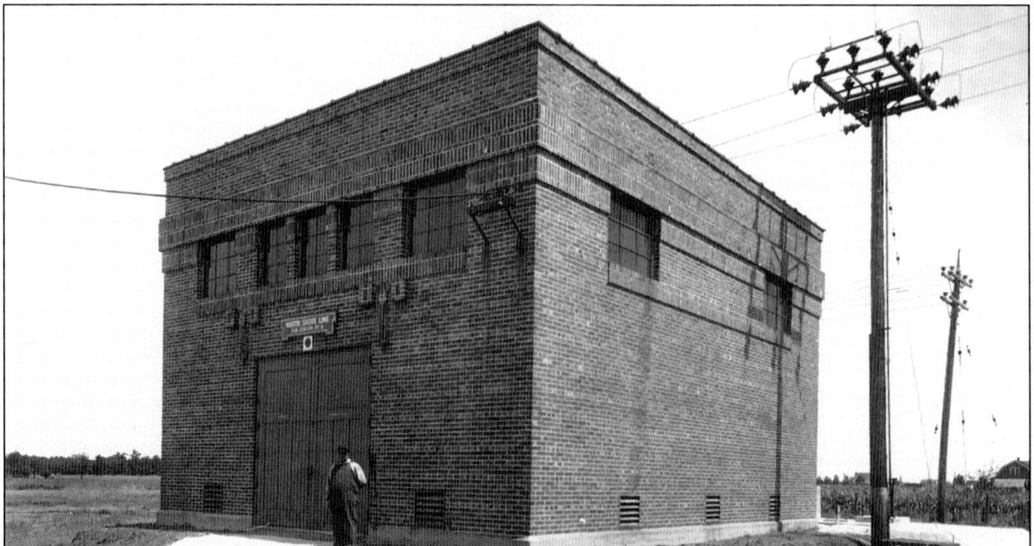

On August 15, 1932, the corn is high behind the new automated North Shore substation. Providing power for the rail line, this building stood at what would later become a through street—Forty-fifth Street just east of Twenty-eighth Avenue. The building was demolished 40 years after the railway was abandoned. Looking southeast, there is scant evidence of housing. (Photograph by AFS, courtesy of TJJ.)

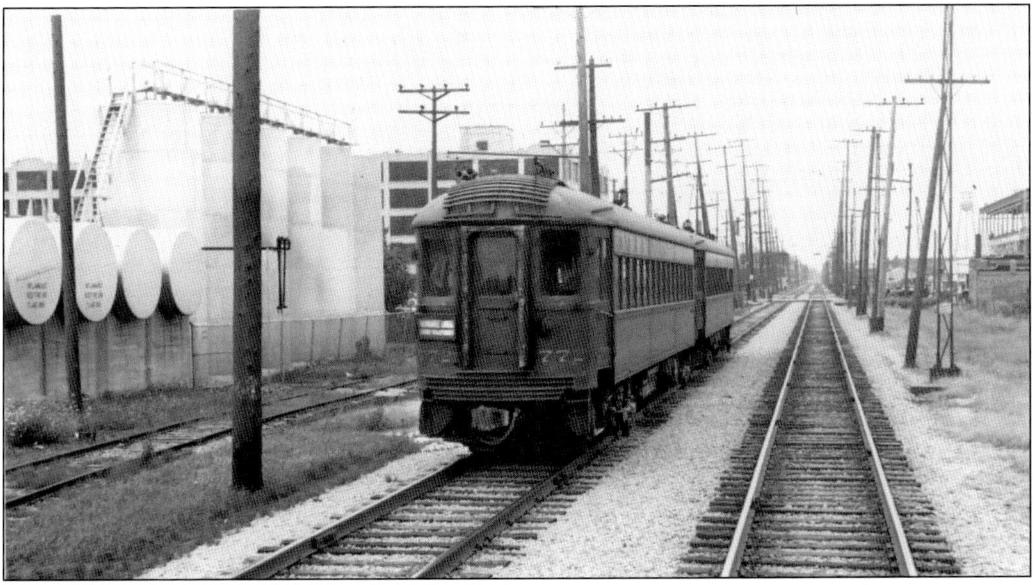

With its motorman standing, a Milwaukee Limited train, led by car No. 772, has just cleared the Fifty-second Street Kenosha crossing of the North Shore Line. With the gates still down in this 1950s scene, it is evident that the photograph was taken from the front platform of a fast-moving southbound train. (Courtesy of JJK, RAE.)

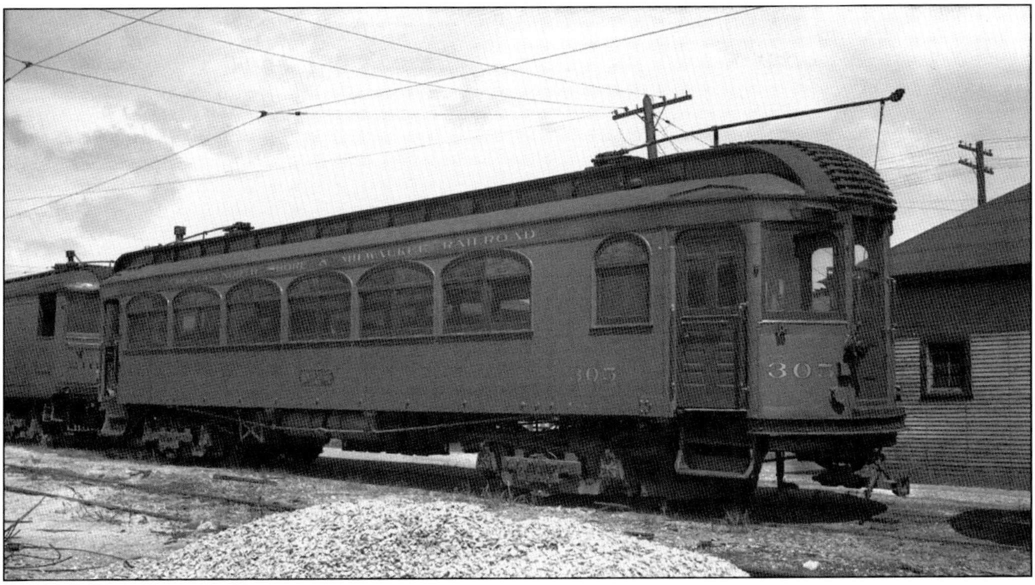

This wooden interurban, built for the Chicago and Milwaukee Electric Railroad by American Car Company in 1910, originally served Kenosha on Chicago/Milwaukee limited runs. Car No. 305, painted orange with maroon doors and letter board and a terra-cotta red roof, is seen here at Highwood, Illinois, on August 22, 1937. After replacement with steel cars in 1915, they served in Chicago–Waukegan suburban service on the Shore Line route. The cars became sleet cutters in 1936 and were scrapped in 1940. (Photograph by JFH, courtesy of RH.)

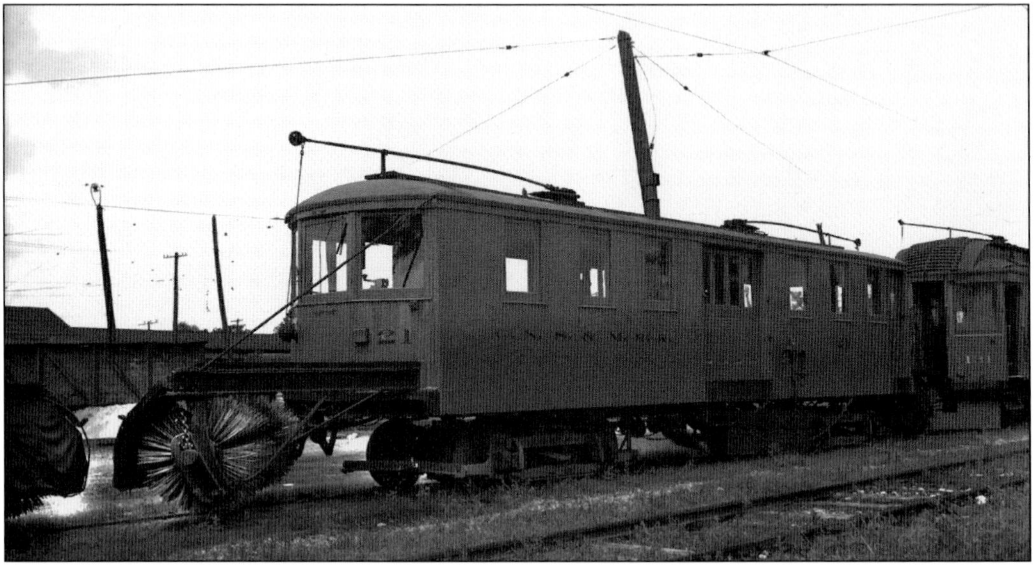

When the snow came, the North Shore Line was ready. The large snow sweeper was built for the Chicago and Milwaukee Electric Railroad in 1908 by the Maguire Car and Manufacturing Company. Seen here at Highwood, Illinois, on August 22, 1937, the car had removable brooms and could be used in work service. Sweeper No. 21 was retired in 1950. (Photograph by JFH, courtesy of RH.)

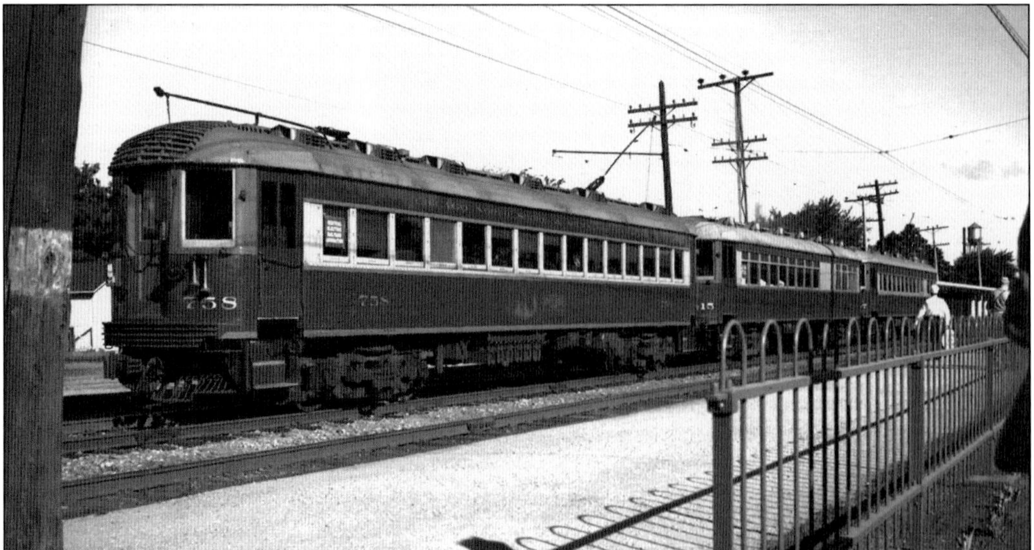

A three-car North Shore train on charter No. 16 of the CERA is seen here at the Kenosha depot on September 17, 1939. Southbound cars Nos. 758, 415, and 757 are splendid in their new paint livery of green, light gray-green, red trim, and gray roof. (Photograph by JFH, courtesy of RH.)

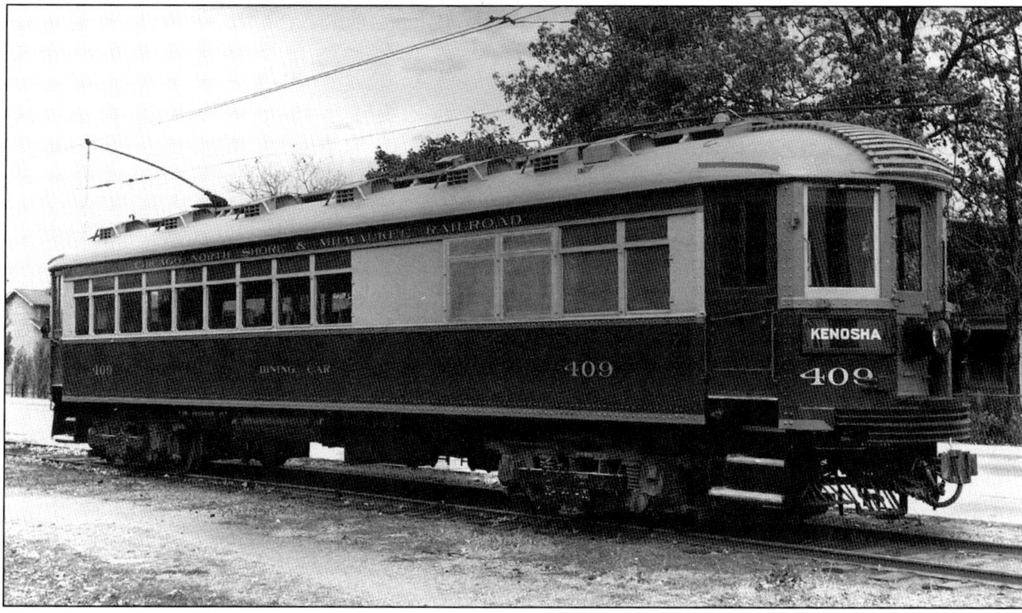

Chicago, North Shore and Milwaukee Railroad diner car No. 409 stands freshly painted at Highwood, Illinois, in the new livery on October 8, 1939. The colors of the car were light gray roof, light gray-green upper body with dark green doors, upper letter board, and lower body. The front window trim, train end doors, and body striping were painted in brilliant red. Notice that the car is signed for Kenosha. In 1942, car No. 409 would be converted to a coach and in 1955, painted as a Silverliner. (Photograph by GK, courtesy of KPA.)

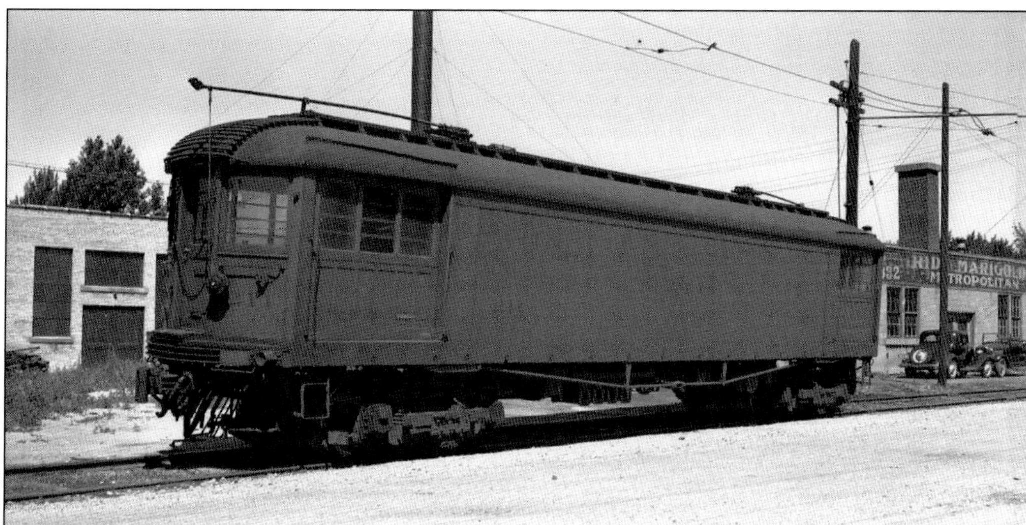

North Shore merchandise dispatch car No. 211, painted bright orange with a dark terra-cotta red roof, sits on the Kenosha team track just south of Sixty-fourth Street looking northwest on July 16, 1939. The building on the right still stands today and was the North Shore Line's Kenosha bus garage; later it would be the garage for Marigold and Metropolitan Coach Lines. (Photograph by JFH, courtesy of RH.)

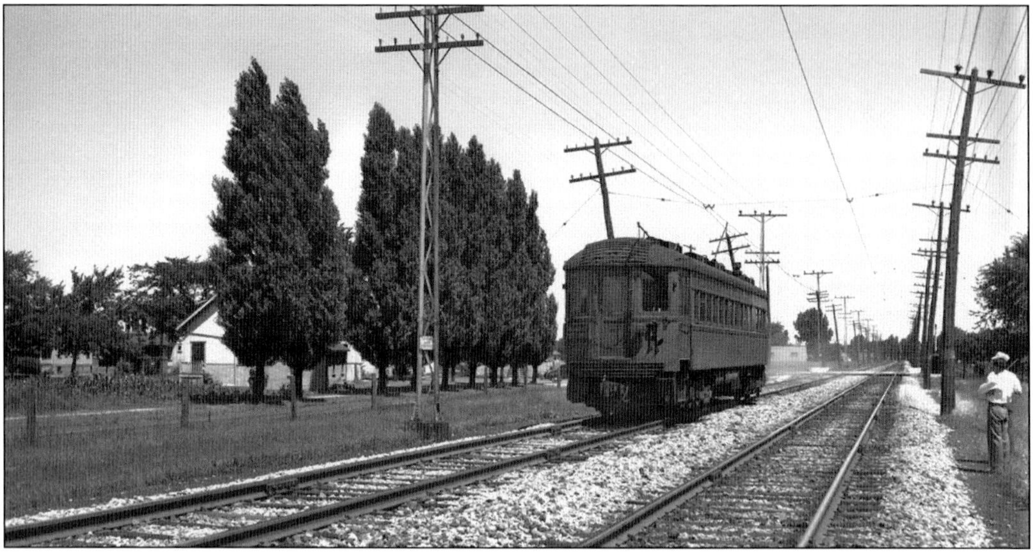

The motorman of North Shore train No. 412 has car No. 752 kicking up dust as he leaves the south end of Kenosha at high speed. This Chicago Limited train is operating here on the Milwaukee Division on July 16, 1939, and is painted orange with maroon trim. (Photograph by JFH, courtesy of RH.)

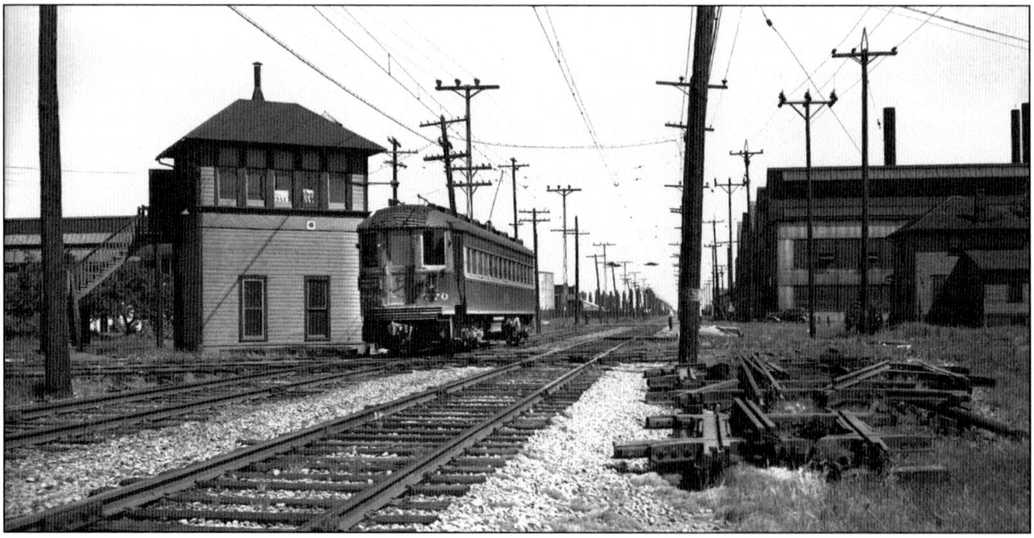

The gates on Sixtieth Street are starting to go up as Chicago, North Shore and Milwaukee Railroad southbound train No. 410 has just run through the middle of the Nash plant on July 16, 1939. Racing across the tracks of the North Western Railroad's KD Line, car No. 770 will start braking for the Kenosha stop three blocks away at Sixty-third Street. (Photograph by JFH, photograph by RH.)

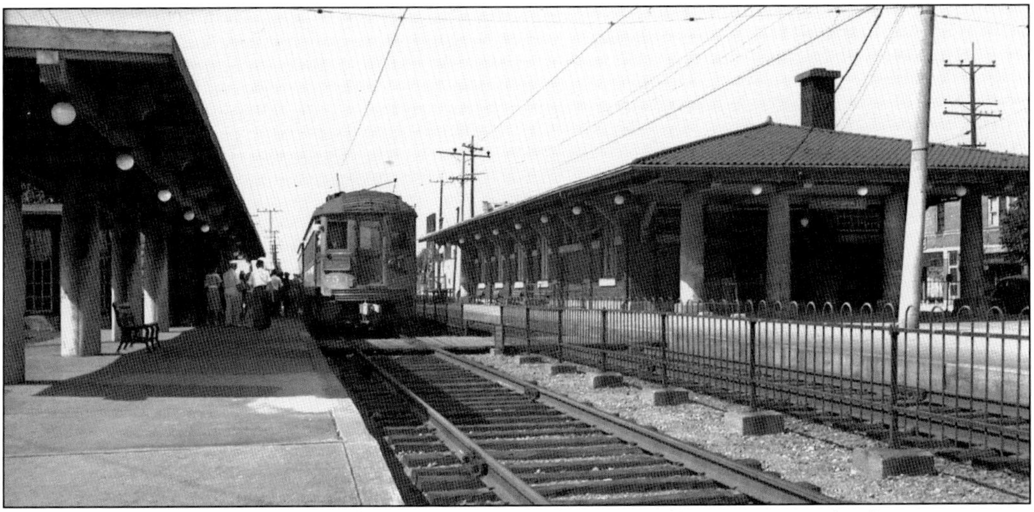

While the motorman peers out the cab window, North Shore train No. 420 loads passengers at the Kenosha train station on July 16, 1939. After the passengers are aboard this two-car train, led by car No. 754, the conductor will signal the motorman; the train will quickly accelerate south away from the Kenosha train station with the next stop being Zion, Illinois. (Photograph by JHF, courtesy of RH.)

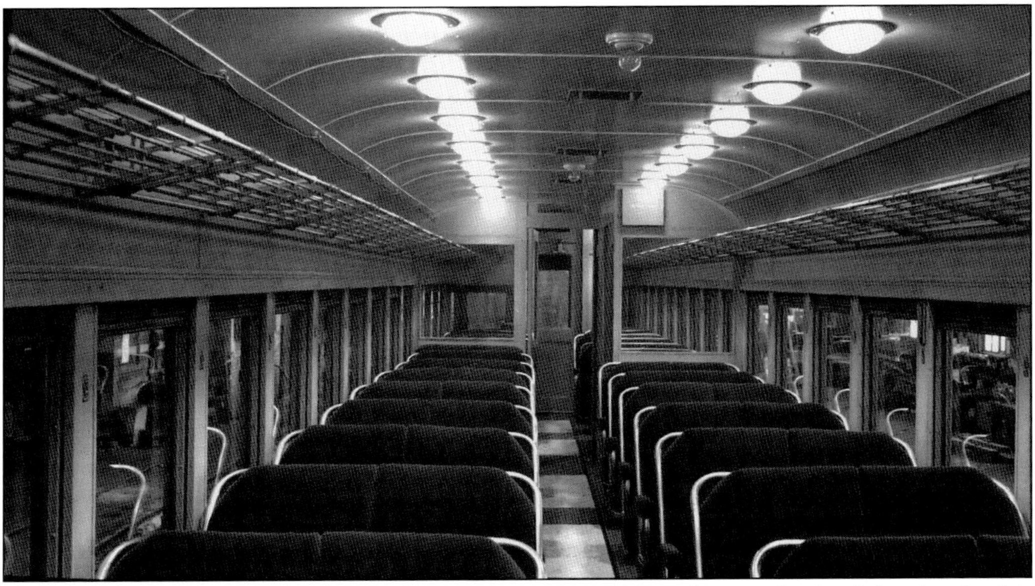

The North Shore modernized several cars starting in 1939 to the standards of the day. In this picture taken on April 20, 1941, the interior of coach No. 739 can be seen, built by Pullman Standard in 1928 and remodeled in 1940. By August 1950, the car would be modernized one more time into a Silverliner. (Photograph by JHF, courtesy of RH.)

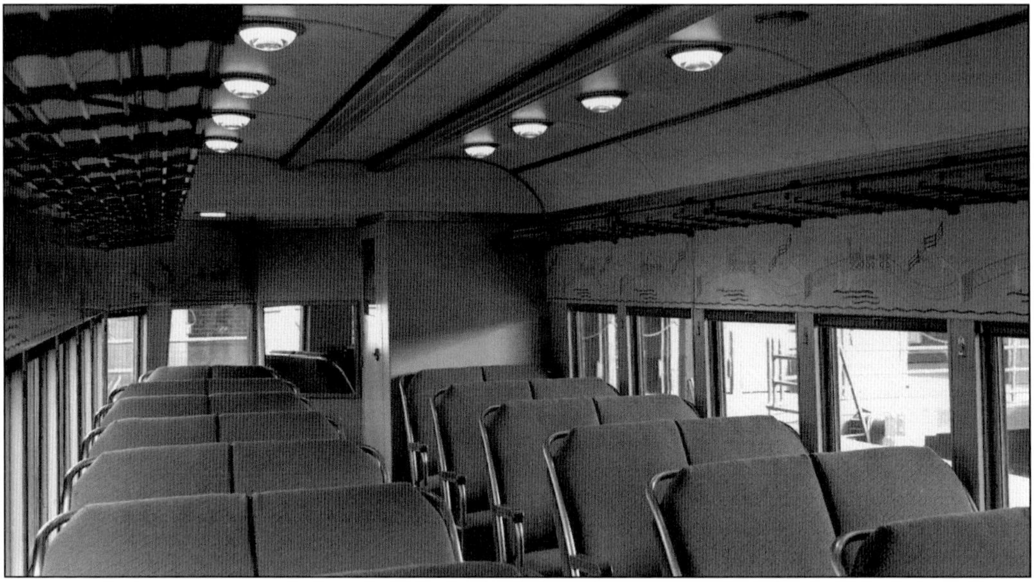

This interior view of Electroliner No. 804A was taken on February 23, 1941, when the two streamliners were new. This view is looking toward the motorman's cab to the right. The interiors of the four units comprising this articulated train were painted separately in shades of pastel coral, silver gray, and apricot, complemented by murals painted on the walls. (Photograph by JFH, courtesy of RH.)

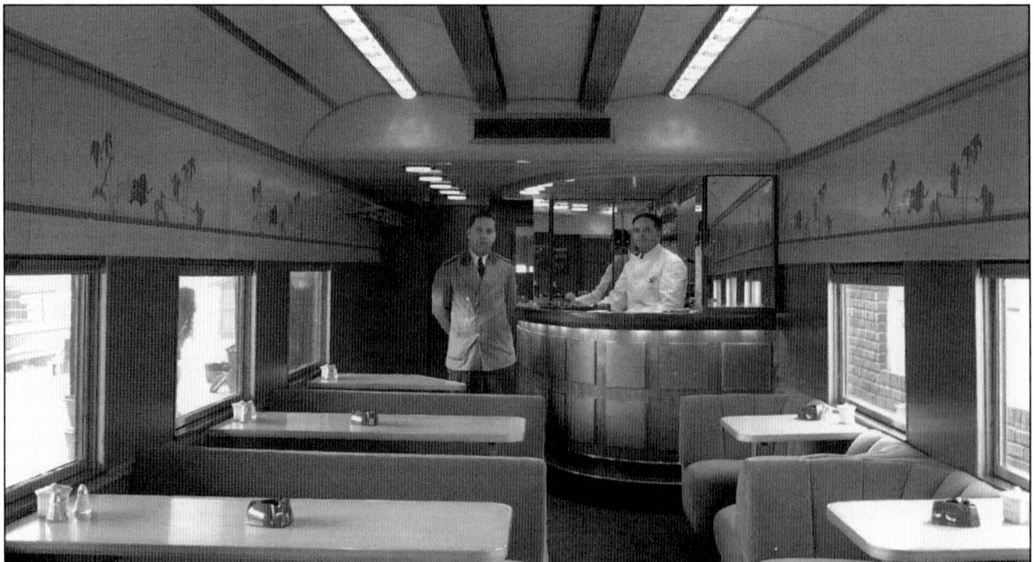

As small as it appears behind the bar of the tavern lounge car, there was adequate space and equipment to prepare food and drink for the passengers aboard the Electroliner. (Photograph by JFH, courtesy of RH.)

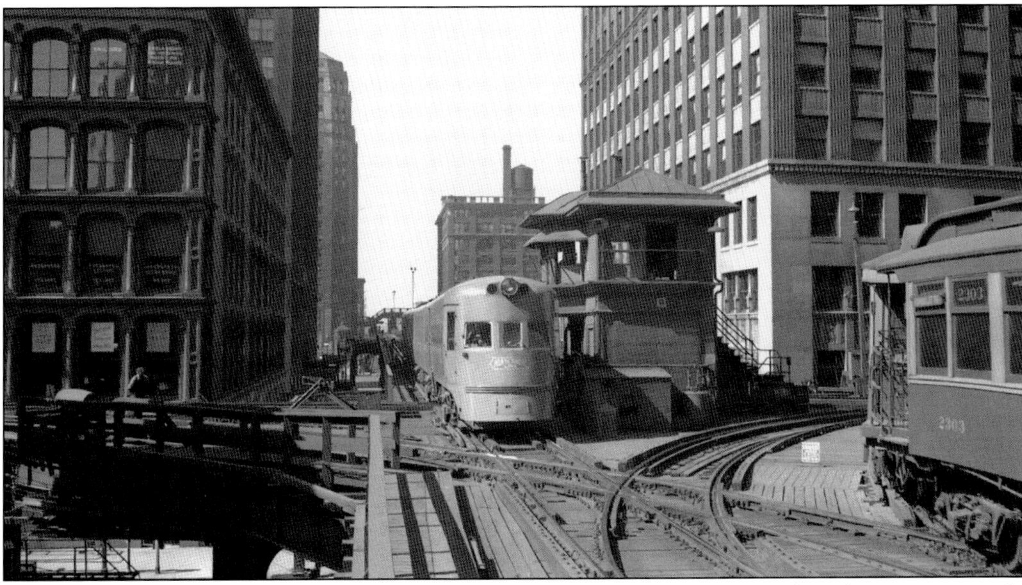

A new North Shore Electroliner has just crossed the Chicago River and is about to enter the Chicago Elevated Loop at the Lake and Wells Streets tower. The scene is looking north on May 24, 1941. This excellent railroad provided Kenosha riders with direct access to the Chicago Loop. Note in the right of the picture is a Humboldt Park "L" gate car No. 2303 of the Chicago Rapid Transit Company. (Photograph by JFH, courtesy of RH.)

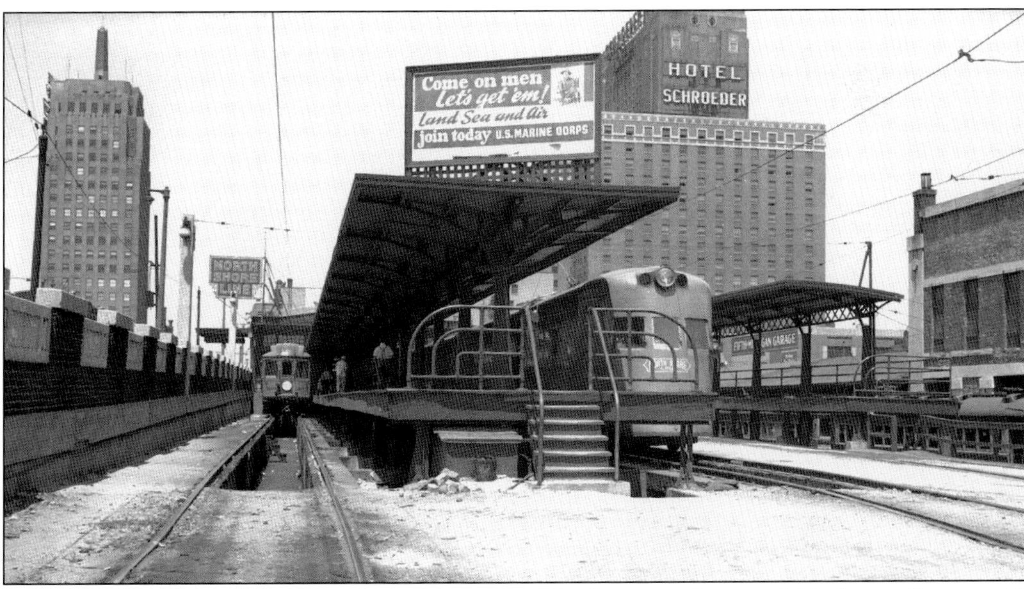

At the North Shore Milwaukee depot, this view is looking north toward Michigan Street, with Sixth Street to the left. The photograph was taken on July 12, 1942. Electroliner train No. 804 is made up and awaiting its southbound running time. To the left, North Shore wood interurban car No. 300 is seen here on a special charter of the CERA. The rail fans are probably having lunch in the depot. (Photograph by JFH, courtesy of RH.)

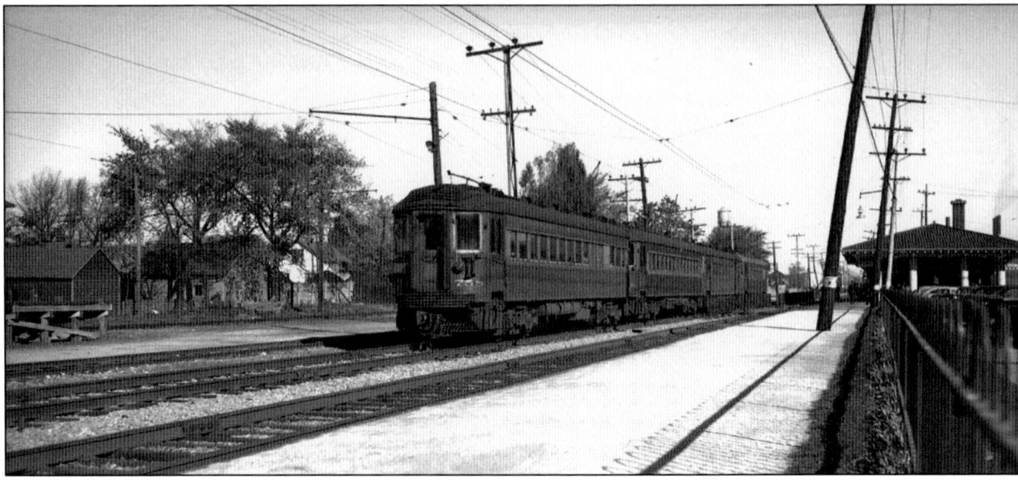

While the motorman is notching up the controller, one can almost hear the whining of the traction motors as train No. 408 leaves the Kenosha train station on October 22, 1944. Led by car No. 758, this four-car train is about to cross Sixty-fourth Street. With the conductor and collectors taking tickets, this southbound train will soon be running at a speed of over 75 miles per hour. (Photograph by JFH, courtesy of RH.)

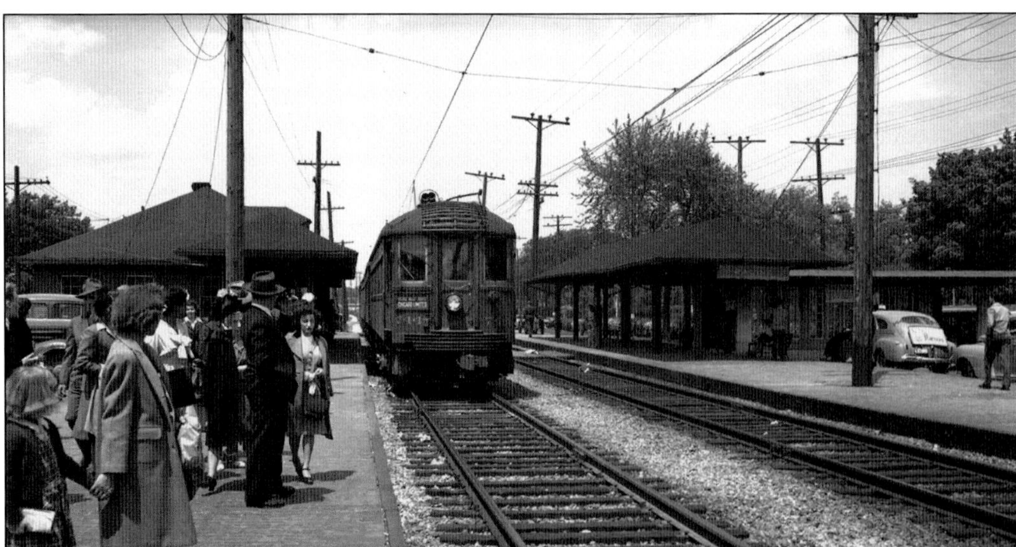

Chicago, North Shore and Milwaukee Railroad train No. 414 is about to load passengers at the busy Racine station on May 30, 1946. Led by car No. 751, the next stop for this Chicago Limited Skokie Valley train will be Kenosha. One can see that traffic on the North Shore Line following World War II was still very heavy. Once the train leaves Racine, the Kenosha station is only 10 minutes away. (Photograph by JFH, courtesy of RH.)

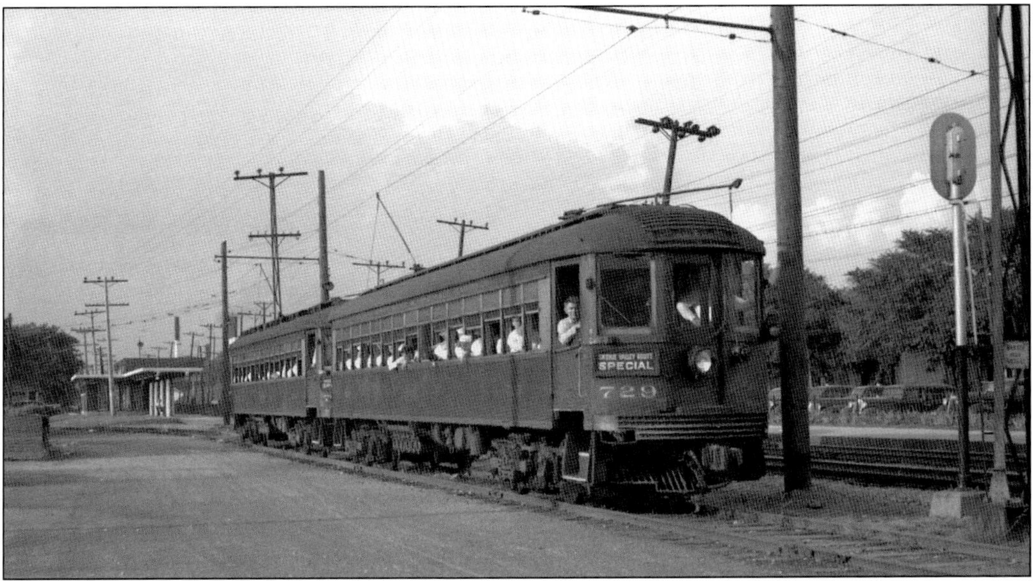

A military special is seen here at the Kenosha siding looking northeast on August 24, 1947. Apparently the sailor in the fifth window of the second car had too much of Milwaukee's finest. The Great Lakes Naval Base would charter trains on a regular basis for recruits going on liberty to either Milwaukee or Chicago. This train is waiting on the Kenosha Siding, possibly a Chicago Limited has to get in front of train X729. (Photograph by JFH, courtesy of RH.)

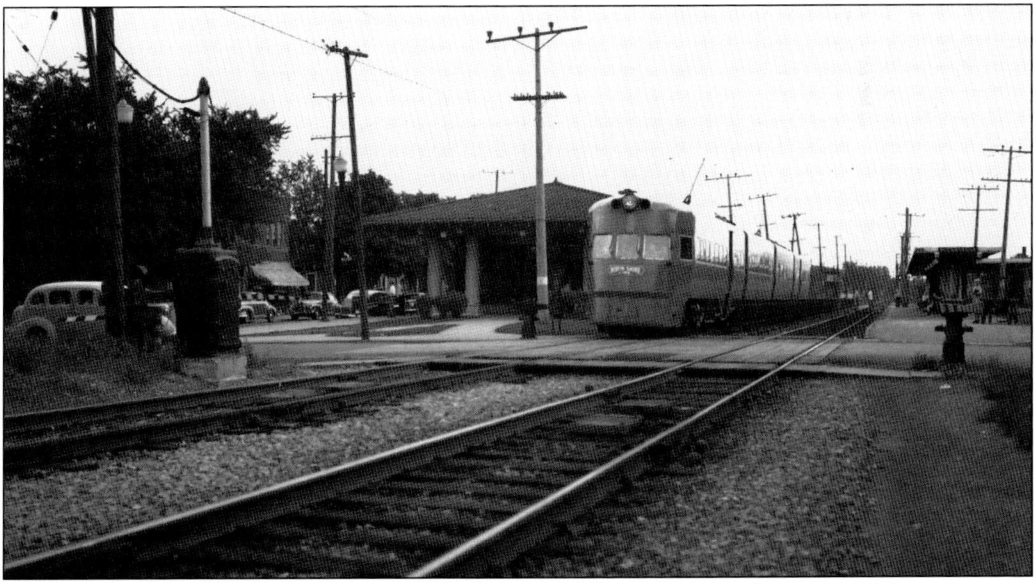

Gates are down and Electroliner No. 802-801 is starting to accelerate northbound across Sixty-third Street from the Kenosha Station on August 24, 1947. The day is likely hot, but this streamlined marvel was fully air-conditioned. Although the Electroliner was capable of traveling 105 miles per hour, the speed was governed down to 78 miles per hour with a full load of passengers. (Photograph by JFH, courtesy of RH.)

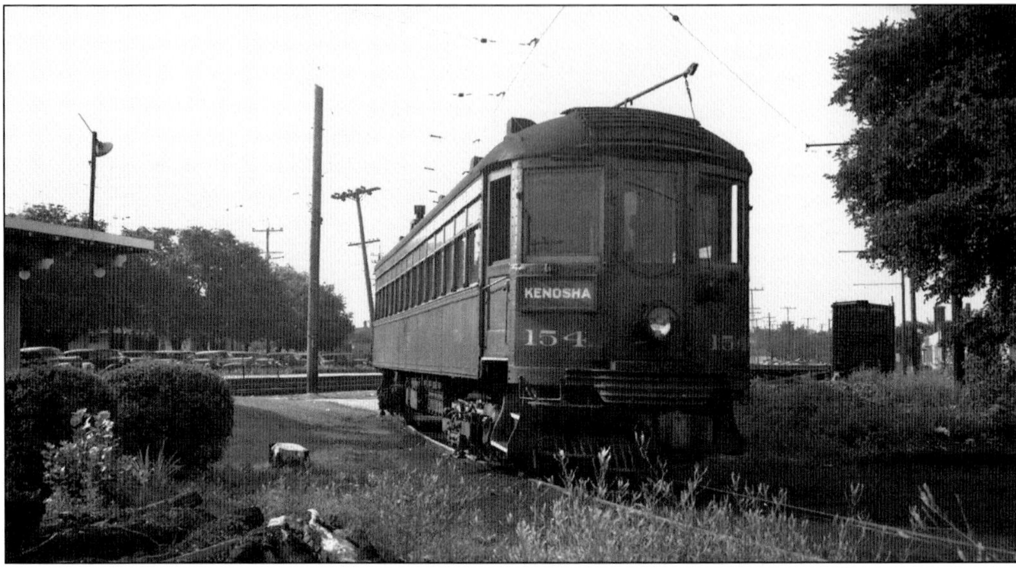

Besides the Electroliner and Chicago and Milwaukee Limited trains, there was local service with trains running between Waukegan or North Chicago junction to Kenosha. North Shore car No. 154, a Kenosha local, is seen here on August 9, 1947, on the sidetrack at Kenosha looking southeast. Depending on the time frame, there also was some local service between Kenosha and Milwaukee. (Photograph by JFH, courtesy of RH.)

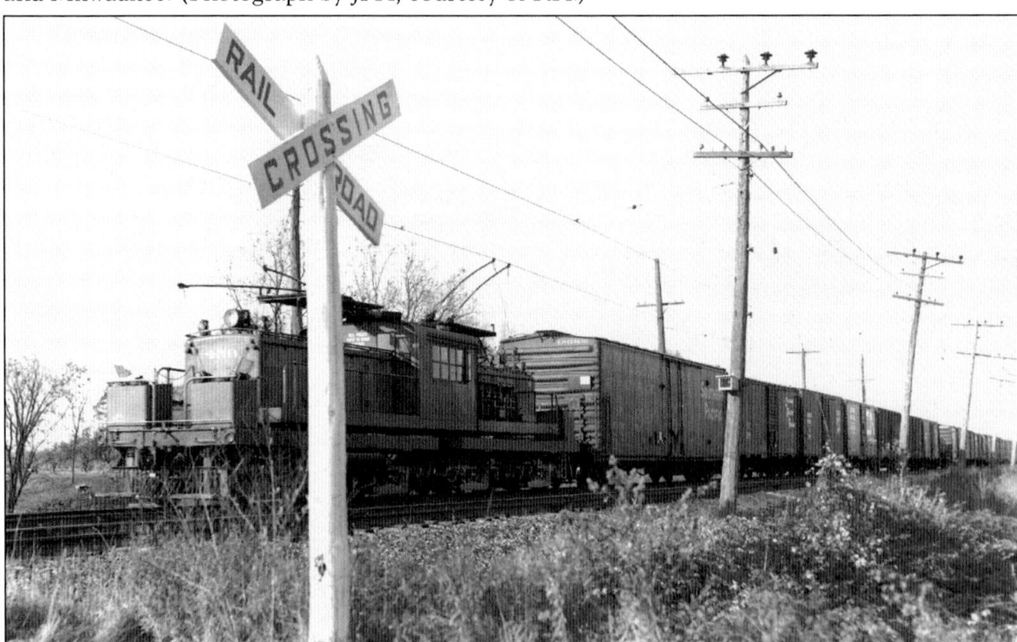

North Shore electric articulated locomotive No. 459 is shown pulling a freight train southbound near the Kenosha-Racine county line. This huge locomotive was built in 1941 by the Spokane Portland and Seattle Railway for the Oregon Electric and was sold along with its companion locomotive No. 458 to the North Shore Line in December 1947. This locomotive weighed 199,500 pounds and was 59 feet long. Locomotive No. 459 also served one day in passenger service in 1961 when it pulled two coaches on a CERA extra charter. (Photograph by EM.)

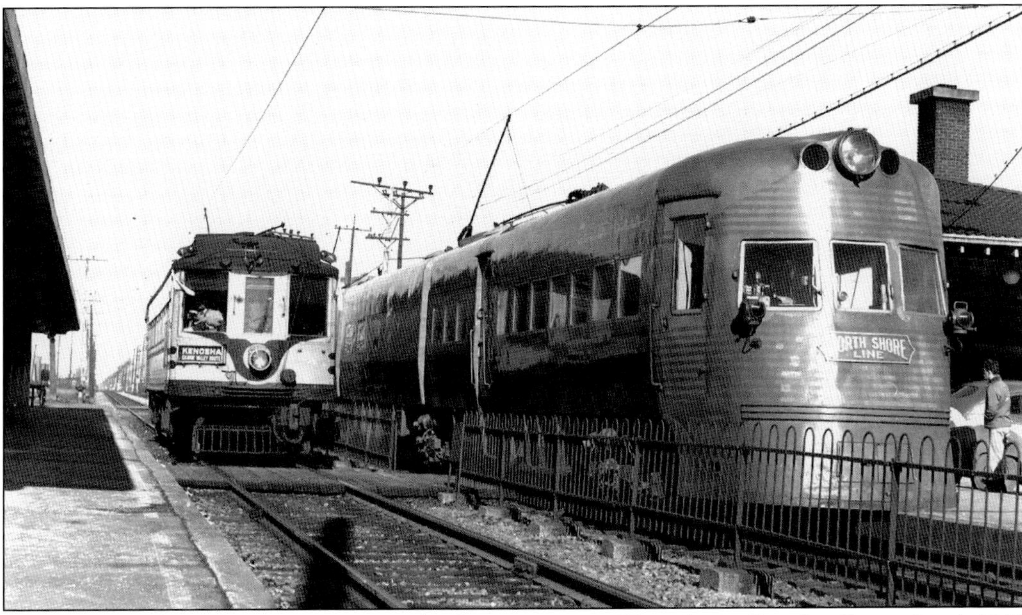

North Shore Electroliner train No. 803 loads passengers at Kenosha on Sunday, December 4, 1949. Operating over foreign rail to the left is Milwaukee Rapid Transit and Speedrail car No. 1121. This interurban, under its fourth ownership, is on a special rail fan excursion with North Shore motorman Howard A. Odinius at the controls. It was 27 months since the last KMCL interurban ran to downtown Kenosha over the now abandoned MRK line. (Photograph by RWG, courtesy of JFD, GEK.)

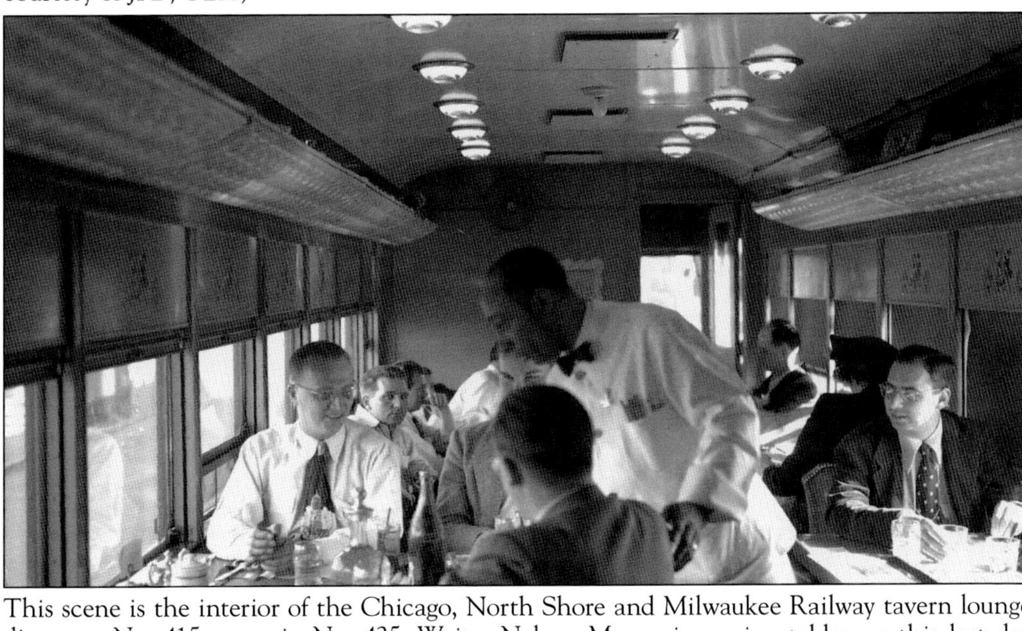

This scene is the interior of the Chicago, North Shore and Milwaukee Railway tavern lounge diner car No. 415 on train No. 425. Waiter Nelson Mason is serving tables on this last day of dining car operation on the North Shore Line, Saturday, June 4, 1949. This car would be converted to a Silverliner by October 1950. Club car service would still be provided on all Electroliner runs, with one set of older cars as a fill-in until the North Shore was abandoned. (Photograph by JFH, courtesy of RH.)

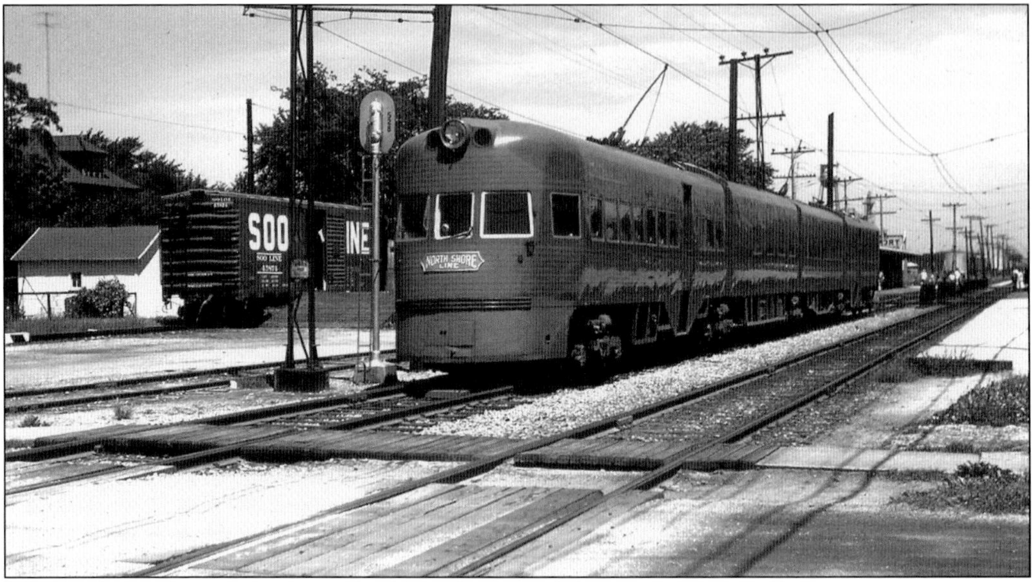

Electroliner train Nos. 801 and 802 is at Sixty-fourth Street accelerating south, away from the Kenosha train station on Saturday, June 20, 1953. The paint livery on this four-section articulated streamliner was aqua green with salmon-red striping to the anti-climbers; below that line was solid salmon-red. Lettering was in silver, outlined in black, and the North Shore Line plate on the front was red with silver letters and outline. (Photograph by JFH, courtesy of RH.)

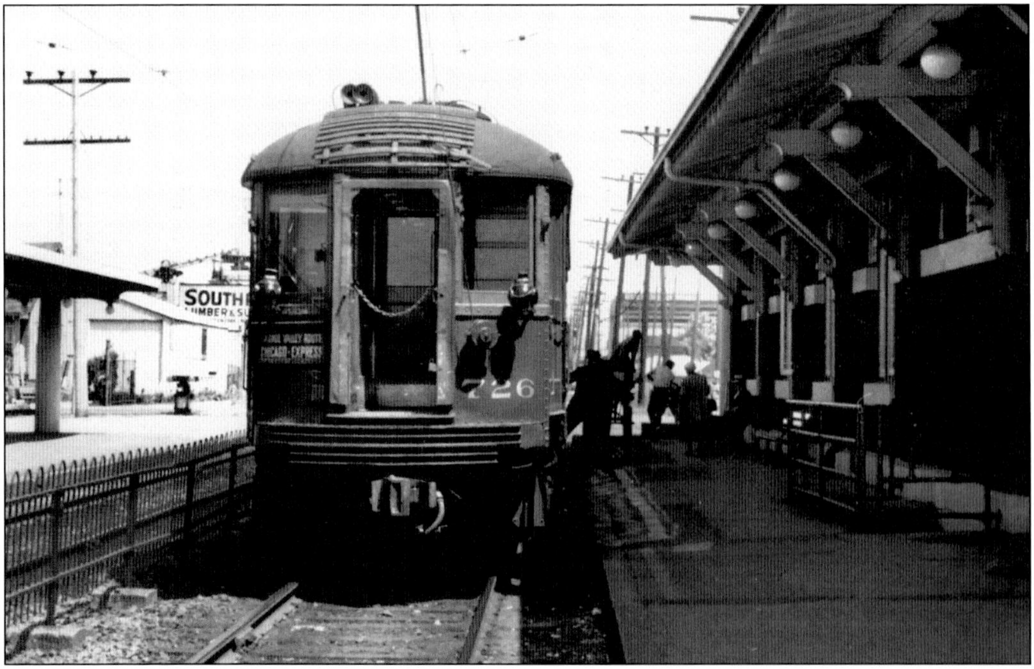

North Shore car No. 726 was built by the Cincinnati Car Company in 1926 and wrecked at Burlington Road in Kenosha on February 23, 1930. The car was rebuilt, and by 1940, it was modernized. Shown here northbound at Kenosha in 1956, the car is painted in a simple but good-looking livery of dark grass green and bright red with a charcoal roof. Note the packages being loaded and unloaded. (Courtesy of JJK, RAE.)

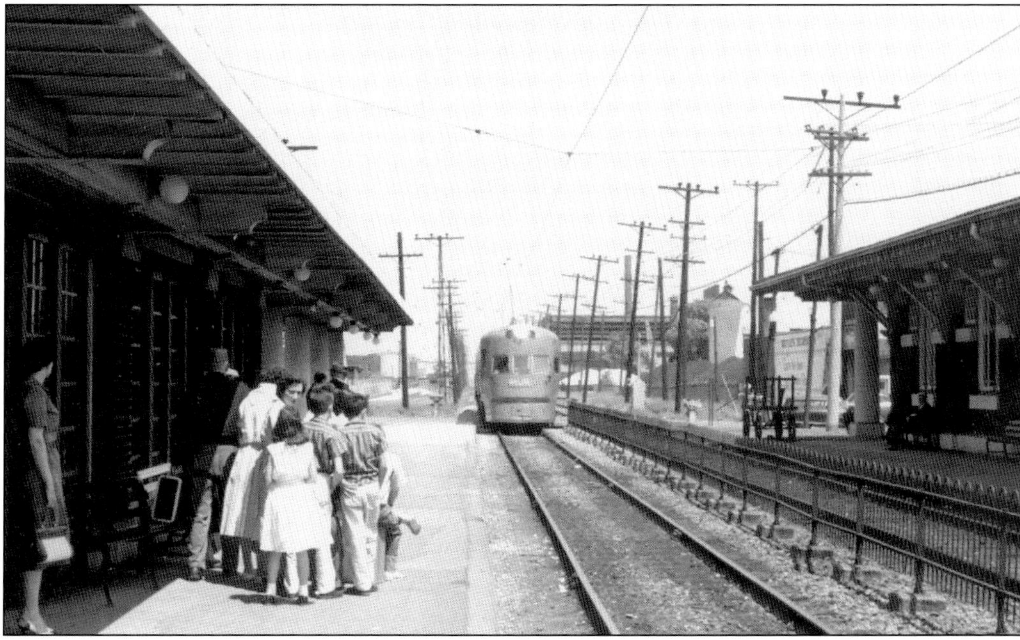

The kids are all dolled up and mother is wondering who the photographer is as a North Shore Electroliner after running through the Nash plant is about to clear Sixty-third Street in Kenosha, looking north in 1956. Soon the conductor and collector will gather their passengers and with a signal to the motorman, the train will rapidly leave the station for its next scheduled stop at Zion, Illinois. (Courtesy of JJK, RAE.)

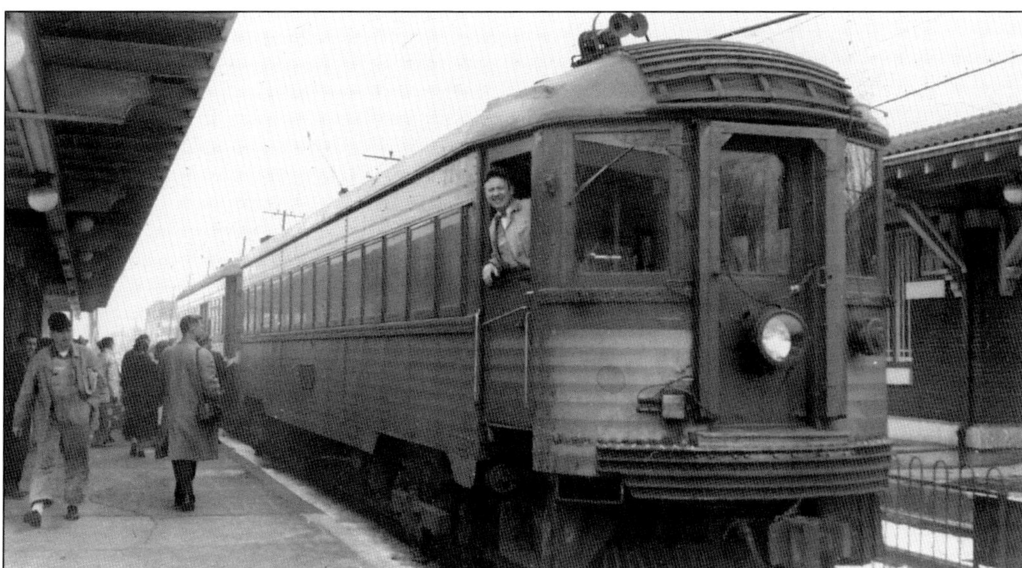

With the North Shore only months away from abandonment, motorman Howard A. Odinius looks down from the motor cab of his two-car Silverliner train standing at the Kenosha station. Odinius was one of the original founders of the Illinois Railway Museum. Note the off-duty North Shore motorman in his pin-striped overalls to the left of the photograph; he is probably a citizen of Kenosha. (Courtesy of RK.)

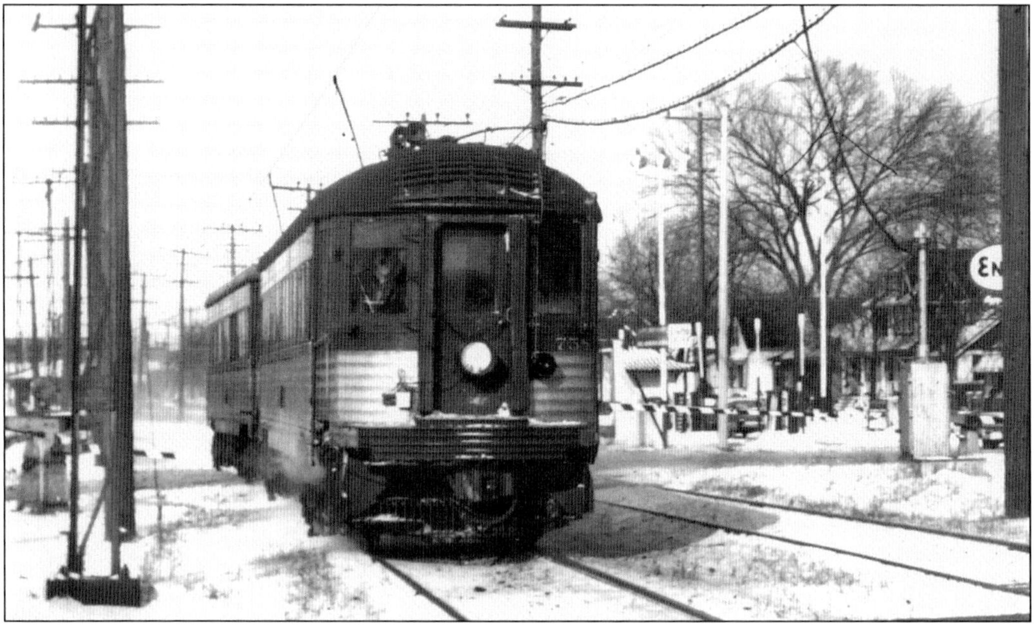

North Shore conductor Bob Johnson and Gary Filbert are attending to passengers who boarded Silverliner car Nos. 758 and 755 when train No. 416 made its brief, but busy, 1:45 p.m. station stop at Kenosha on Sunday, January 13, 1963. In just one week, the North Shore Line will pass into history. Motorman Kenneth E. Brown has his controller wound to the full parallel position and is crossing Roosevelt Road southbound fast enough that his train begins to kick up plumes of snow. (Photograph by JDH.)

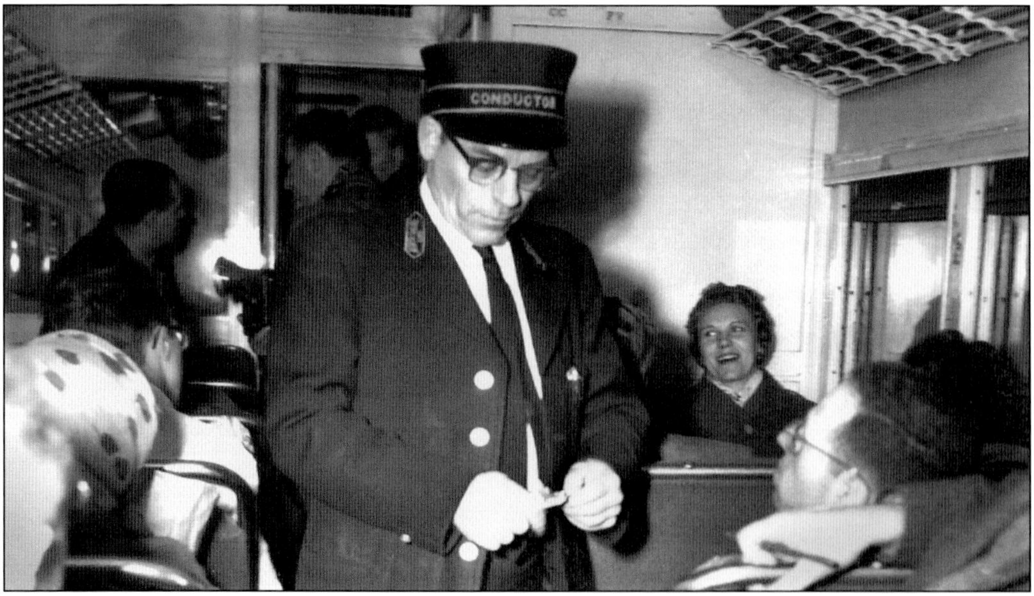

On a freezing winter night, conductor Joe McGrath of Kenosha punches tickets on train No. 437 that originated at Roosevelt Road in Chicago at 12:00 a.m. With his motorman Francis T. Murray of Cudahy, Wisconsin, and his collector Charles Wussow of Appleton, Wisconsin, they would make the last scheduled Kenosha stop on the North Shore Line in the early morning hours of January 21, 1963. (Photograph by JDH.)

Four

The Chicago and North Western Railroad

On May 19, 1855, the last rail of the Milwaukee and Chicago Railroad Company was connected at West Main Street in Kenosha, and rail service commenced between Chicago and Milwaukee. There was a grand opening celebration with speeches from the mayors of Chicago and Milwaukee. Cannons were fired, church bells rang, and Mayor Michael Frank of Kenosha presided over the ceremonies. A seven-car train with guests from Chicago, Waukegan, and Kenosha rode to Milwaukee over the new line.

Business interests in Kenosha did not want economic development in the region west of the city to be diverted to other port cities in the area. The plank roads were inadequate, and the Kenosha and Beloit Railroad Company was incorporated in March 1853. After financial difficulties, the railroad, through a merger with another railroad, eventually reached Rockford, Illinois. Like the Milwaukee and Chicago Railroad, the line would become part of the Chicago and North Western Railroad and become known as the KD Line.

The North Western became the primary railroad for Kenosha, making the industrial expansion of the early 20th century possible.

Accidents were always a problem for the railroad running at grade through Kenosha. On the first day of city streetcar service, February 1, 1903, a streetcar derailed on the Elizabeth Street crossing (Sixty-third Street). Before the car could be rerailed, a steam train reduced the little four-wheeler to kindling wood. No one was hurt, but other accidents were fatal. At 8:15 p.m. on Saturday, December 29, 1928, five teenagers (the sons and daughters of prominent Kenosha residents) were killed at the Seventy-fifth Street crossing. This in turn led to a nine-year public works project that elevated the railroad through Kenosha from Thirty-fifth Street to Eightieth Street.

Today the Union Pacific Railroad still operates a 4.2-mile section of the KD Line between the Union Pacific's Kenosha depot and the bypass line at Bain in Pleasant Prairie.

Vulcan Materials is the KD Line's primary customer. During construction season, two trains a day are operated between Ives Quarry in Racine County and the Vulcan Materials site at Bain and Gurnee, Illinois. On rare occasions, the KD Line can be used for freight trains changing from one main line to another.

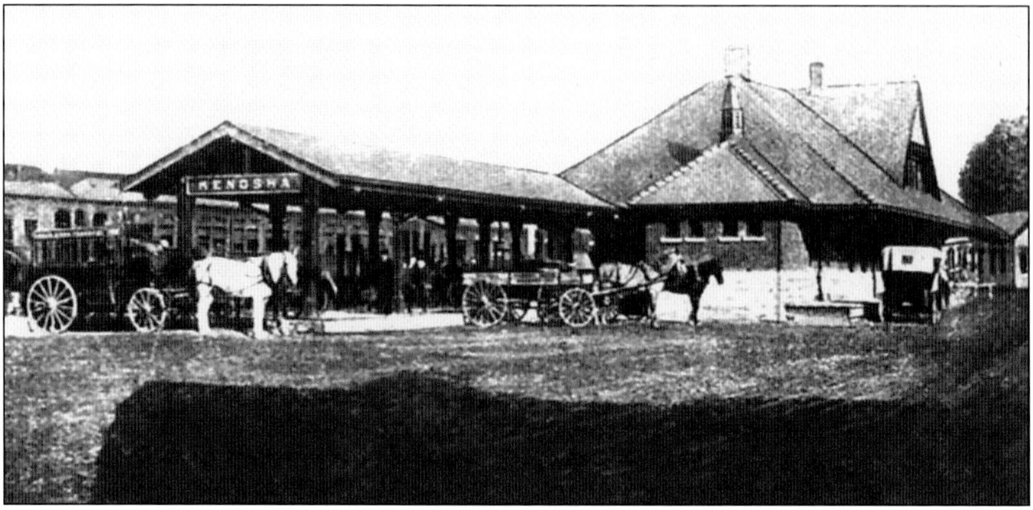

This photograph, taken in 1909 with a North Western passenger train in the background, was taken facing northwest from Pearl Street (Fifty-fifth Street) and West Main Street (Thirteenth Avenue). The train is on the inbound track (left side) to Chicago. (Courtesy of JP, C&NWRHS.)

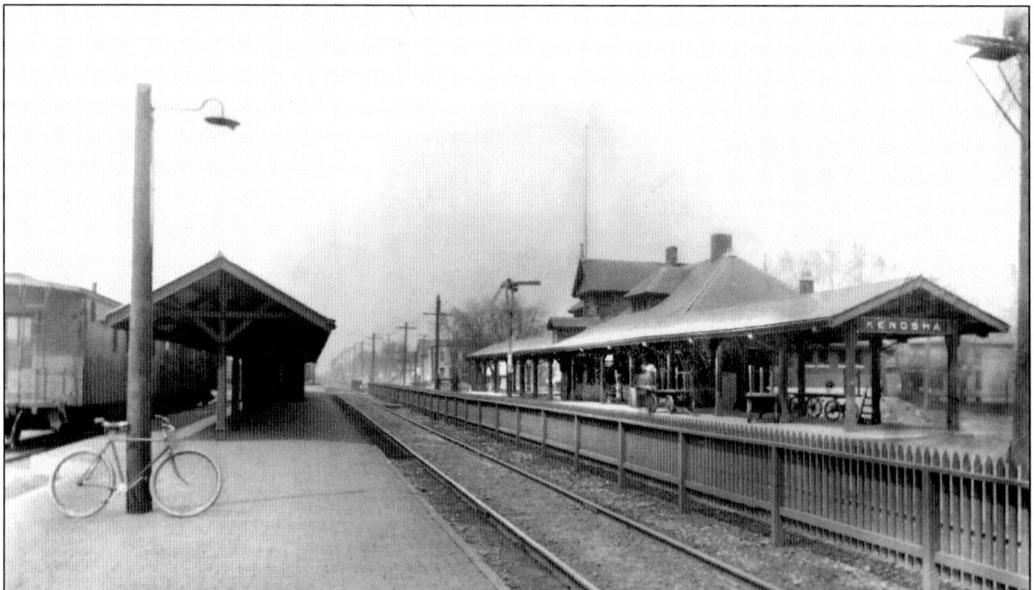

This trackside view of the North Western Railroad's Kenosha station is looking north. The station is located on West Main Street (Thirteenth Avenue) and York Street, which would later become Garden Street and, after 1926, Fifty-fourth Street. (Courtesy of WS.)

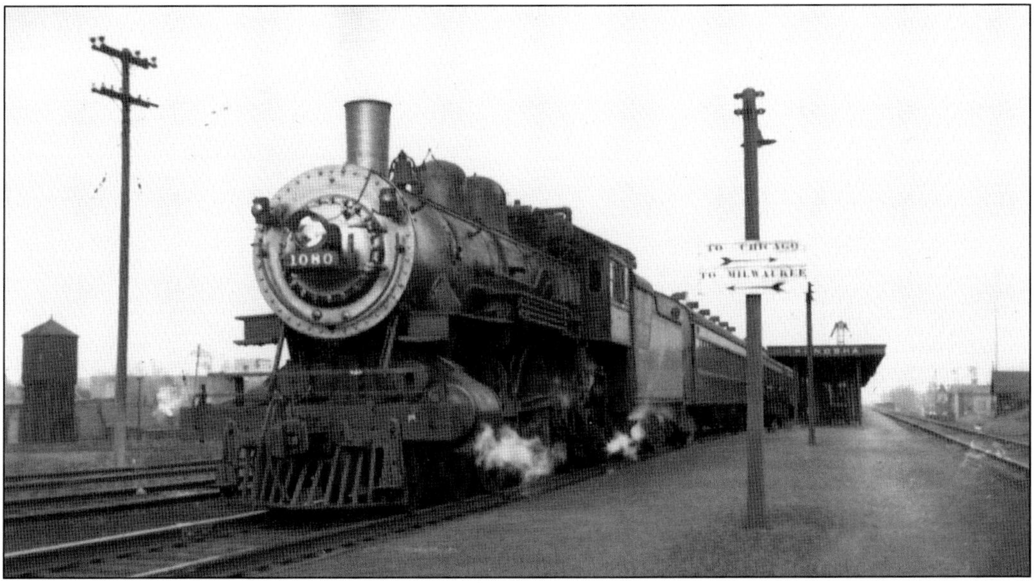

This Chicago and North Western commuter train is about to depart the Kenosha train station for Chicago and stops in between around 1940. On the head end is a class D 4-4-2 Atlantic steam locomotive No. 1080. It was built by the American Locomotive Company (ALCO) at Schenectady, New York. The D class engines were built between 1900 and 1908. (Courtesy of WS.)

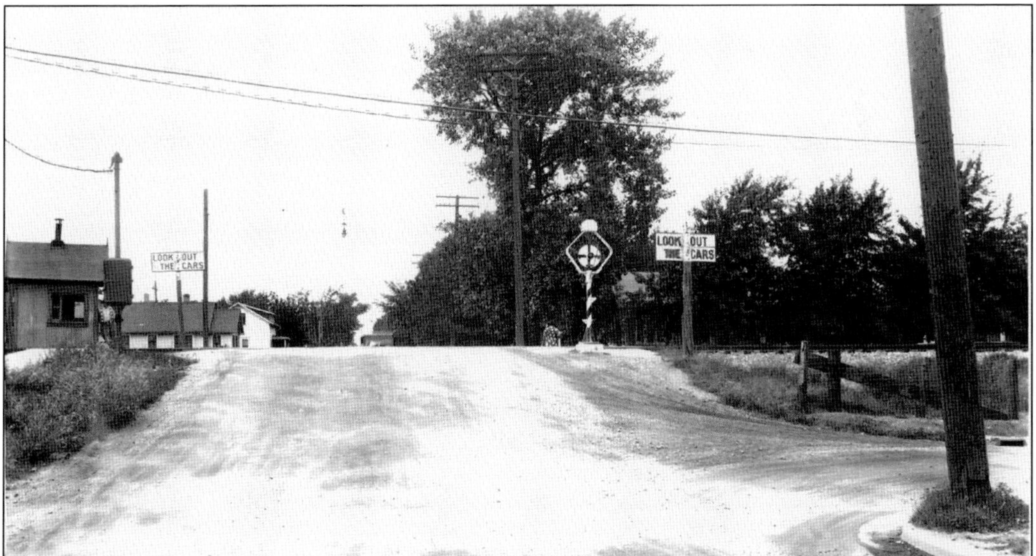

Looking west on Seventy-fifth Street at Eleventh Avenue, this was the scene of a tragic accident on December 29, 1928, that took the lives of five teenagers. A standing northbound freight train on the right track (west) was obstructing the view of a southbound train's headlight operating on the left-hand track (east). All was dark except for the flashing signal light. The first eastbound automobile got across, but the second two were hit. This in turn led to raising the railroad above grade through Kenosha. (Courtesy of RES.)

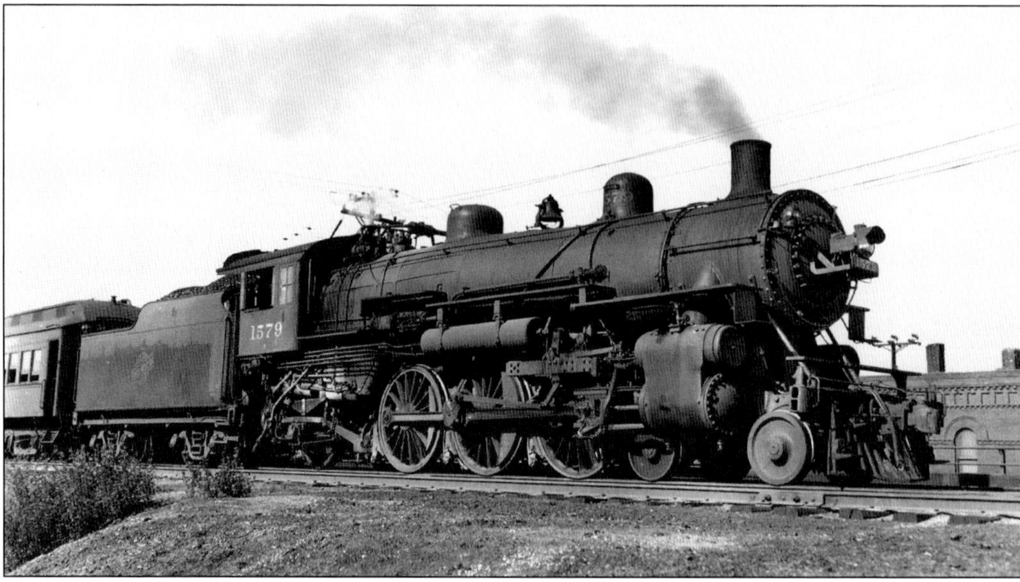

Chicago and North Western Railroad 4-6-2 class E Pacific steam locomotive No. 1579 is about to leave the elevated Kenosha depot at Fifty-fourth Street and Thirteenth Avenue on June 28, 1947, for an inbound trip to Chicago. Built between 1910 and 1912 by ALCO, this steam locomotive operated into the mid-1950s on the North Western's commuter lines. (Courtesy of JK.)

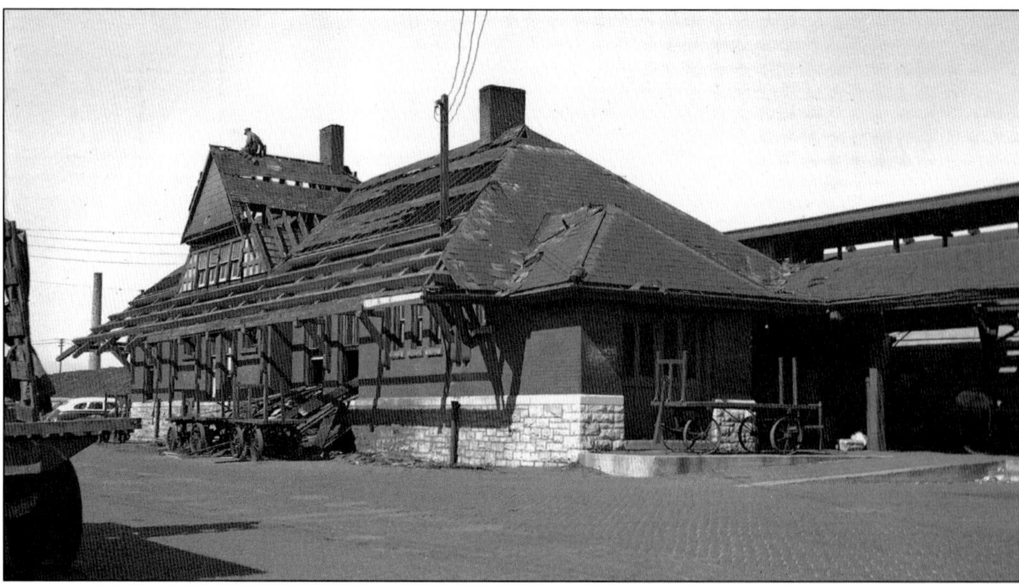

This beautiful Queen Anne–style Kenosha train station is unfortunately being dismantled down to the Ashler cut limestone foundation in December 1947. The demolition was probably due to reducing upkeep costs and a desire to create a modern station. (Courtesy of JP, C&NWRHS.)

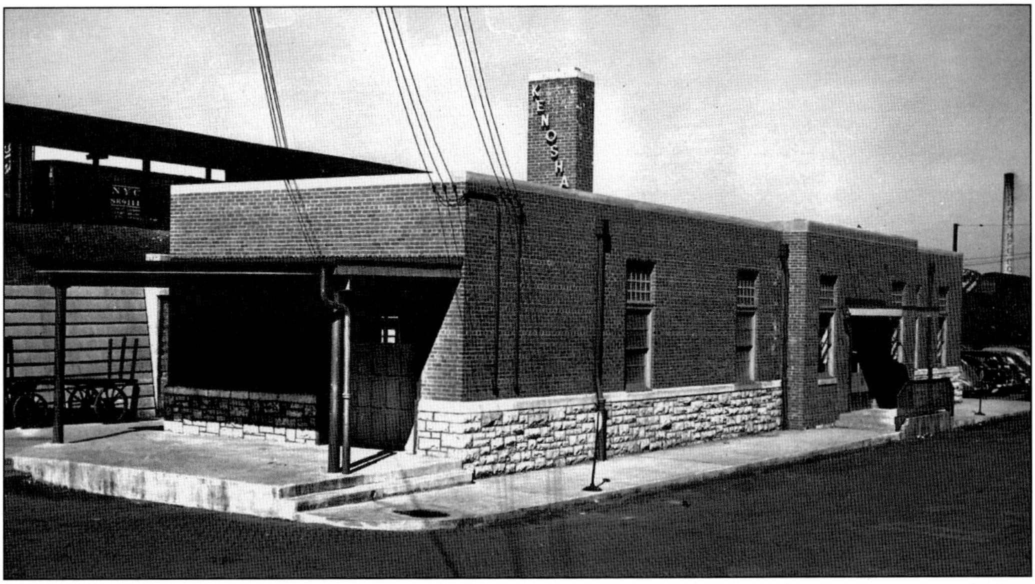

The new Kenosha train station looking northwest from Thirteenth Avenue near Fifty-fourth Street still retains its limestone foundation in December 1948. This modern art deco building would later get an addition to the south end and be remodeled again in 1984. (Courtesy of JP, C&NWRHS.)

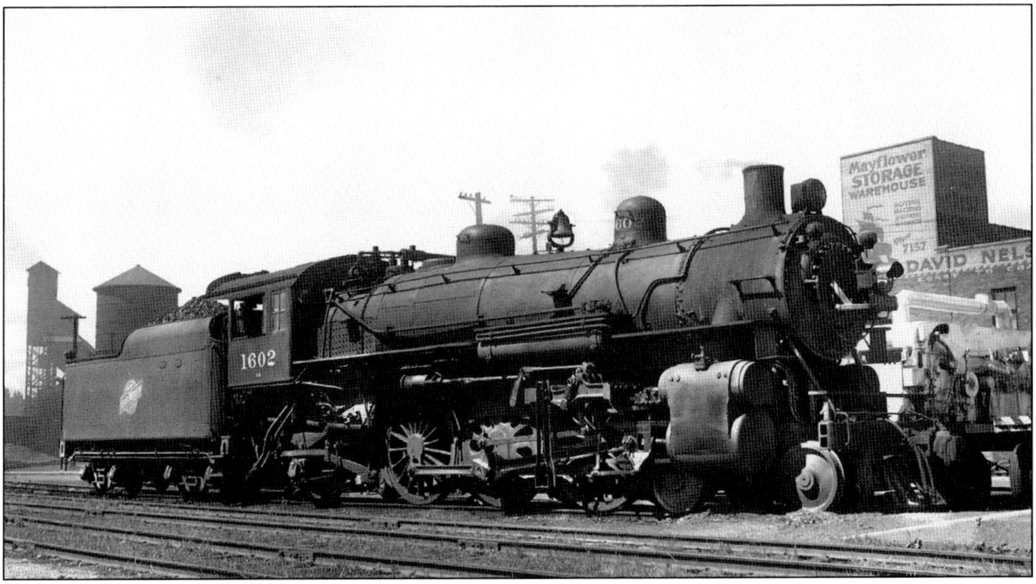

Chicago and North Western Railroad 4-6-2 class ES Pacific steam locomotive No. 1602 idles, facing north, in the Kenosha coach yard on May 14, 1949. Built between 1913 and 1915 by ALCO at Schenectady, New York, this steam engine pulled commuter passenger coaches between Chicago's North Western station and the Kenosha train depot at Fifty-fourth Street and Thirteenth Avenue. (Courtesy of JK.)

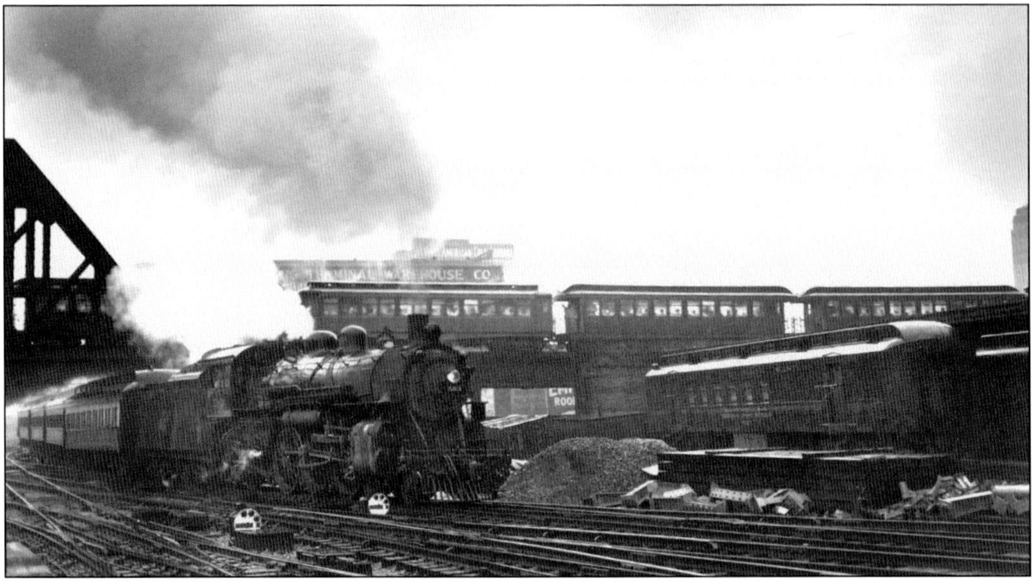

On a rainy day, a commuter train on the Wisconsin Division tracks is pulling into the North Western train station in Chicago, looking northeast on June 1, 1954. This train, which originated at Kenosha, is being pulled by a 4-6-2 Pacific class E hand-fired steam locomotive. The diverted Douglass Park el train on the Lake Street el, passing over the North Western consists of wood gate cars and at least one wood closed-end deck-roof car. Note the Railroad Post Office (RPO) car to the right. (Photograph by PAW.)

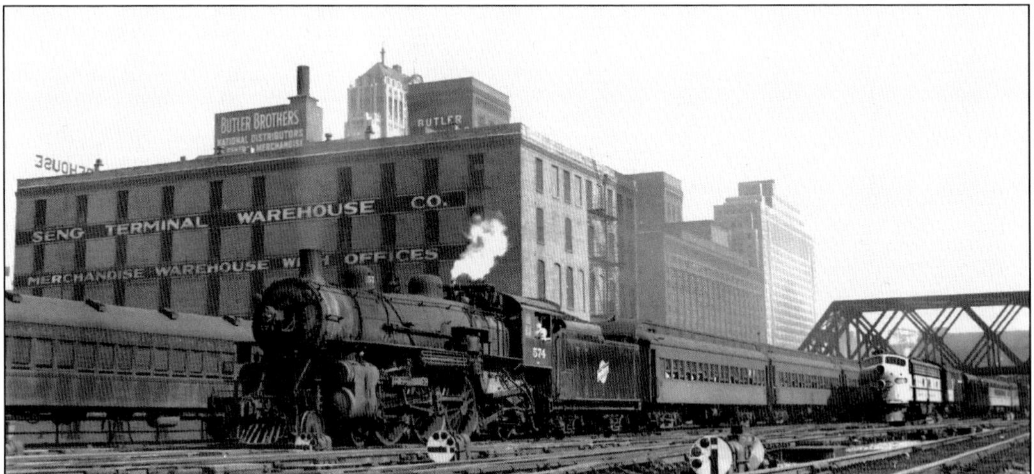

This Kenosha-bound commuter train, led by a 4-6-2 Pacific class ES steam engine No. 574, is about to clear the Lake Street "L" in Chicago, looking southeast in July 1955. To the right is a Peninsula 400 passenger train scheduled to leave the North Western Railroad terminal at 4:10 p.m. With Kenosha as a stop, this streamliner will arrive in Green Bay, Wisconsin, at 8:35 p.m. (Photograph by PAW.)

Dressed in the working clothes of the day, a North Western engineer can be seen in his steam locomotive at the Kenosha coach yard in the summer of 1955. One of the largest producers of bib overalls and their accessories was Oshkosh of Oshkosh, Wisconsin. With many of their customers being Irish, the company honored them by having shamrocks trimmed in Kelly green on their product's brass buttons. (Photograph by EM.)

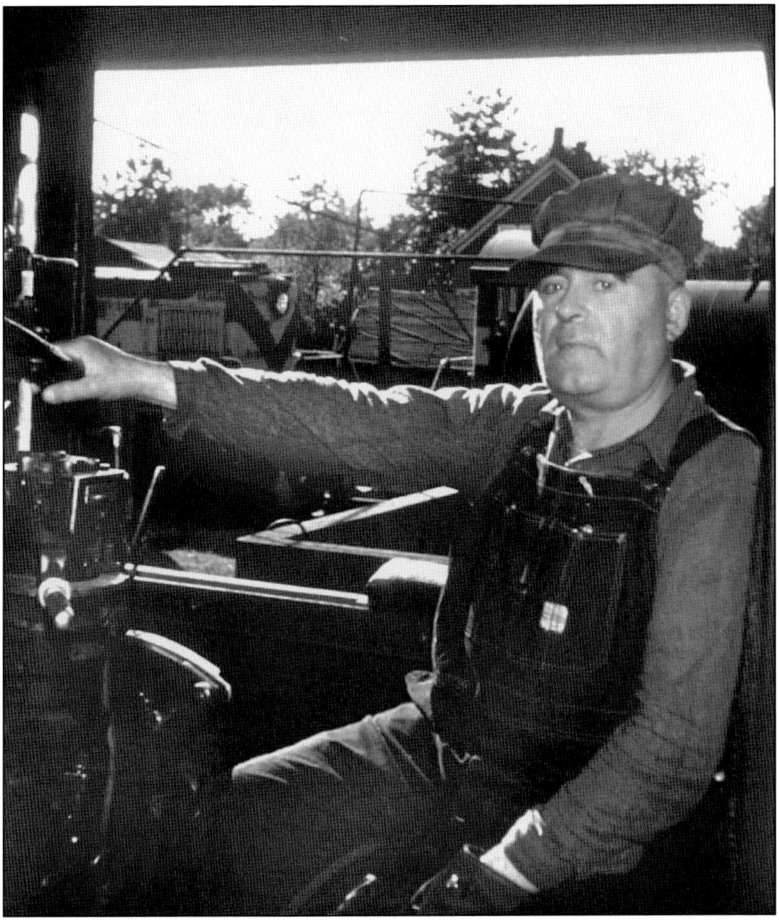

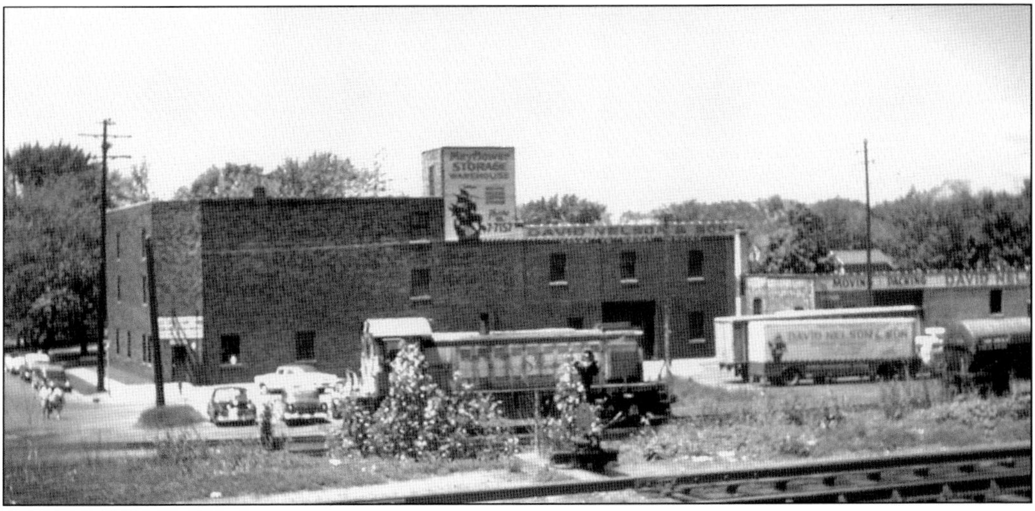

A North Western Railroad ALCO diesel switch engine idles in the Kenosha North Western coach yard at Thirteenth Court and Fifty-third Street in June 1959. The Mayflower storage and moving building still stands today. Note the kerosene switch lamp in the foreground. (Photograph by EM.)

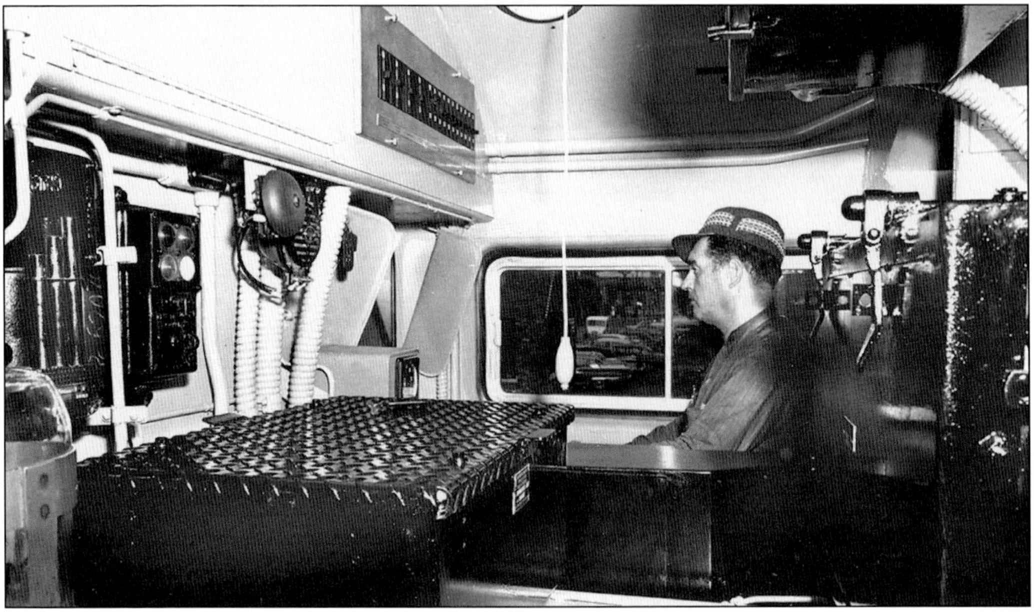

The North Western pioneered the "push-pull" train concept, which eliminated the need to turn locomotives and move them from one end of the train to the other at their terminals. A control cab, as seen here in 1959, was installed in a number of bi-level coaches allowing the engineer to control power from the locomotive at the rear of his train. The train would now be pushed. To move in the opposite direction, the engineer would operate from the locomotive thus pulling the train. (Courtesy of JP, C&NWRHS.)

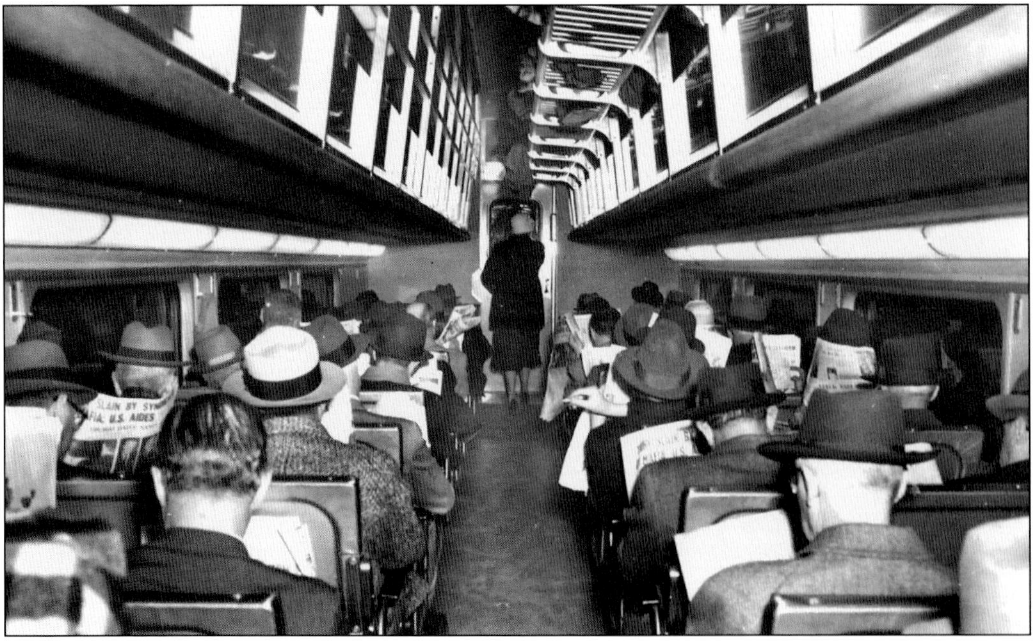

This company photograph shows the lower interior of a North Western Railroad's new bi-level coach in 1959. This type of modern coach built by Pullman Standard would be used on the 1-hour-and-30-minute commute to Kenosha from downtown Chicago. (Courtesy of JP, C&NWRHS.)

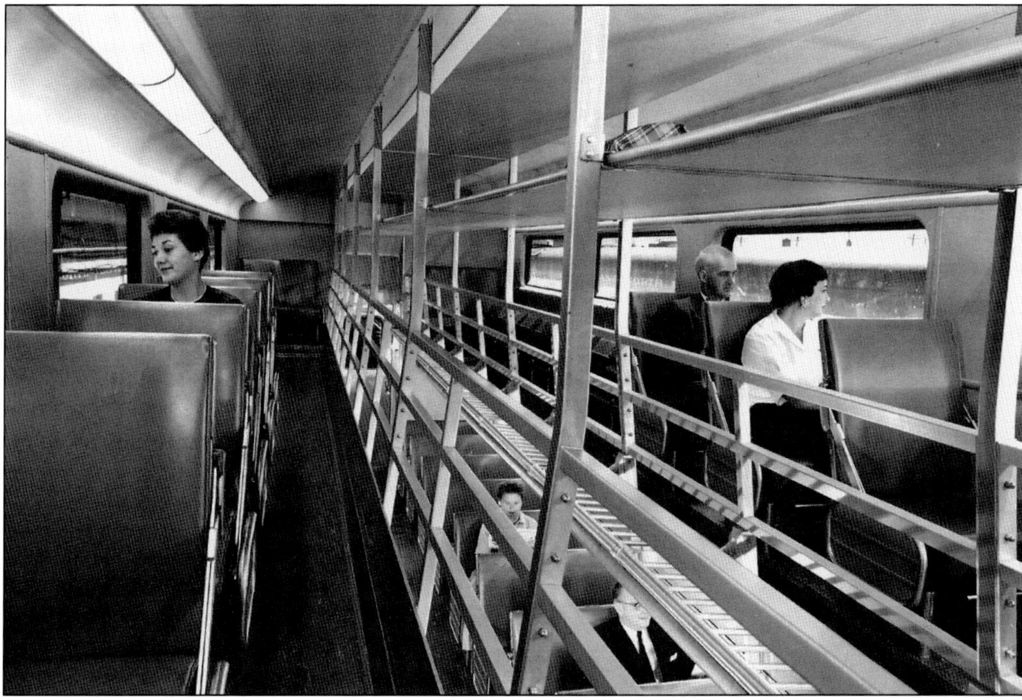

In this other company interior view taken in 1959 of a new interior of a North Western Railroad bi-level coach, the upper single-seat section is seen. The train conductor and collectors could easily move up and down the lower isle collecting fares or tickets from the passengers on the upper level. (Courtesy of JP, C&NWRHS.)

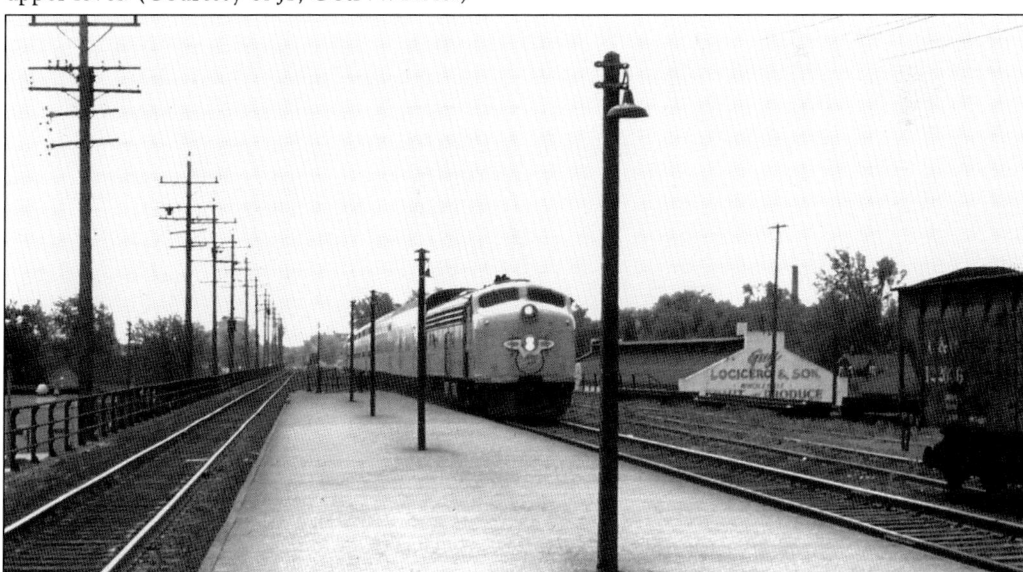

On this August day in 1962, it is 5:03 p.m. as a Peninsula 400 train arrives at Kenosha. On the head end, an Electro-Motive Division (EMD) E-8 streamline engine is being followed by a baggage-mail-tavern car and a full dining car. The bi-level passenger coaches also had parlor accommodations. This train will terminate at Ishpeming, Michigan, in the Upper Peninsula at 1:25 a.m. The distinctive building to the right still stands today. (Photograph by RM.)

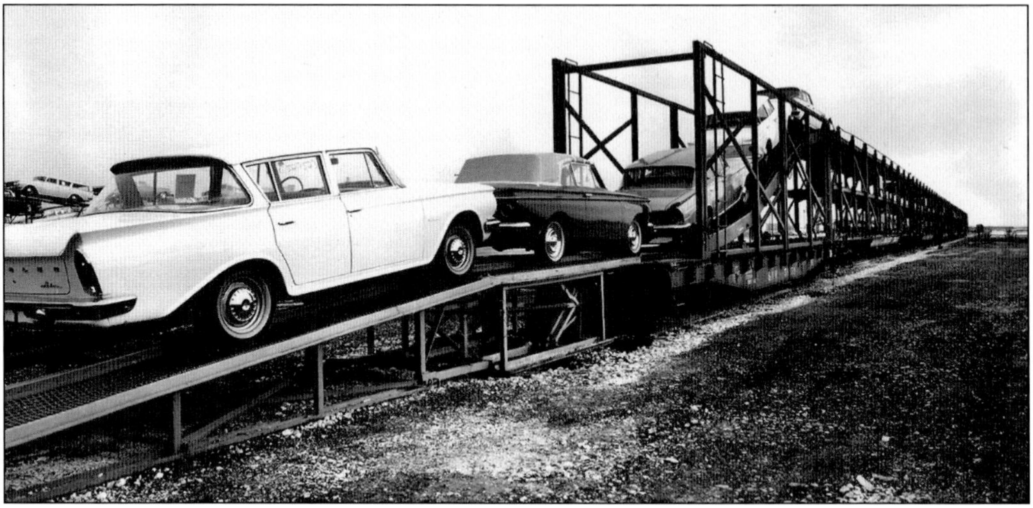

Seen here at Bain, a short distance southwest of Kenosha in 1961, new Ramblers are being loaded aboard auto-rack freight cars for shipment throughout the country. Today all that remains of the vast automobile production that Kenosha once enjoyed is a Chrysler engine plant. (Courtesy of JP, C&NWRHS.)

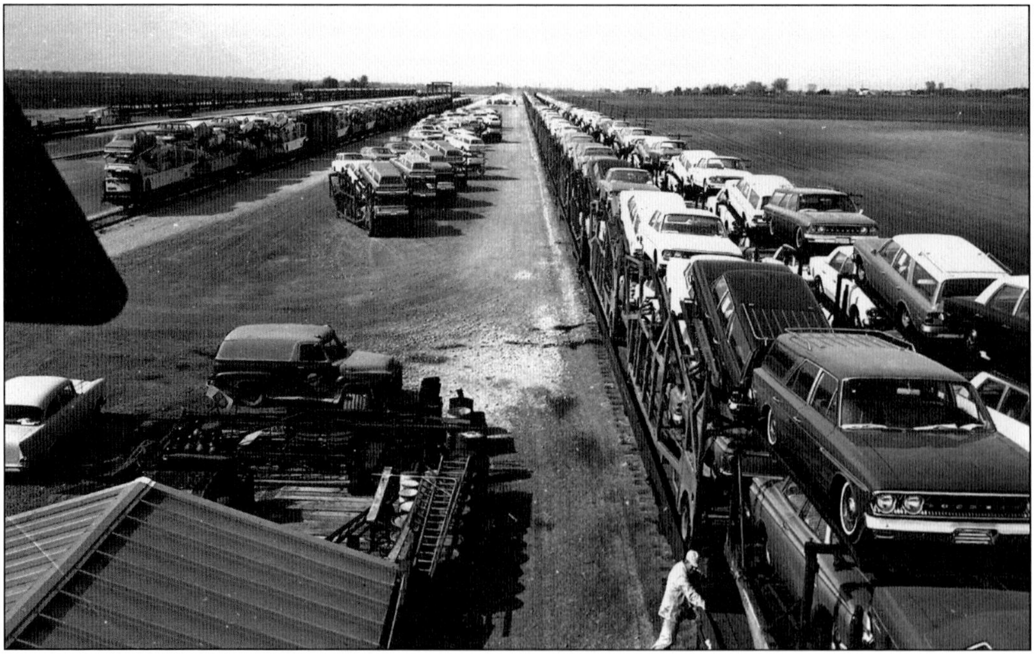

American Motors would become the primary customer on the North Western Railroad's KD Line. Most of the KD Line was abandoned west of Bain by 1939. Trailers filled with new cars in the center of the photograph will be delivered by the Kenosha Auto Transport Company and await loading at Bain in 1963. (Courtesy of JP, C&NWRHS.)

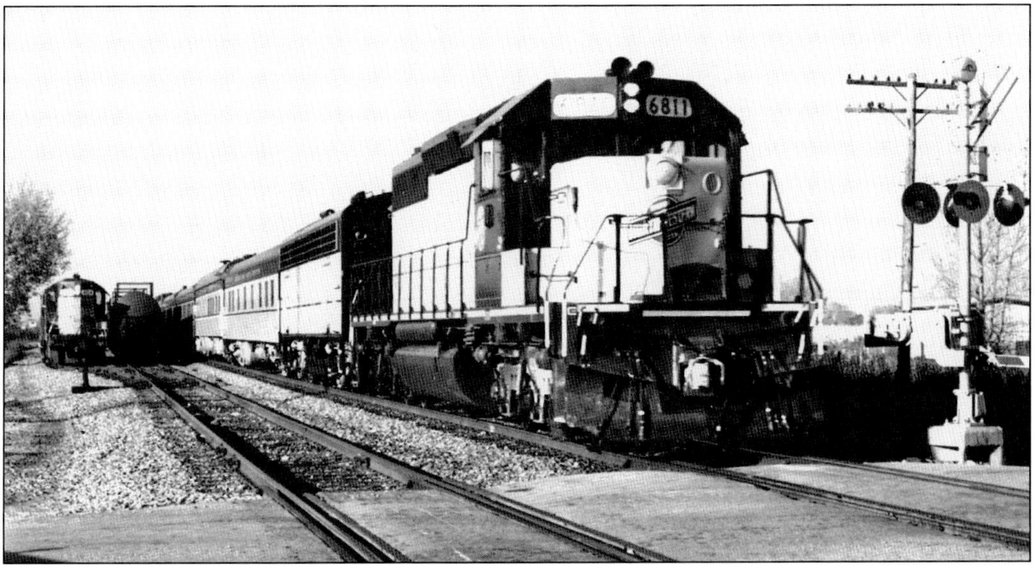

Southbound at Bain, EMD SD (special duty) 40-2 diesel locomotive No. 6811, built in 1974, is seen at the head end of a business train operating on the bypass line (New Line). The locomotive is trailed by the power car Oak Creek that will provide electricity to the company cars. The North Western livery was bright yellow and dark grass green with a red and white logo trimmed in black. (Courtesy of JP, C&NWRHS.)

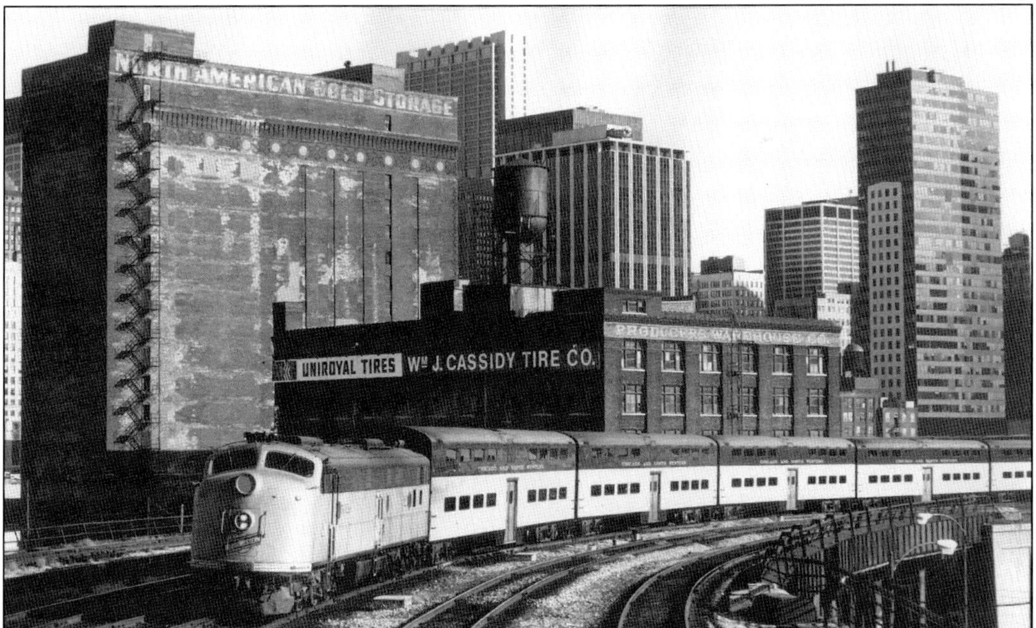

A push-pull bi-level commuter train is headed by EMD E-8 diesel locomotive No. 5031A on its way to Kenosha as it crosses above the Milwaukee Road tracks north of Kinzie Street in Chicago in May 1977. With the loss of the North Shore Line in January 1963, Kenosha still had train service to Chicago provided by the North Western. Unfortunately Kenosha lost all train service north of the city on May 1, 1971, after the government (Amtrak) took over passenger service. (Photograph by PAW.)

WAUKEGAN
ZION
WINTHROP HARBOR
KENOSHA

SEPTEMBER 1, 1973

- **FAST, DEPENDABLE RUSH-HOUR SERVICE**
- **CONVENIENT HOURLY OFF-PEAK SERVICE**

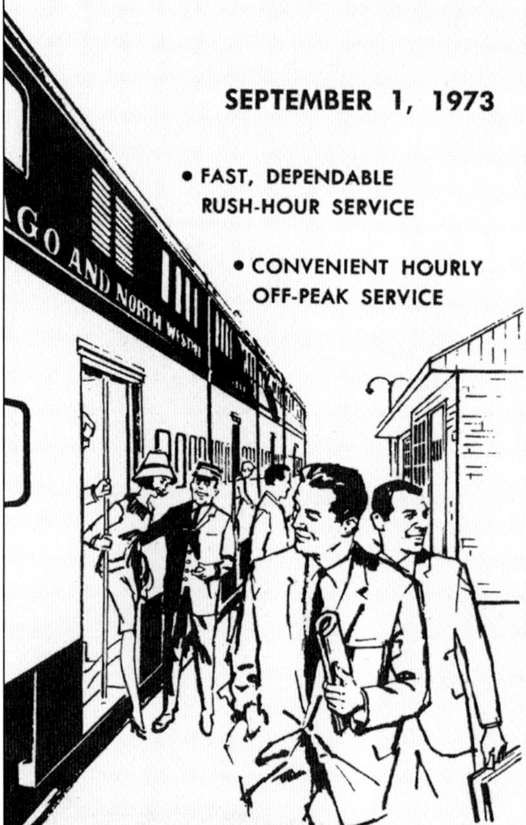

CHICAGO AND NORTH WESTERN RAILROAD

AMERICA'S FINEST SUBURBAN SERVICE FOR YOU

TO CHICAGO

MONDAYS through FRIDAYS

Leave Kenosha	Leave Winthrop Harbor	Leave Zion	Leave Waukegan	Arrive Chicago (See Note)
AM	AM	AM	AM	AM
....	....	....	5.05	6.20
....	....	....	6.00	7.10
6.00	6.08	6.12	6.20	7.35
6.20	6.28	6.33	6.41	8.00
....	....	....	7.10	8.15
6.55	....	7.06	7.15	8.20
....	....	....	7.20	8.32
....	....	....	7.30	8.38
• 7.15	• 7.24	• 7.28	• J7.37	8.41
....	....	....	7.53	9.05
7.53	8.01	8.06	8.14	9.15
8.47	8.55	9.00	9.08	10.25
....	....	....	10.10	11.25
				PM
....	....	....	11.10	**12.25**
PM	**PM**	**PM**	**PM**	
....	....	....	**12.10**	**1.25**
....	....	....	**1.10**	**2.25**
....	....	....	**2.10**	**3.25**
2.49	**2.57**	**3.02**	**3.10**	**4.25**
....	....	....	**4.05**	**5.25**
....	....	....	**5.10**	**6.25**
5.49	....	**6.01**	**6.10**	**7.25**
....	....	....	**7.10**	**8.25**
....	....	....	**8.10**	**9.25**
....	....	....	**9.10**	**10.25**
....	....	....	**10.10**	**11.25**
				AM
11.30	....	**11.41**	**11.50**	1.05
....	....	....	....	....
....	....	....	....	....
PM	**PM**	**PM**	**PM**	AM

SATURDAYS ONLY

Leave Kenosha	Leave Winthrop Harbor	Leave Zion	Leave Waukegan	Arrive Chicago (See Note)
AM	AM	AM	AM	AM
....	....	....	5.05	6.20
....	....	....	6.00	7.10
6.20	6.28	6.33	6.41	8.00
....	....	....	7.10	8.30
• 7.20	• 7.28	• 7.33	• 7.42	8.45
....	....	....	7.50	9.10
8.47	8.55	9.00	9.08	10.25
....	....	....	10.10	11.25
PM	**PM**	**PM**	**PM**	
....	....	....	**12.05**	**1.25**
1.50	....	**2.01**	**2.10**	**3.25**
....	....	....	**4.05**	**5.25**
....	....	....	**5.10**	**6.25**
....	....	....	**7.10**	**8.25**
....	....	....	**8.10**	**9.25**
8.50	....	**9.01**	**9.10**	**10.25**
				AM
11.30	....	**11.41**	**11.50**	1.05
....	....	....	....	....
....	....	....	....	....
....	....	....	....	....
PM	**PM**	**PM**	**PM**	AM

This schedule was made for commuters in 1973. (Courtesy of DOE.)

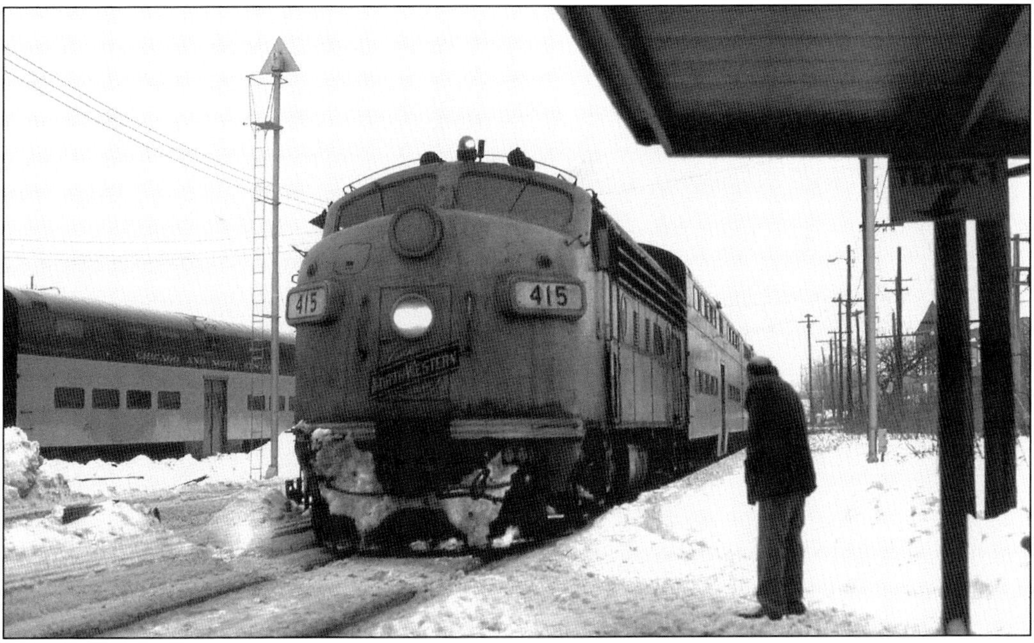

The second Saturday in January 1979 marked the second major blizzard in many weeks, the first being New Year's Eve day, 1978. This North Western Railroad commuter train is arriving at Waukegan and will soon be underway to Kenosha. Many local residents will remember walking in the streets, as snowdrifts covered the sidewalks for some time. (Photograph by DOE.)

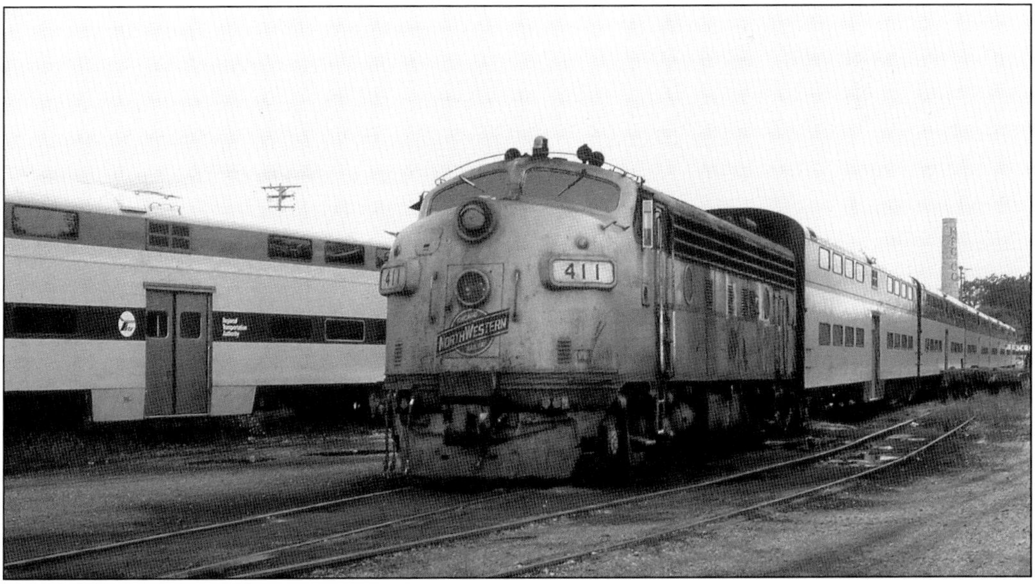

By October 1980, there is evidence of change as the Regional Transit Authority (RTA) has begun painting its equipment. The passenger coach to the side is painted a silver gray with brown striping with the RTA logo next to the loading door. The train, along with its diesel locomotive sitting in the Kenosha coach yard, is still painted in the North Western Railroad's chrome yellow and green. (Photograph by DOE.)

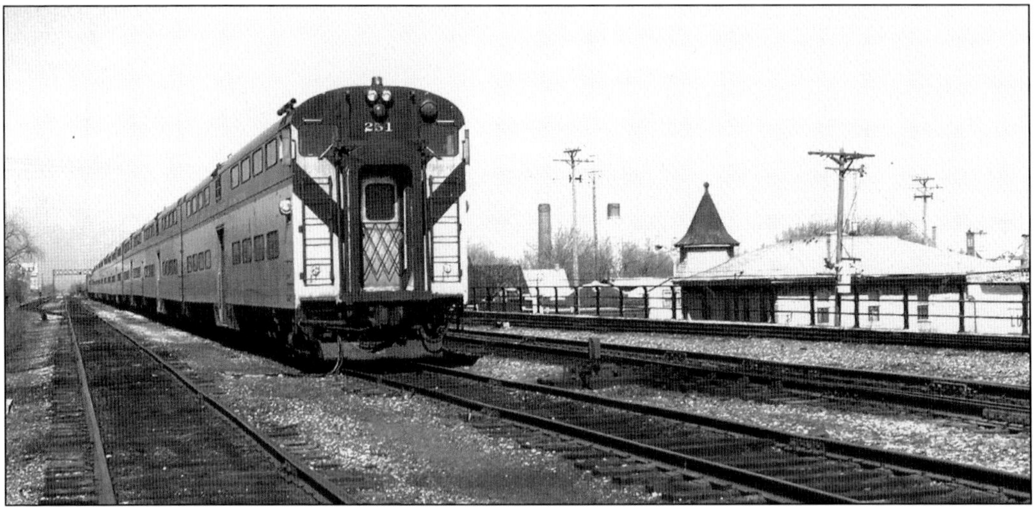

This April 1981 scene at Kenosha is typical of the North Western Railroad commuter service that served Kenosha for many years. RTA was formed in 1974 in northeast Illinois and by this time has contracted with the North Western to provide rail service. Although not a part of the RTA taxing district, Kenosha continued to see commuter service due to its history of providing needed storage space for trains awaiting their next scheduled run. (Photograph by DOE.)

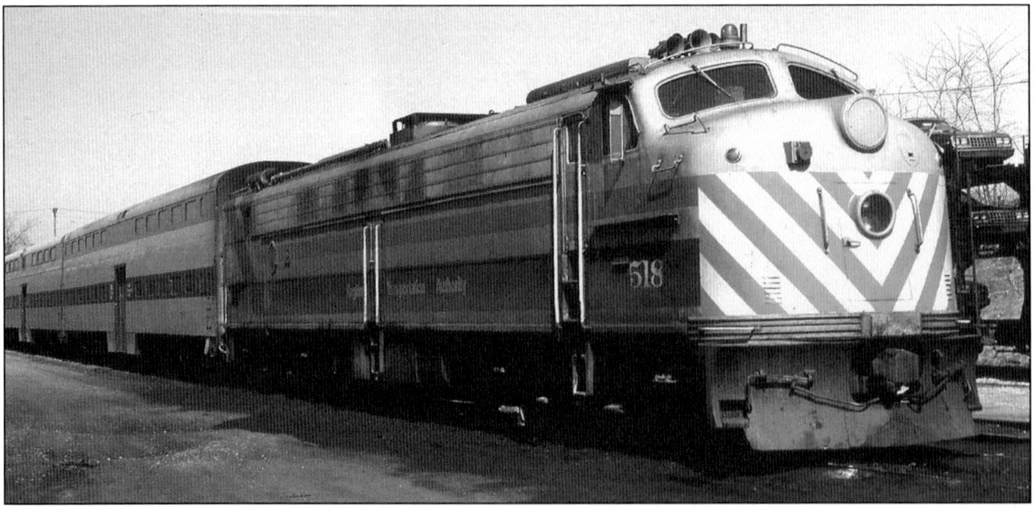

By April 1981, commuter engines were beginning to be painted in the RTA's colors of brown and light blue with red trim. The safety stripes were red on a white background. Former Chicago and North Western Railroad diesel locomotive No. 518 is seen here in the Kenosha coach yard between runs. At one time, this EMD F-7 diesel locomotive ran passenger trains to Williams Bay and needed a snowplow pilot as seen in the photograph. (Photograph by DOE.)

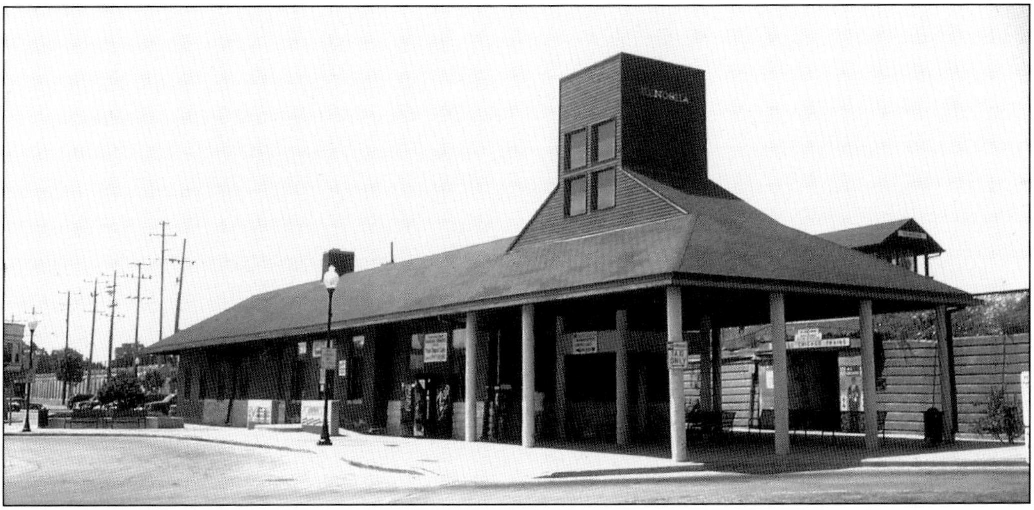

With Thirteenth Avenue eliminated up to Fifty-fifth Street, the modern Kenosha train station is seen here on July 22, 1999, looking southwest. In less than 11 months, this commuter train station would be served by Kenosha's new streetcar line. (Photograph by WS.)

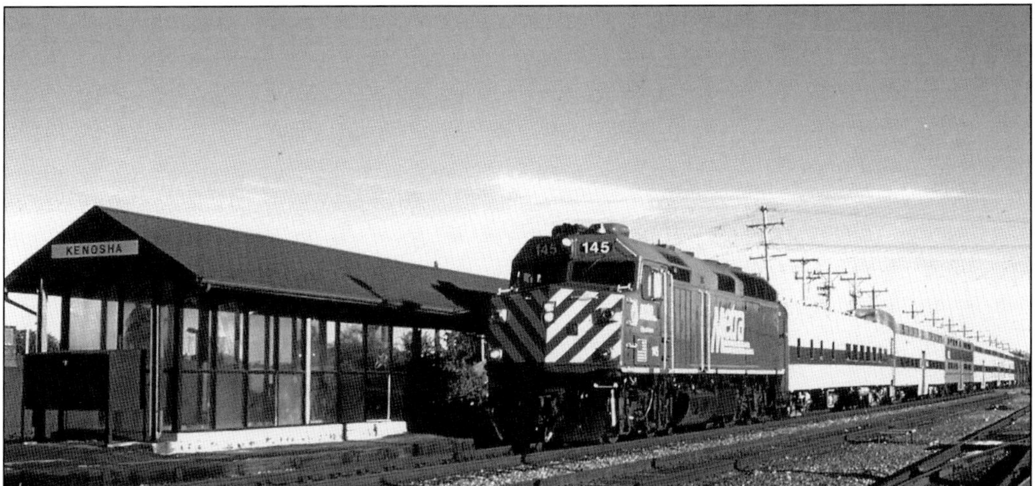

During a weekday evening in August 2005, Metra train No. 335 has departed downtown Chicago at 5:07 p.m. and eases to the platform at precisely 6:32 p.m., ending its 51.5 mile trip in just 1 hour and 25 minutes. This train is commonly known as the "Club Run." The single-level car directly behind the lead engine is unique, as it is the only one on the entire Metra system. A select group of riders from south Lake Country pay extra for the privilege of riding this car. (Photograph by DOE.)

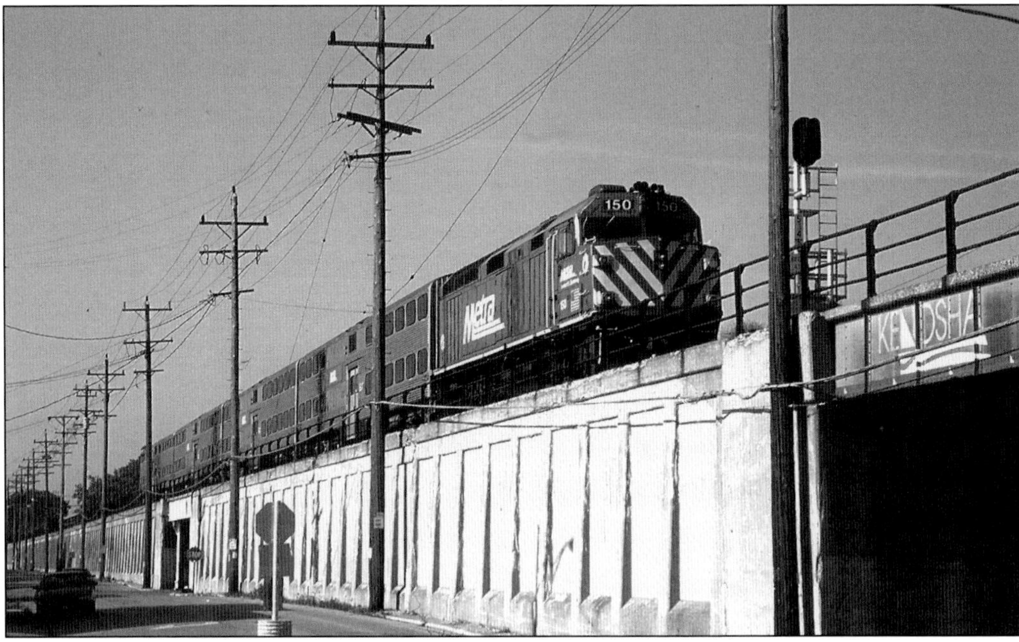

The scene is looking south from Fifty-sixth Street along Thirteenth Avenue. An RTA Metra train leaves Kenosha for Chicago on a weekday morning in July 2006. Note the southbound train is operating on the left side, a practice adopted from the North Western Railroad. (Photograph by DOE.)

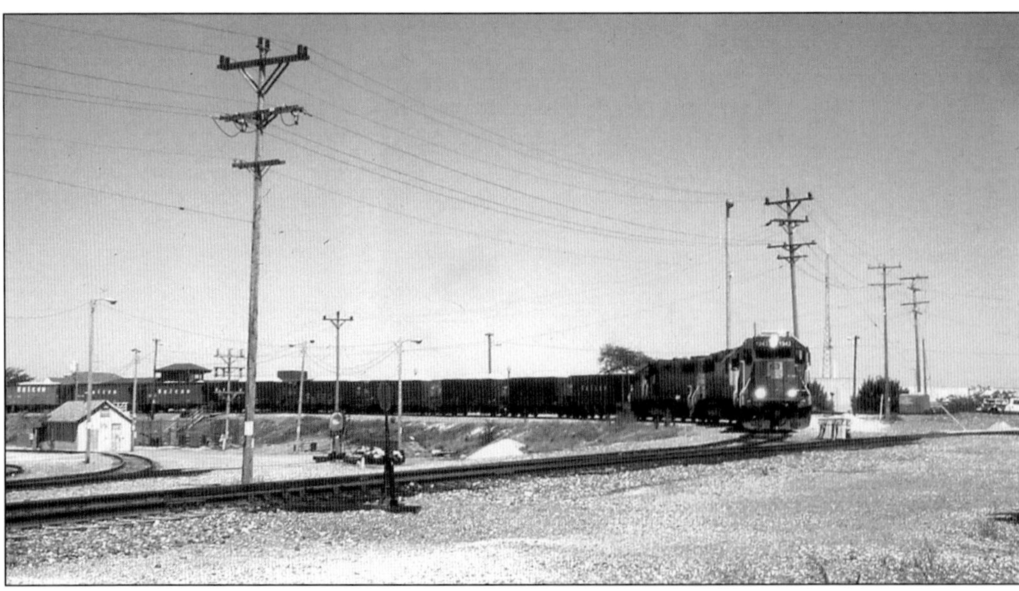

Vulcan Materials is today the KD Line's primary customer. Looking northeast from Fourteenth Avenue, a loaded Union Pacific rock train can be seen leaving the former North Western main line at Kenosha on August 4, 2006. In season, two trains a day are operated between Ives Quarry in Racine County and the Vulcan site at Bain and Gurnee, Illinois. (Photograph by WS.)

Five

STREETCARS RETURN

Joseph McCarthy, the late director of Kenosha Transit, had an idea. Because of that idea, on Saturday, June 17, 2000, streetcars returned to Kenosha after a 68-year absence. When the city decided to redevelop Kenosha's lakefront, McCarthy received approval to build a 1.9-mile streetcar loop to serve this former factory area that would become HarborPark.

A streetcar barn and transit center was built at Fifty-fourth Street and Eighth Avenue; it would become a terminal for both city buses and streetcars. The new line would run west over Fifty-fourth Street to the Metra commuter train station and turn south into Eleventh Avenue. At Fifty-sixth Street, the line would turn east running on parkway in the middle of this two-way street through downtown and entering HarborPark at Fifth Avenue. Passing townhomes, parks, and the Kenosha Museum, the line would turn north at Ring Road, running on private right-of-way and then west next to Fifty-fourth Street. Paralleling Pike Creek inlet, the line would re-enter street running at Sixth Avenue to the terminal at Eighth Avenue.

Kenosha's five former Toronto Transit Commission (TTC) A-8 class President's Conference Committee (PCC) streetcars were assembled by the Canadian Car and Foundry Company in 1950 with components and body shells provided by the St. Louis Car Company. Between 1987 and 1990, the TTC rebuilt 19 A-8 class PCC cars for a new line. All but two of those cars became surplus and were sold in 1995. The cars for Kenosha were later purchased, reconditioned, and painted in liveries of five North American street railways.

The name PCC is derived from the Electric Railway President's Conference Committee (ERPCC). The ERPCC was formed by presidents of privately owned street railways in 1930 for the purpose of creating superior technology for modern electric rolling stock. A triumph of United States know-how, 5,000 units were produced for North America between 1936 and 1951, and 16,000 were produced in Europe under license from the ERPCC. Thousands more were built in the Soviet Union without license. North American streetcar operations gave way to oil interests and only a handful of systems survived. Thanks to the vision of McCarthy, PCC streetcars are running today on the streets of Kenosha.

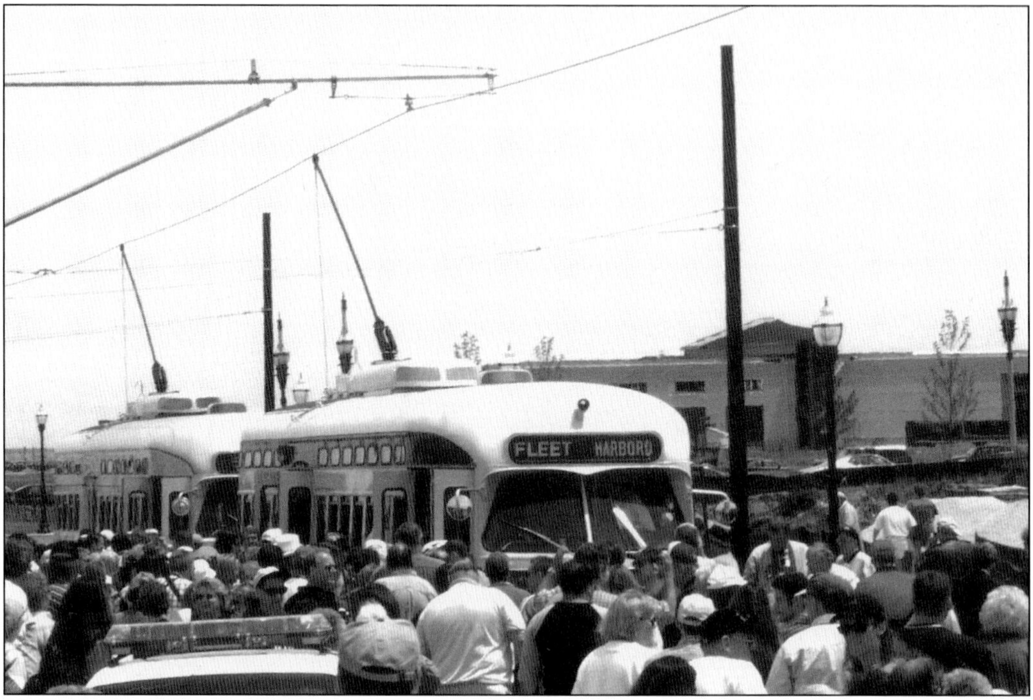

The first two PCC streetcars to go into service on June 17, 2000, were the Kenosha Toronto and the Kenosha Cincinnati. The other three cars would arrive at a later date. Large crowds of people attest to this grand celebration, a very special event for the city of Kenosha. (Photograph by SCC.)

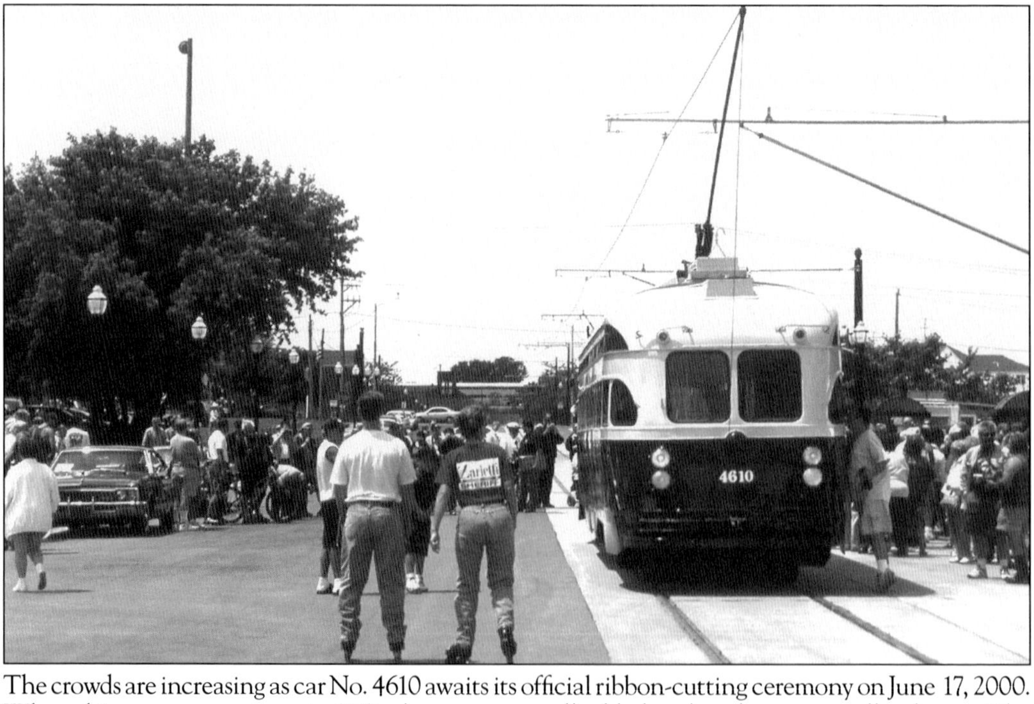

The crowds are increasing as car No. 4610 awaits its official ribbon-cutting ceremony on June 17, 2000. When this streetcar was new in 1951, there were no roller bladers, but there were roller skaters. The scene is looking west on Fifty-fourth Street across Eighth Avenue. (Photograph by DOE.)

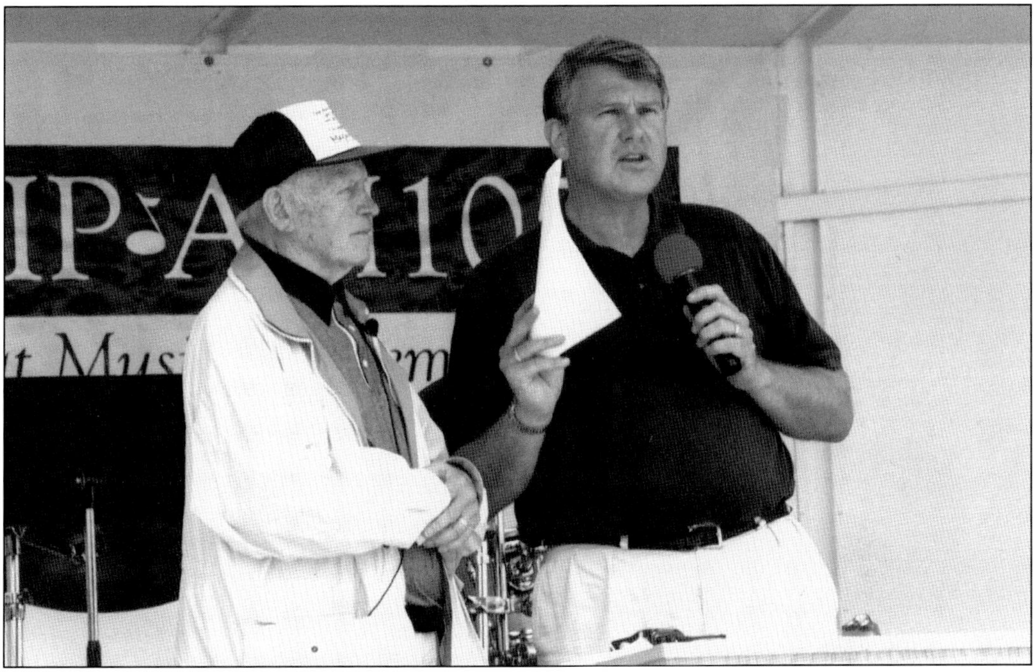

Joseph McCarthy (right), director of Kenosha Transit, introduces Richard Lindgren (left) to the crowd on opening day, June 17, 2000. Lindgren, born in Sweden on May 17, 1908, started working for WG&E in 1926 at age 18 doing custodial work; later he managed the streetcar barn. One of his other jobs was to flag one-man operated streetcars across railway tracks. (Photograph by EF.)

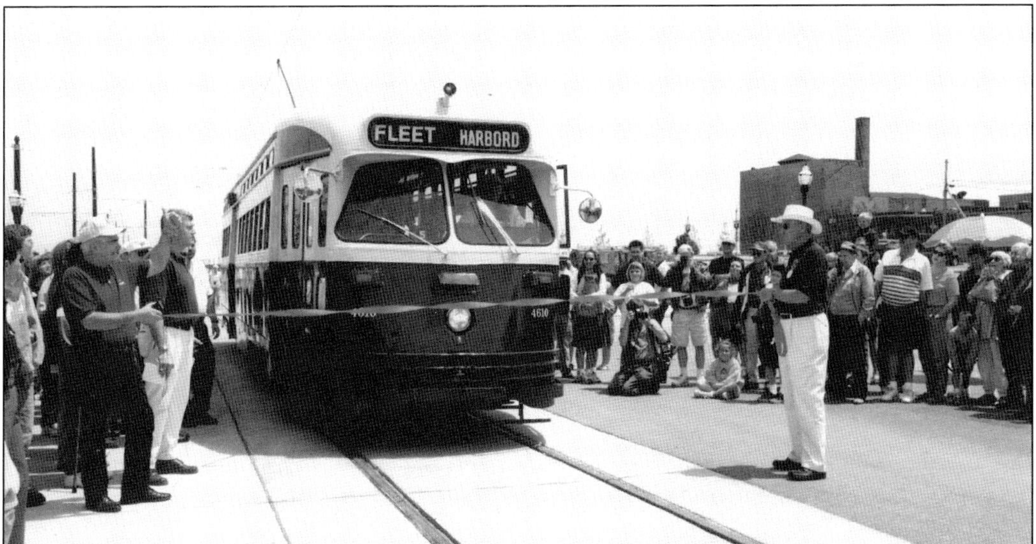

Kenosha Transit Commission board member Louis Rugani (front left) and board chairman Donald K. Holland (front right) tighten the ribbon as Lindgren, honorary streetcar operator, is about to run through the grand opening ribbon on Saturday, June 17, 2000. Rugani would later become cofounder of the Kenosha Streetcar Society. (Photograph by EF.)

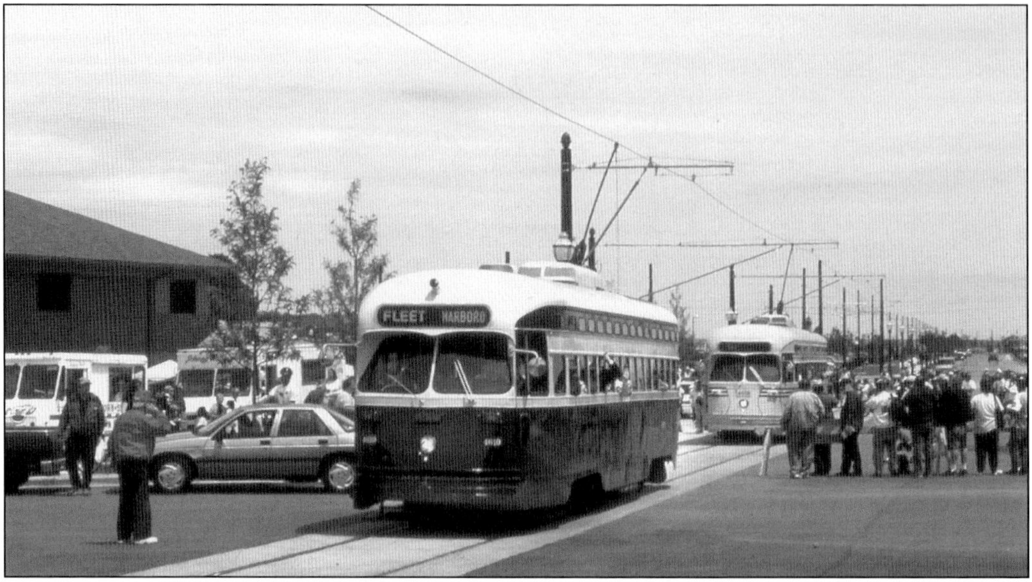

Toronto car No. 4610 crosses Eighth Avenue and is carrying invited guests on the first official streetcar to go into service in Kenosha on Saturday, June 17, 2000. Earlier in the day, TTC streetcar operator Raymond Madden and Patrick Lavallee from the Halton County Radial Museum in Ontario installed a historic destination curtain in the Kenosha Toronto car. Appropriately signed for Fleet Harbord, at day's end, the curtain would be removed and taken back to Toronto. (Photograph by DOE.)

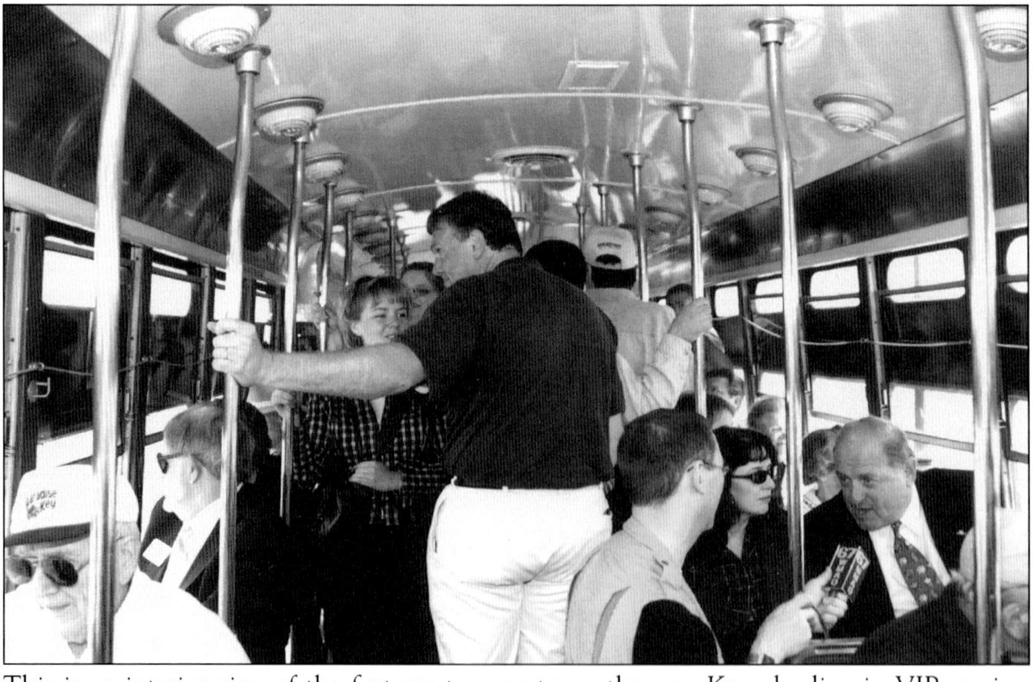

This is an interior view of the first car to operate on the new Kenosha line in VIP service, Saturday, June 17, 2000. Joseph McCarthy is seen here (center, back to the camera) while John F. Doyle (front right) is being interviewed by WMAQ. Doyle would later become cofounder and the first chairman of the Kenosha Streetcar Society. (Photograph by EF.)

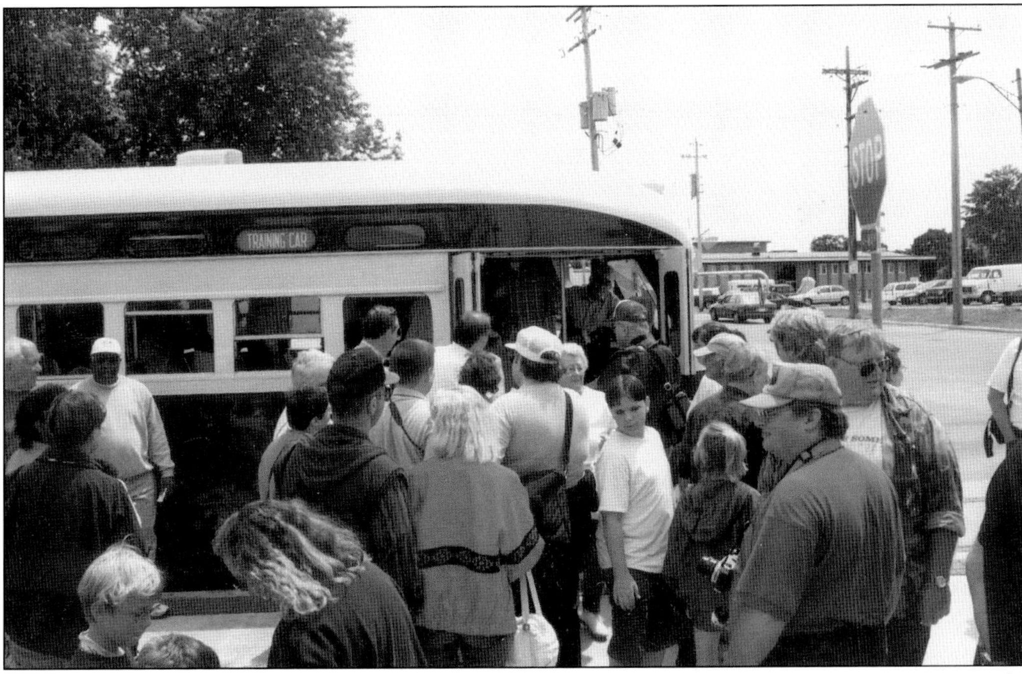

Opening day, Saturday, June 17, 2000, shows the crowds boarding the Toronto car. Among the riders is a future Kenosha Streetcar Society member and contributor to this book, David Stanley (right foreground with baseball hat). The scene is looking south from the Transit Center down Eighth Avenue. The building in the far right background sits on the site of the demolished MRK rapid transit terminal. (Photograph by EF.)

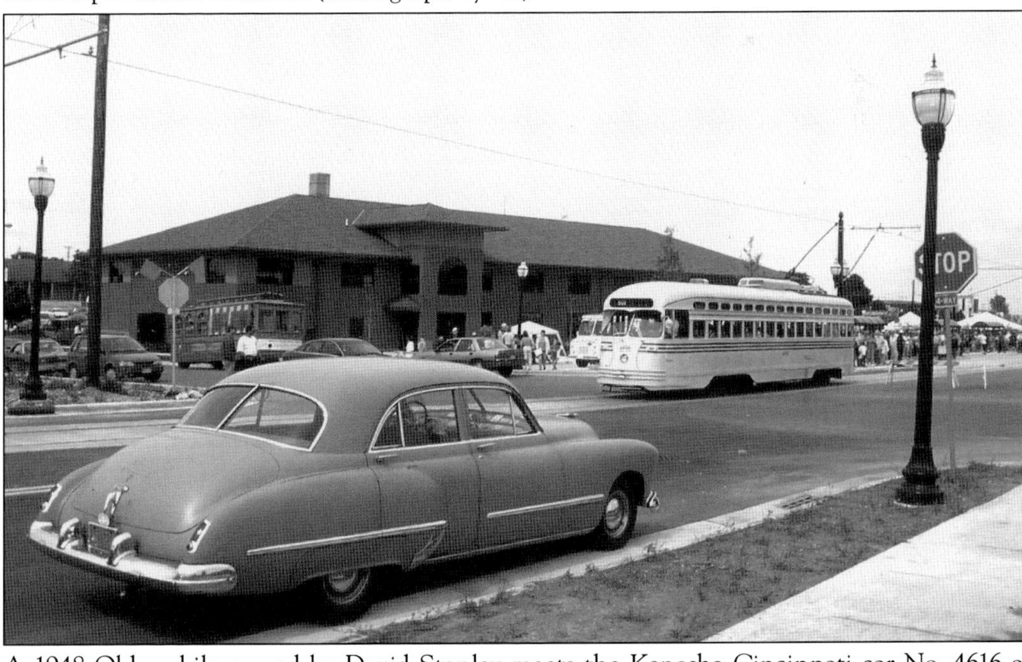

A 1948 Oldsmobile owned by David Stanley meets the Kenosha Cincinnati car No. 4616 as inaugural day runs on the streetcar continue on June 17, 2000. The scene is looking northeast across Eighth Avenue to the carbarn. (Photograph by DOE.)

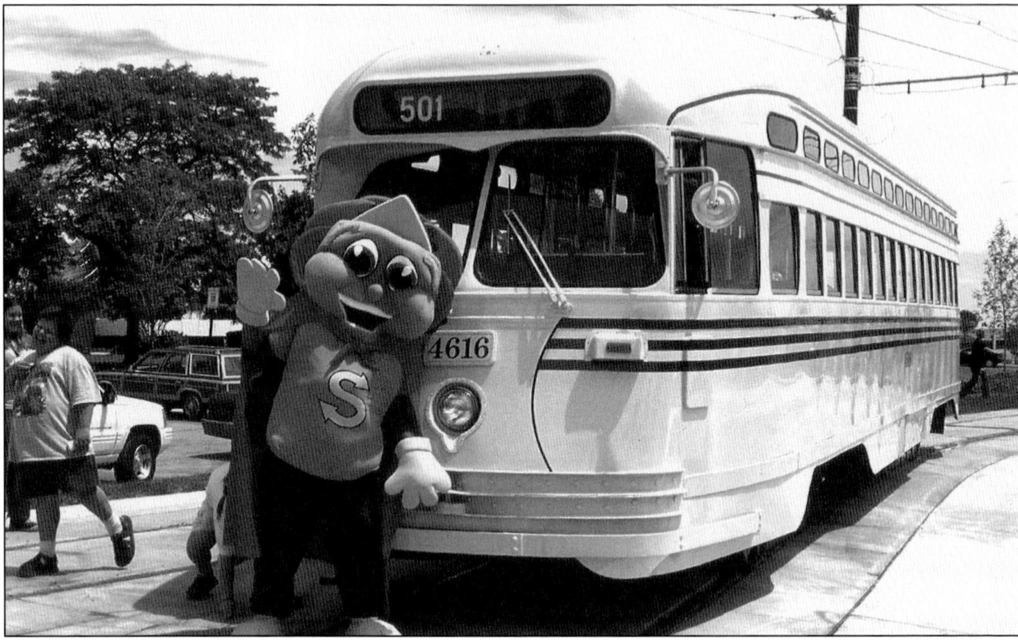

Adding to the excitement on inaugural day is a mascot from a nearby sandwich shop that is attracting customers to the menu specials of the day. Running with blank destination curtains, John F. Doyle would later find the proper cloth material and Andrew W. Maginnis of Philadelphia would paint and letter the destination curtains for all five Kenosha streetcars. (Photograph by DOE.)

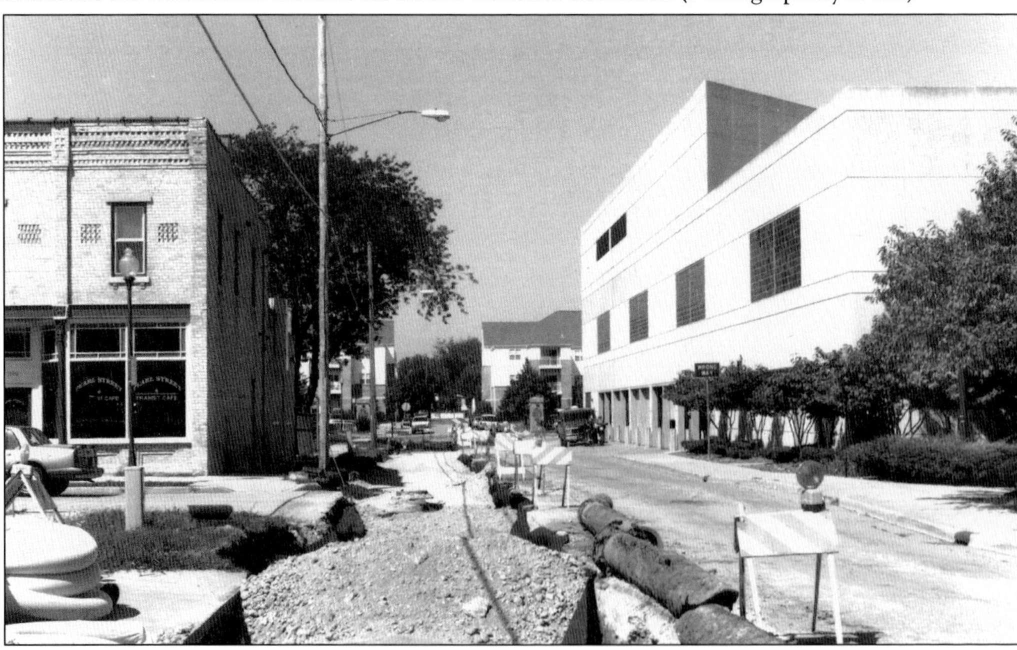

One gets the feeling of a "lost Kenosha" when looking at the building to the left in this new-track construction photograph taken in July 1999. Looking north on Eleventh Avenue from Fifty-fifth Street (named West Street and Pearl Street until 1926), this section of town was a busy marketplace up to Thirteenth Avenue (West Main). The North Western Railroad was at grade, and the KD Line of the North Western came down the middle of Pearl Street. (Photograph by RES.)

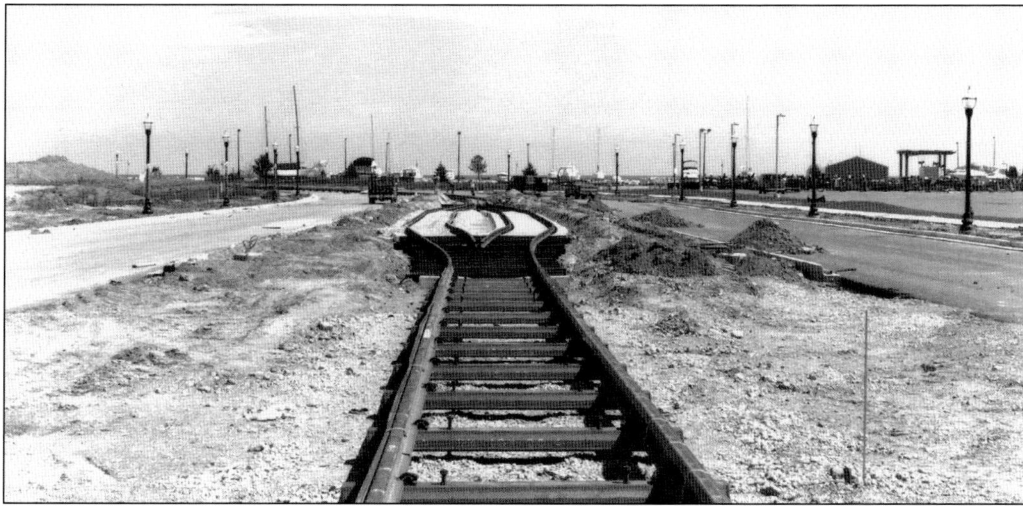

Looking east toward Lake Michigan, track construction in the middle of the brand-new Fifty-sixth Street is well under way in this August 1999 photograph. The passing siding was planned to provide for special events; one car could pass another on this eastbound segment of track. The last streetcar-passing track in Kenosha was built on Grand Avenue (Fifty-second Street) and Fremont Street (Fourteenth Avenue) in 1921. (Photograph by RES.)

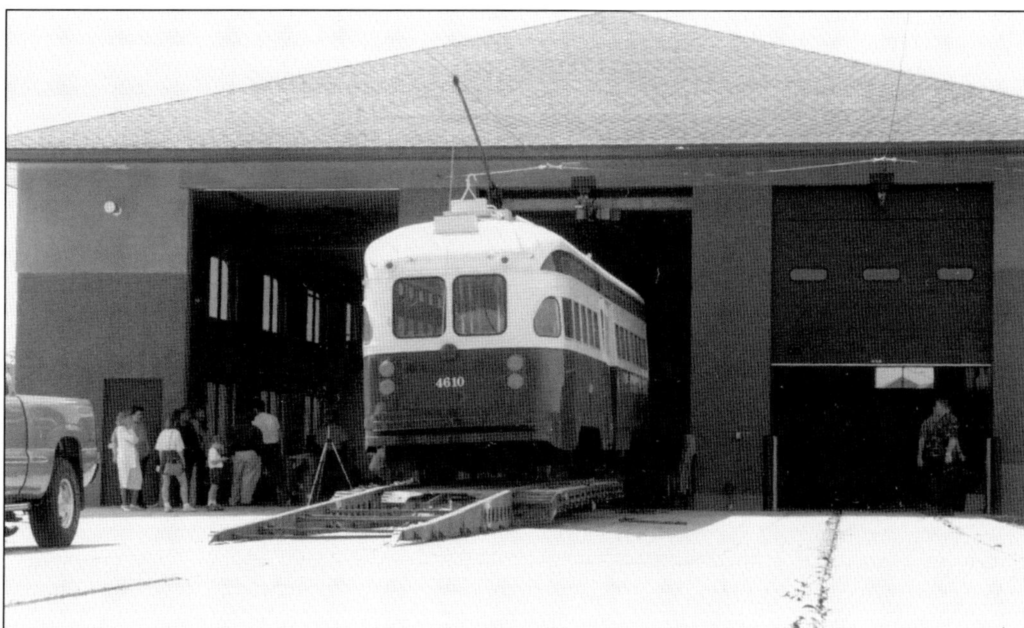

The day is May 5, 2000, and the first streetcar has arrived at the new streetcar barn and transit center in Kenosha. What a very historic event this will be. Within minutes, car No. 4610 will touch the ground of Kenosha, 68 years after streetcar service was abandoned. (Photograph by EF.)

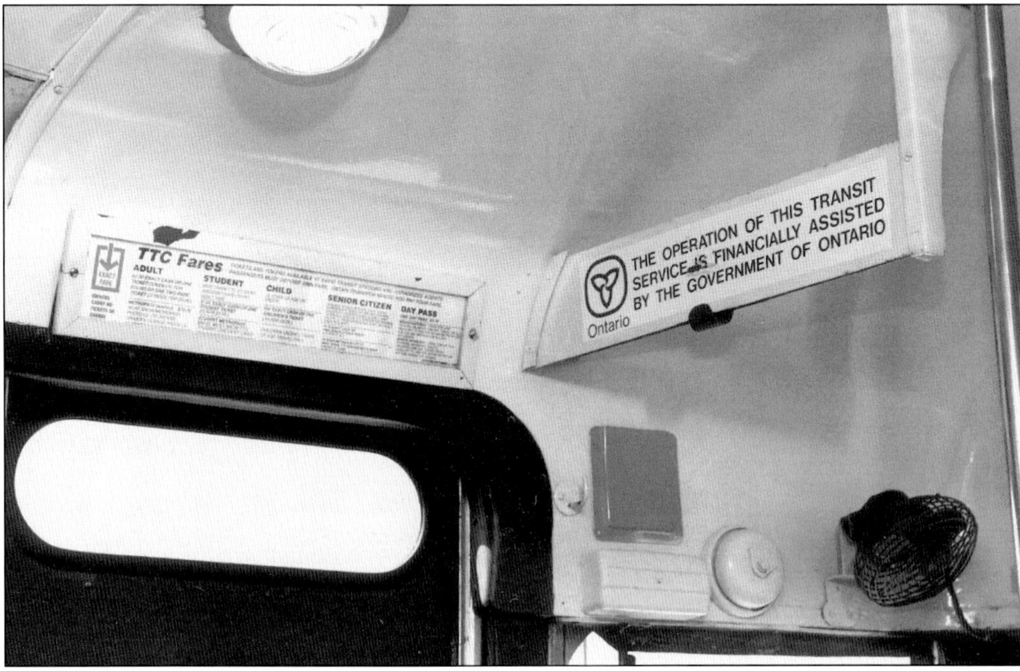

The five PCC streetcars for Kenosha's new line were reconditioned by Minor Rail Services in Donnellson, Iowa. The interiors were in such good condition that they did not have to be repainted. The cars still carry the TTC signage as viewed in this section above and behind the operator. (Photograph by EF.)

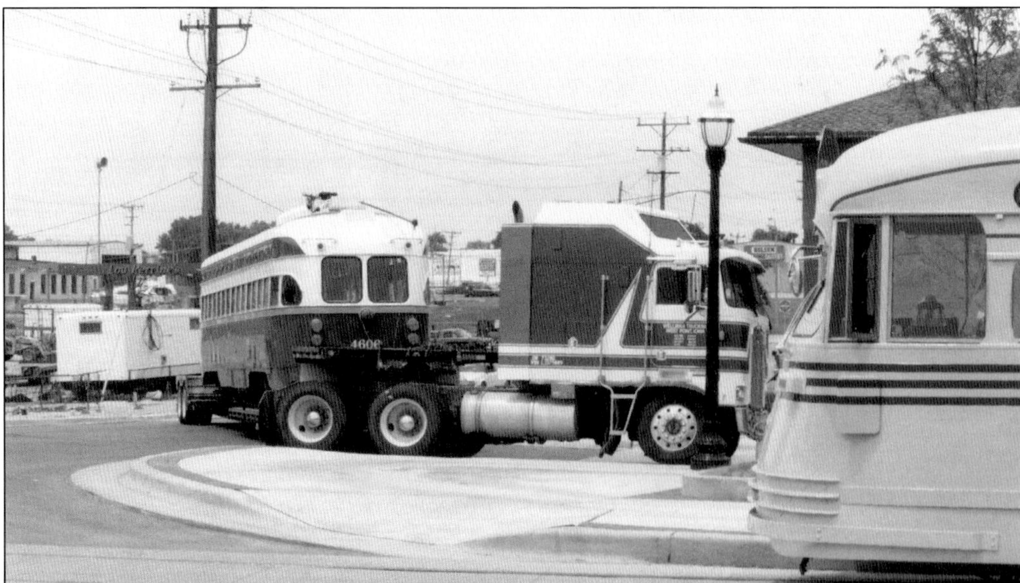

The Chicago painted PCC car No. 4606 is about to be delivered to the Kenosha streetcar barn on June 23, 2000, while Cincinnati painted car No. 4616 in revenue service awaits its departure time. The truck will proceed east through the bus terminal to the back of the carbarn, then back up and unload the streetcar. The scene is looking northwest from Fifty-fourth Street and Eighth Avenue. (Photograph by EF.)

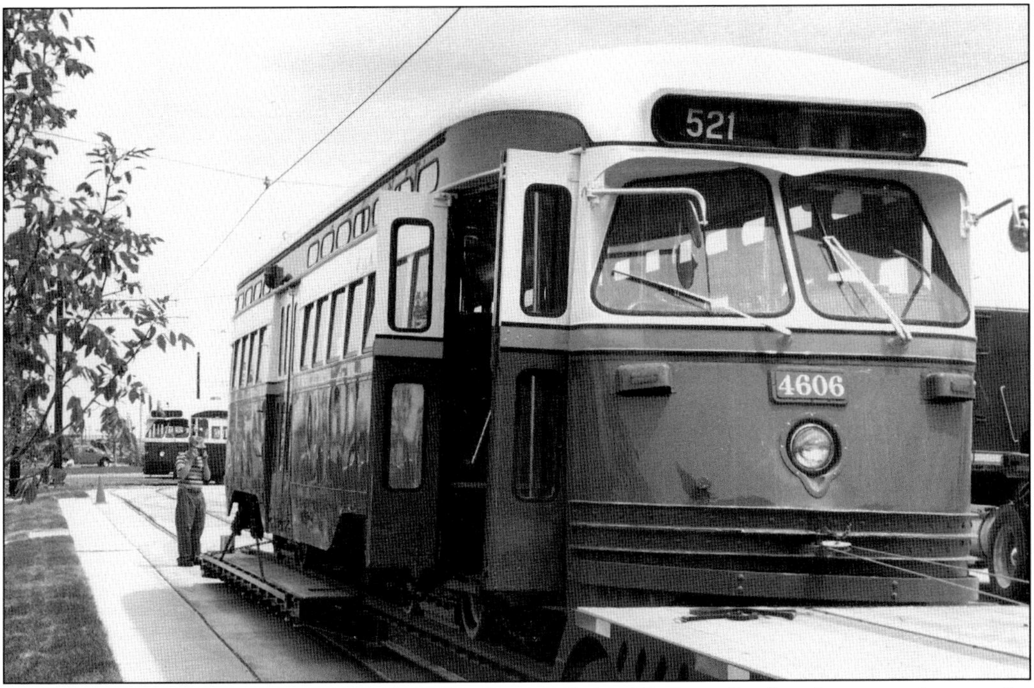

Newly arrived car No. 4606 painted in the livery of the Chicago Surface Lines is about to be moved onto new rail behind the Kenosha Streetcar barn looking east. The colors of the car are aqua green and cream with an orange belt rail. The photographer recording the scene is Frank Sirinek of the Illinois Railway Museum. (Photograph by EF.)

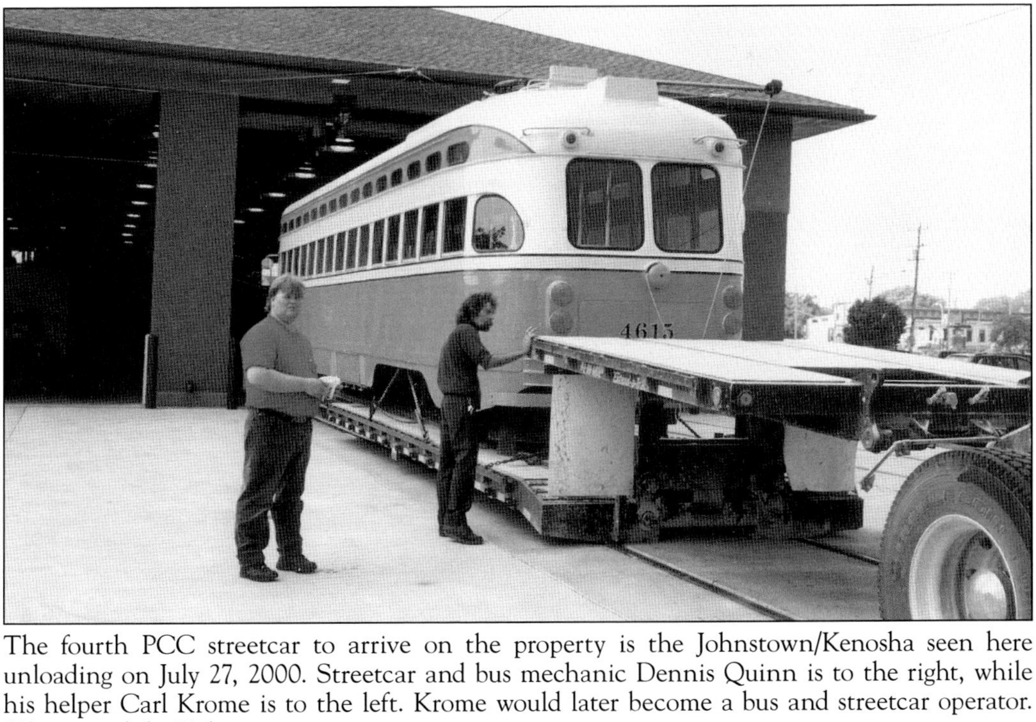

The fourth PCC streetcar to arrive on the property is the Johnstown/Kenosha seen here unloading on July 27, 2000. Streetcar and bus mechanic Dennis Quinn is to the right, while his helper Carl Krome is to the left. Krome would later become a bus and streetcar operator. (Photograph by EF.)

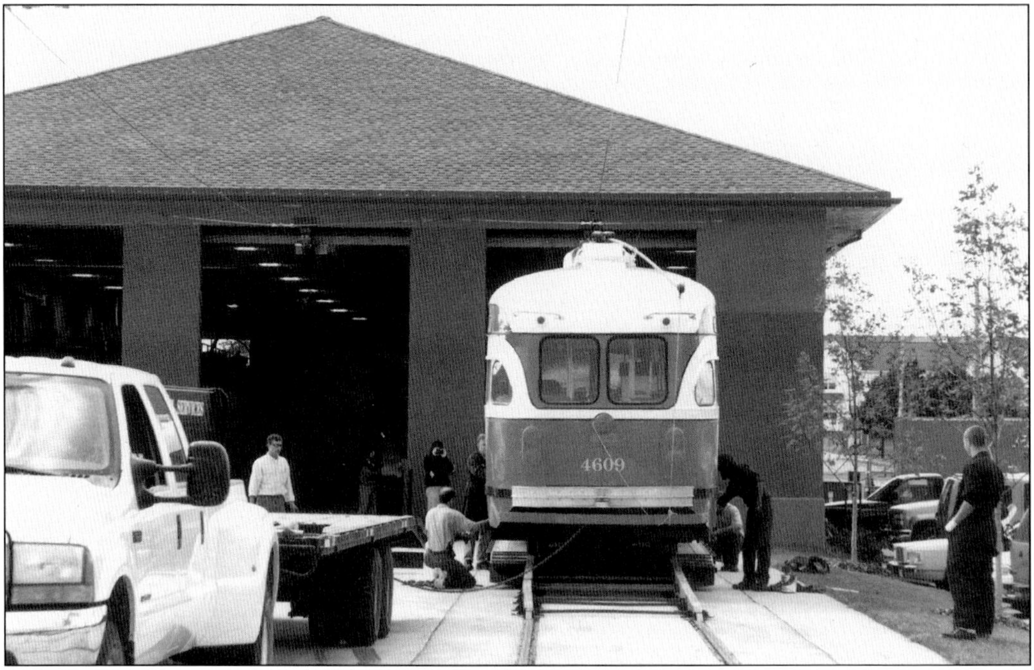

With the arrival of the last streetcar, it was a mystery as to what color the car would be, as Joseph McCarthy had not yet made a decision. John Nicholson, a model importer, presented McCarthy (at this exact same location) a precision model of a Pittsburgh PCC streetcar. Sadly, not long after this meeting, McCarthy unexpectedly passed away. When the streetcar arrived, it was painted in the bright red of Pittsburgh Railways. Only then did everyone realize that the gift to Joe made his color decision. (Photograph by EF.)

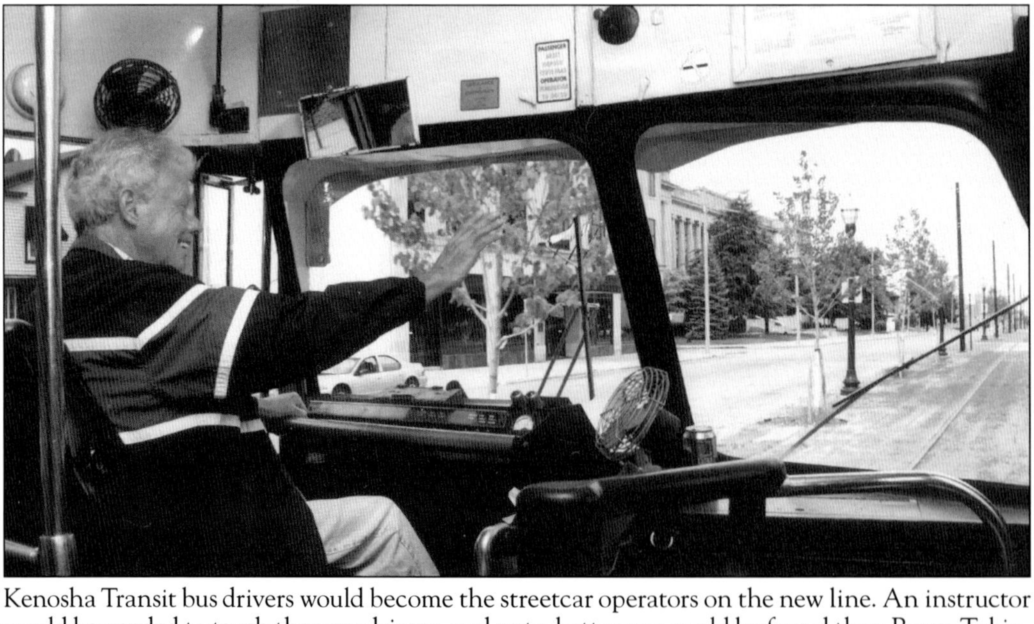

Kenosha Transit bus drivers would become the streetcar operators on the new line. An instructor would be needed to teach the new drivers, and not a better one could be found than Roger Tobin. Tobin, a former streetcar operator and instructor for the Metropolitan Boston Transit Authority (MBTA), is seen here operating on the new line in July 2000. (Photograph by EF.)

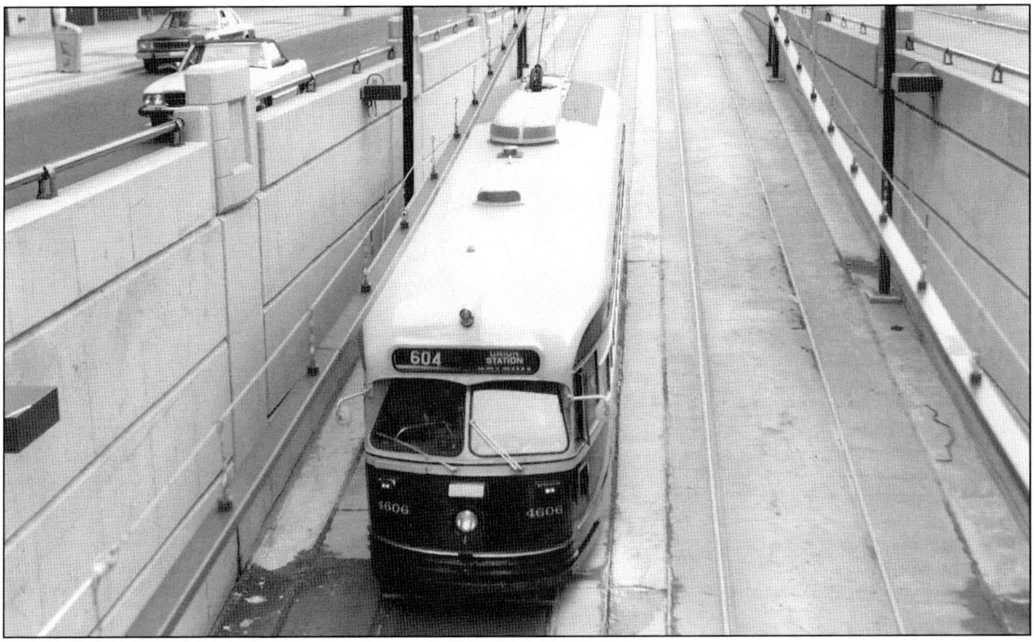

Little did the photographer know, but TTC car No. 4606 would arrive in Kenosha on June 23, 2000, for the new HarborPark streetcar line, almost 10 years to the day from when this photogrpah was taken. Coming off Queens Quay (pronounced "key") on June 25, 1990, on the Harbourfront/Spadina Line, car No. 4606 is descending into the two-stop subway to Union Station. (Photograph by JFD.)

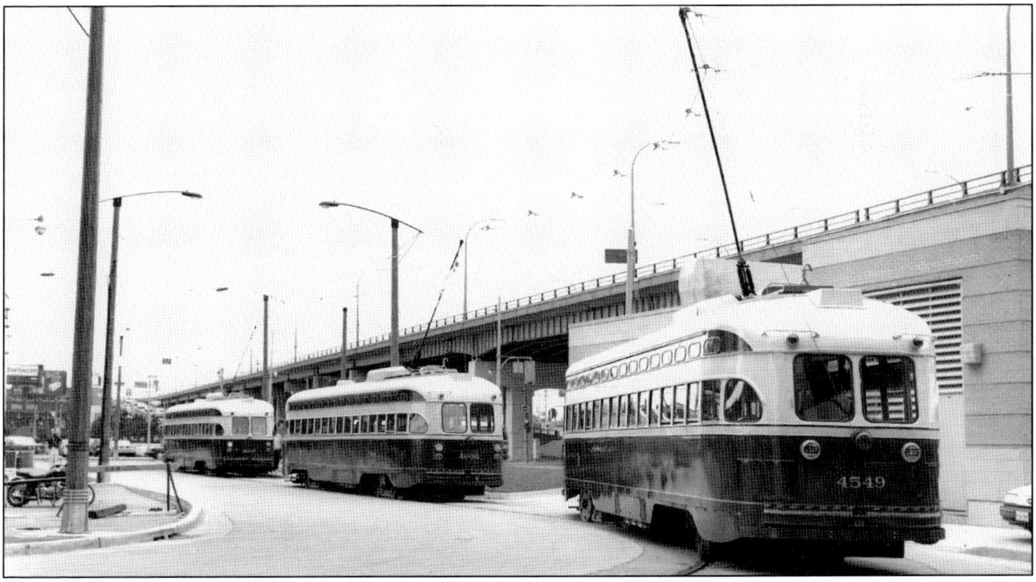

It is grand opening day on the new light rail line, Harbourfront/Spadina, in Toronto on Sunday, June 24, 1990. Car No. 4549, restored as delivered new in 1951 with its operator Raymond Madden, will follow future Kenosha car No. 4606 out of the new Spadina loop. Car No. 4549 on the John F. Doyle and Patrick Lavallee charter will be the first chartered car to operate over the new line. As of 2007, car No. 4549 is still available for private excursions in Toronto as well as car No. 4606 in Kenosha. (Photograph by JFD.)

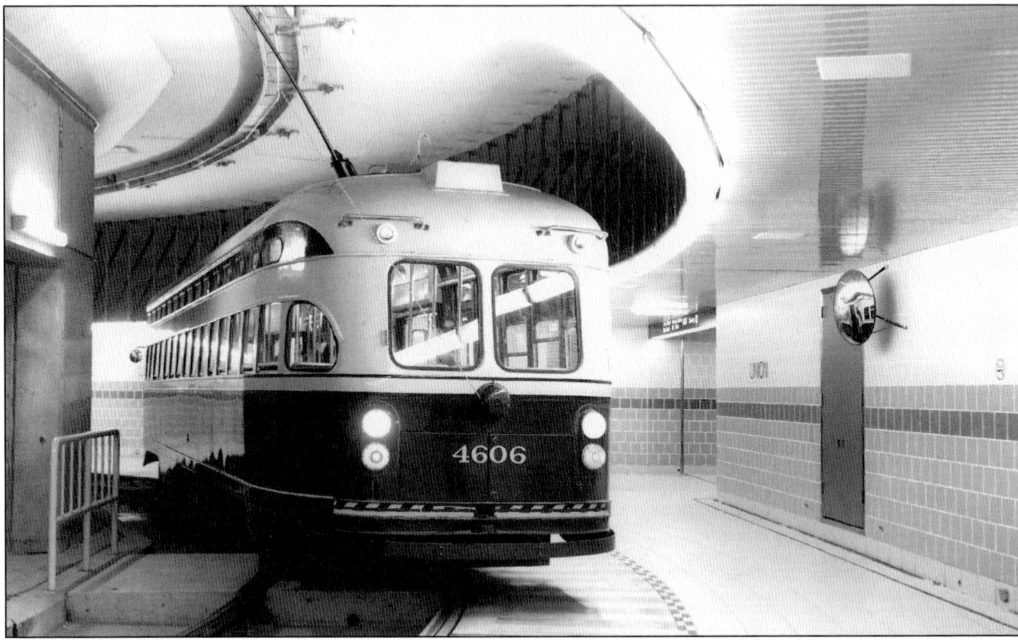

TTC PCC streetcar No. 4606 is at Union Station in Toronto on Monday, June 25, 1990. The car, originally numbered 4528 was one of 19 cars rebuilt in the late 1980s for service on the new light rail line, Harbourfront/Spadina. The car would later become the Kenosha Chicago car and retain its Toronto fleet number. (Photograph by JFD.)

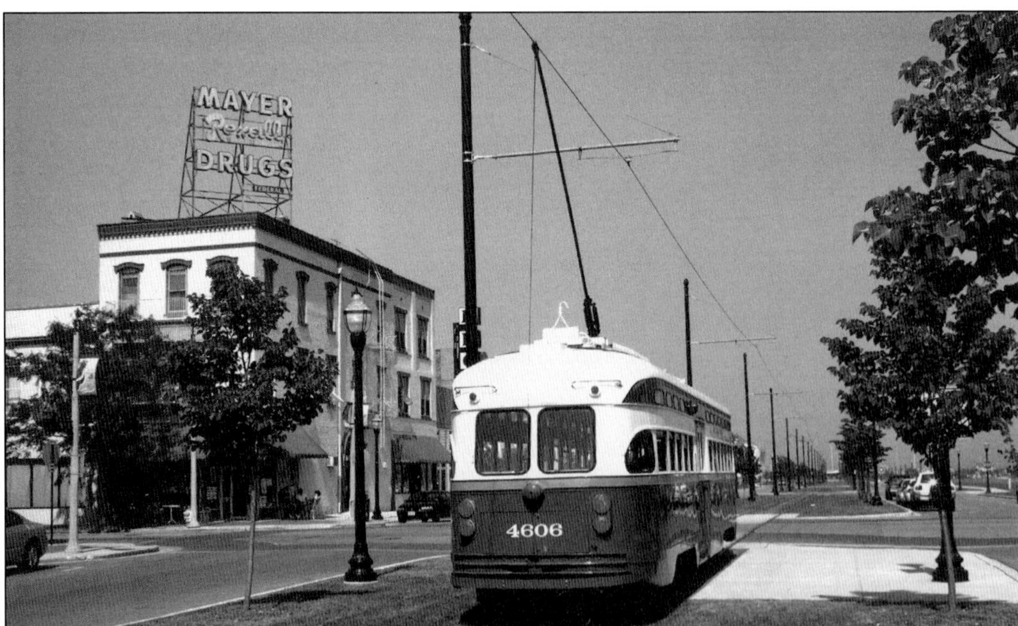

Former TTC PCC streetcar No. 4606 would again operate in a lake setting; only this time, it would be Lake Michigan rather than Lake Ontario. Painted in the livery of the Chicago Surface Lines, the car is seen here on July 24, 2002, about to cross Sixth Avenue on Fifty-sixth Street looking east. (Photograph by JFD, MS.)

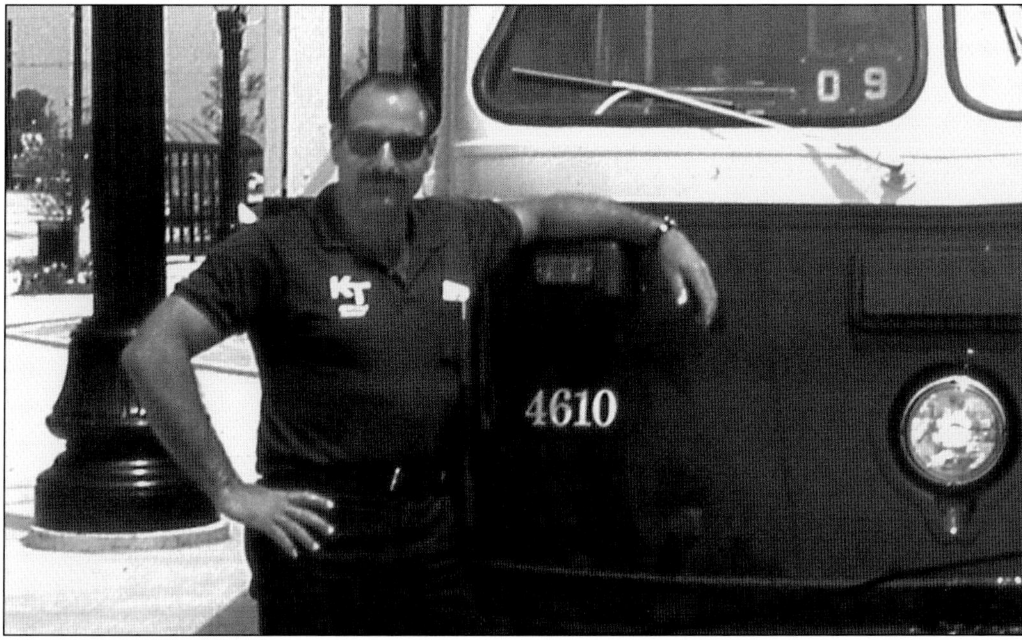

Streetcar operator Sam Lucchetta stands next to Kenosha Transit PCC streetcar No. 4610 painted in the maroon and cream livery of the TTC in July 2000. Lucchetta was well loved and will be missed by all, as he passed away unexpectedly on January 2, 2007. Lucchetta was especially good with the children who rode the streetcars. (Photograph by GEK.)

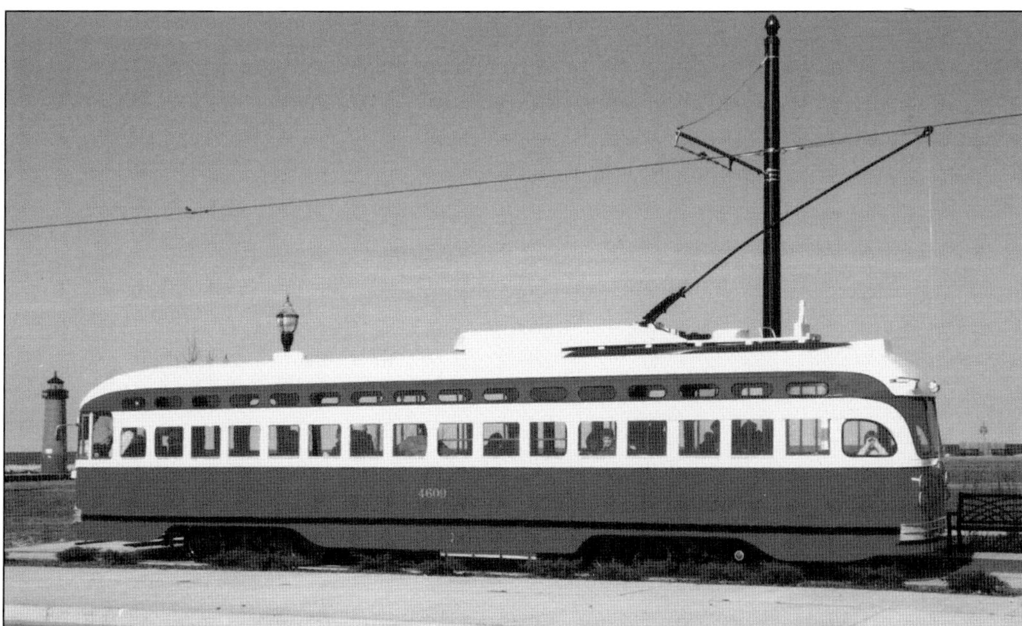

This view is looking east with Lake Michigan as a backdrop for the Kenosha Pittsburgh PCC streetcar No. 4609 in April 2002. While the streetcar drifts northbound on Ring Road, the child in the rear window mimics the photographers by forming a camera with her hands. Note the round mile recorder on the axle end of the rear wheel. (Photograph by JFD, MS.)

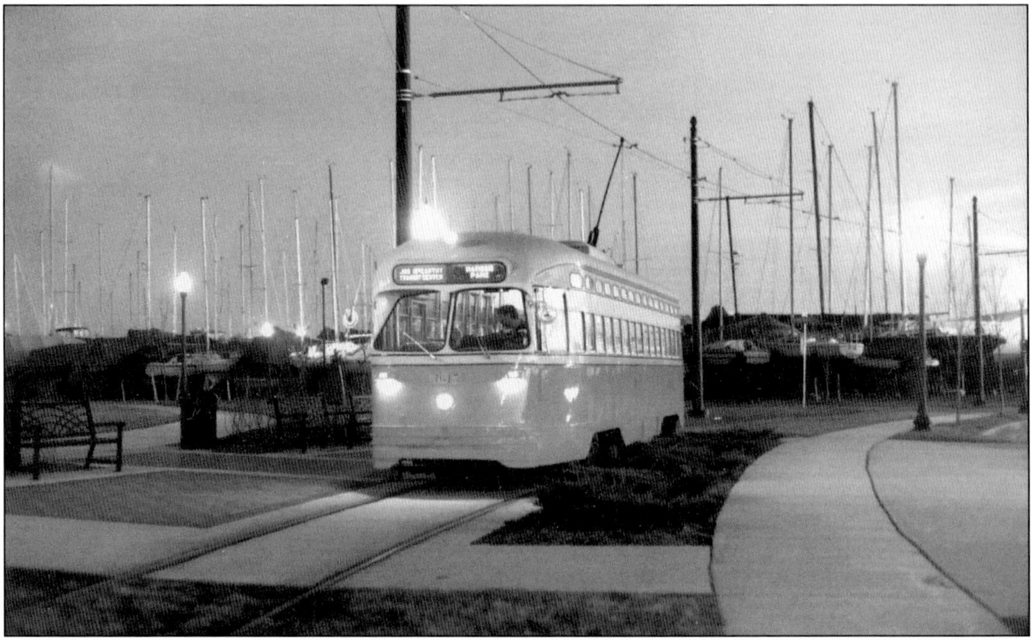

It is twilight in March 2003 as the Kenosha Johnstown PCC streetcar No. 4615 is seen northbound on Ring Road. The tall masts of sailing ships attest to Kenosha's nautical ambience. The area in the rear of the photograph would be the future home of a new boathouse for the Southport Marina. (Photograph by LK.)

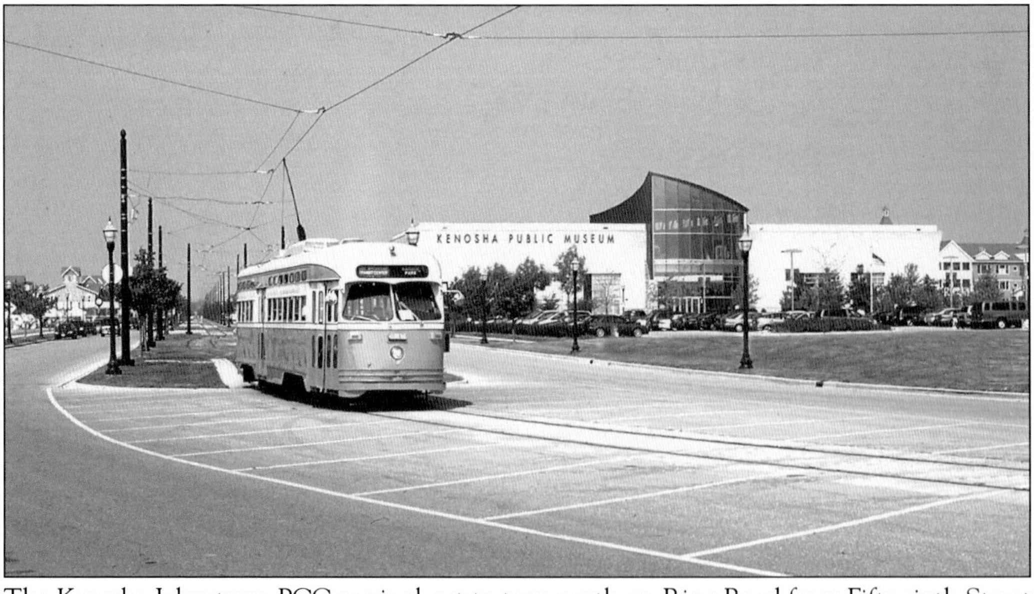

The Kenosha Johnstown PCC car is about to turn north on Ring Road from Fifty-sixth Street with the Kenosha Public Museum in the background on May 10, 2003. The museum houses the skeletal remains of a 12,500-year-old woolly mammoth, butchered by humans and discovered in 1992 on the Schafer Farm west of Kenosha. The bones, along with a life-size replica of the animal, are displayed at the museum. (Photograph by EB.)

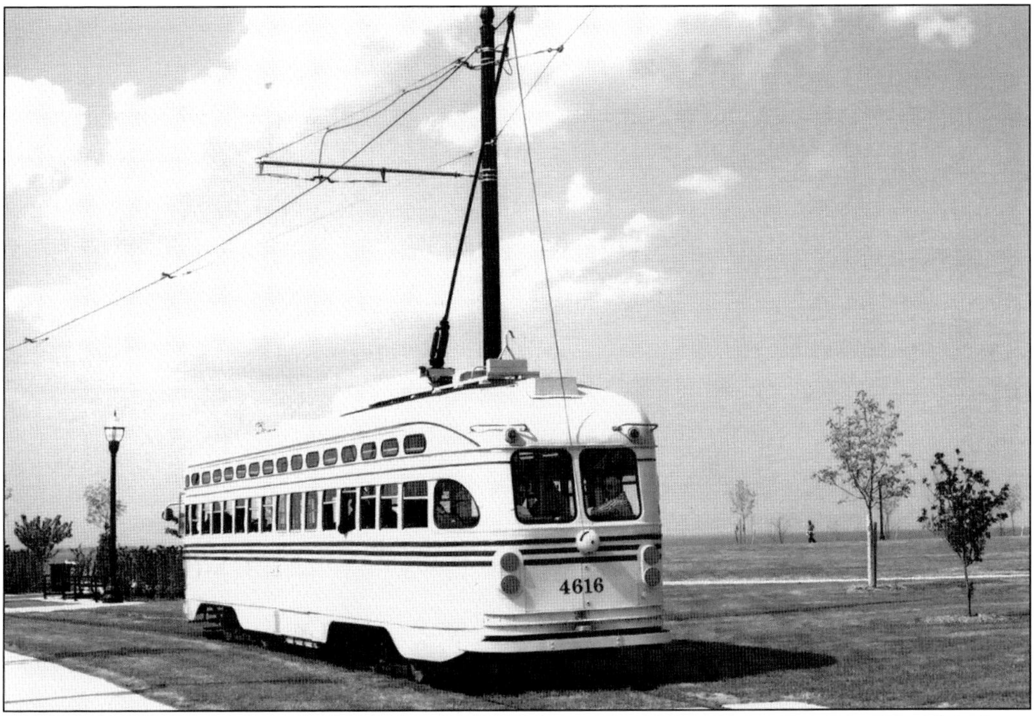

Kenosha Transit PCC streetcar No. 4616 is seen here turning west next to Ring Road looking north toward Lake Michigan on June 5, 2003. Splendid in its bright yellow livery, the car will turn west and run on parkway between Fifty-fourth Street and the Pike Creek inlet. (Photograph by DJD.)

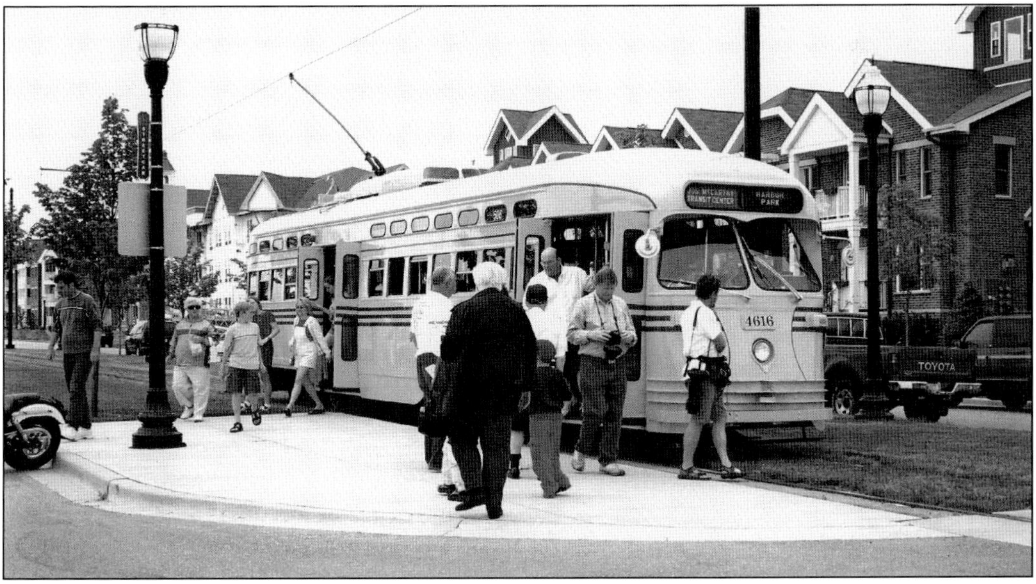

Kenosha Transit PCC streetcar No. 4616 is painted in brilliant yellow with green striping and a gray roof in the livery of the Cincinnati Street Railway. Eastbound on Fifty-sixth Street on June 14, 2003, two Kenosha Streetcar Society members, Larry Konsbruck (far left) and Richard Smyth (right, with camera in hand), are seen. (Photograph by JFD, MS.)

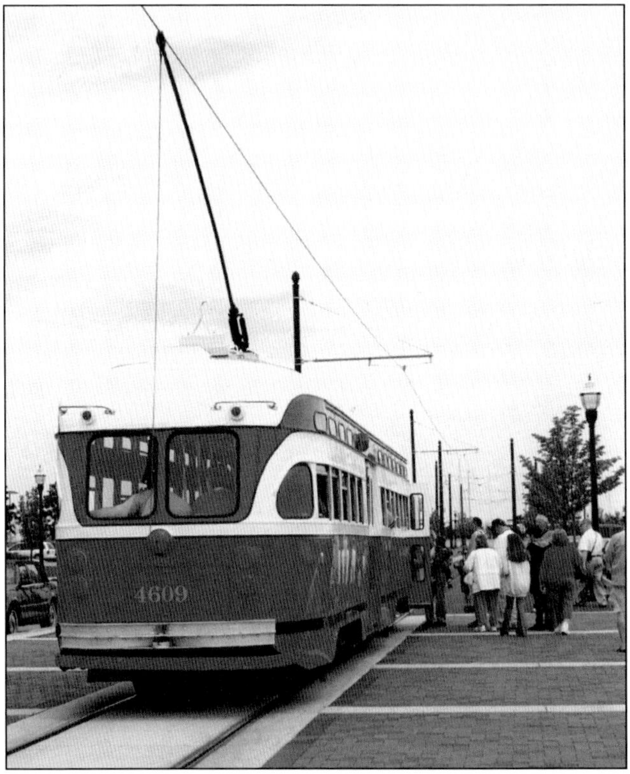

Pittsburgh Railways painted Kenosha Transit PCC car No. 4609 loads passengers from the Kenosha Public Museum stop on Saturday, June 14, 2003. The car, painted in bright red and cream with black striping, gold letters, and silver bumper, is facing east on Fifty-sixth Street. (Photograph by JFD, MS.)

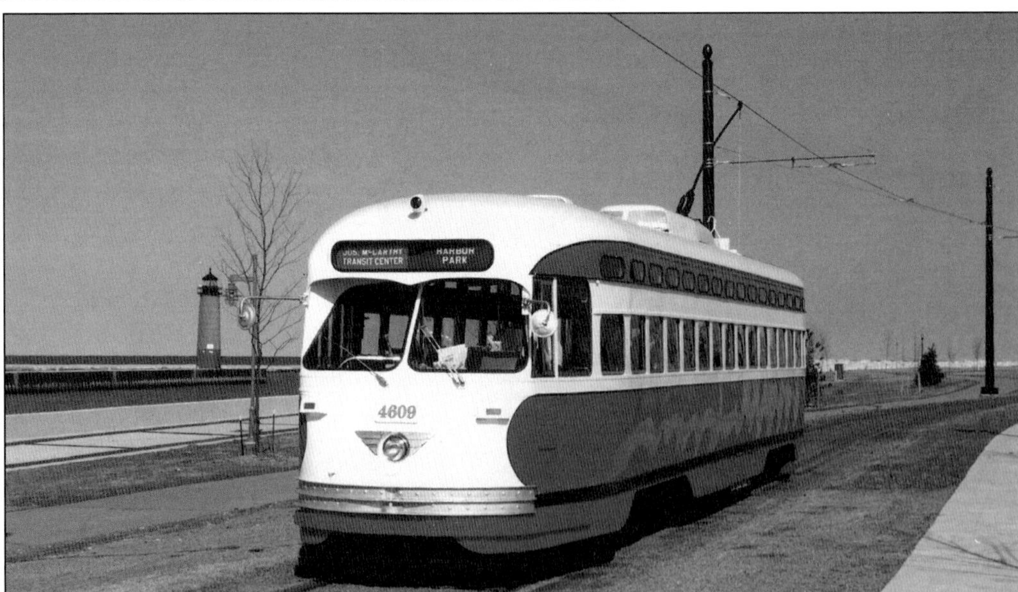

Car No. 4609 shows off its new destination signs and headlight wings. Robert Hughes of Philadelphia donated a set of PCC wings that were needed for the Kenosha, Chicago, and Pittsburgh cars. John F. Doyle personally picked them up, and Louis Rugani had patterns and molds produced from the originals for two new sets of headlight wings. On the other Kenosha liveries, those cities had no wings. (Photograph by JFD, MS.)

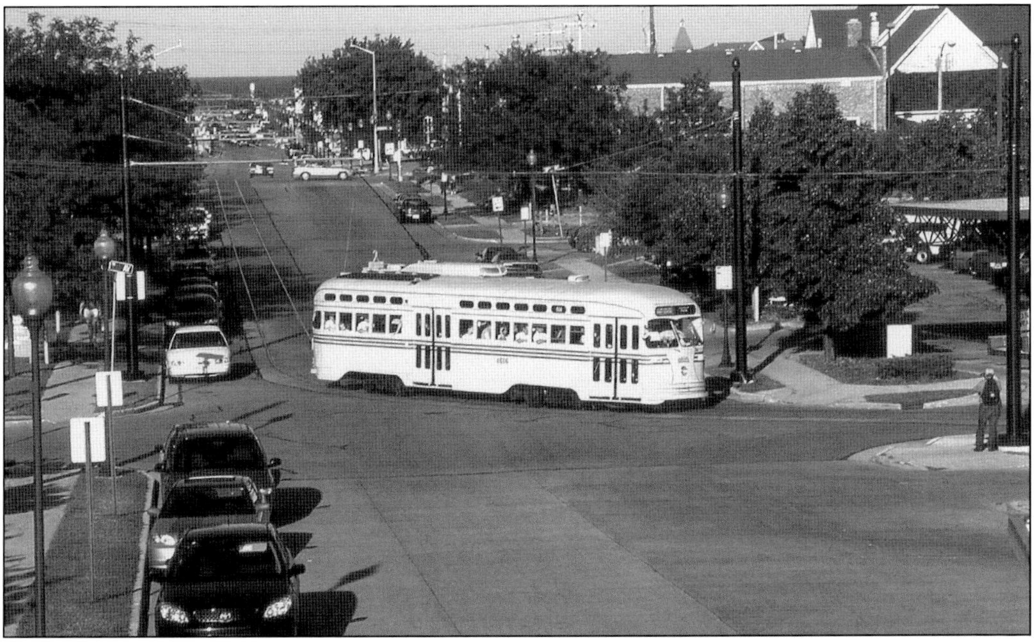

It is the weekend of the tall ships at Kenosha on August 8, 2003. To the thousands of people converging on the lakefront, riding the streetcar was a double treat and to many, a big surprise. The Kenosha Cincinnati PCC streetcar, hauling a full load of passengers, is turning south into Eleventh Avenue, as this view looks east down Fifty-fourth Street to Lake Michigan. (Photograph by EB.)

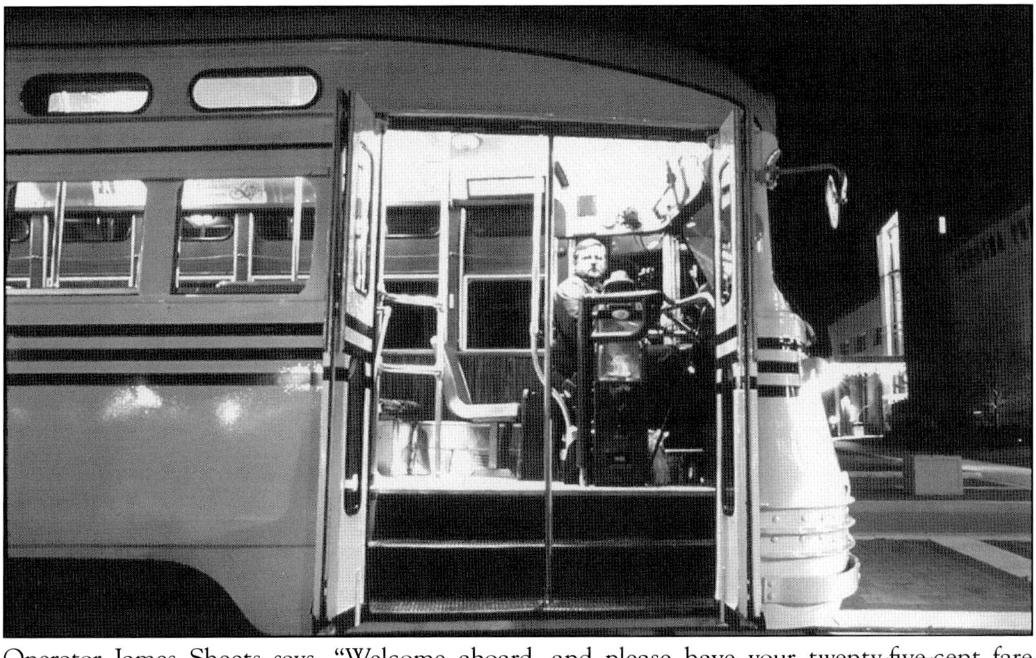

Operator James Sheets says, "Welcome aboard, and please have your twenty-five-cent fare ready." Car No. 4616 is seen here on the last trip of the day at the Kenosha Public Museum in December 2003. (Photograph by EB.)

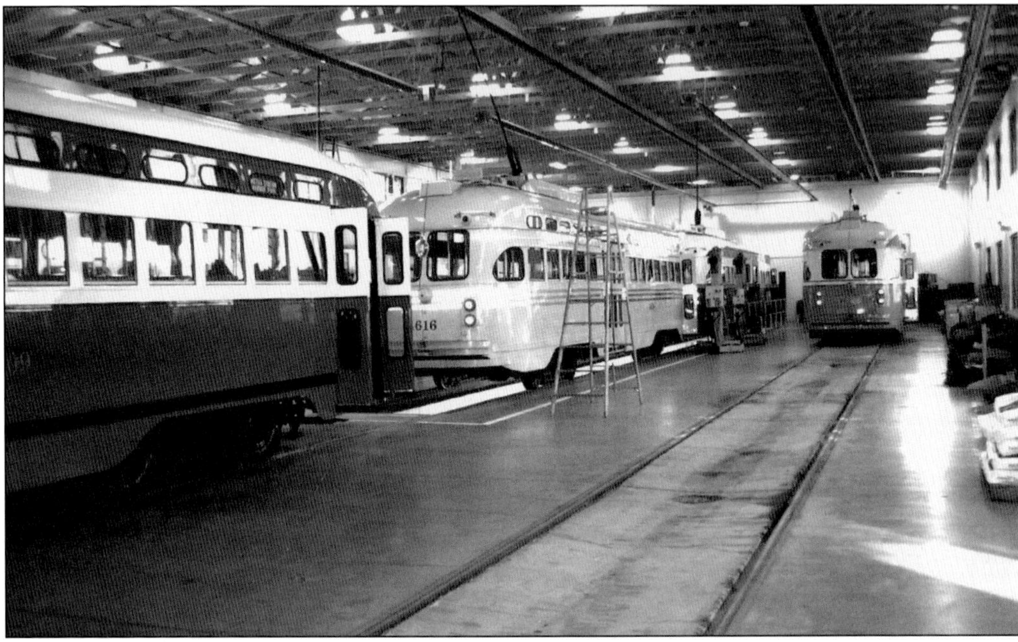

The interior of the Kenosha streetcar barn is seen here on December 27, 2003. The Chicago Cincinnati, Pittsburgh, and Johnstown cars are facing the west end of the barn. To enter service, the cars are backed out of the barn and switched over to the main line. (Photograph by MH.)

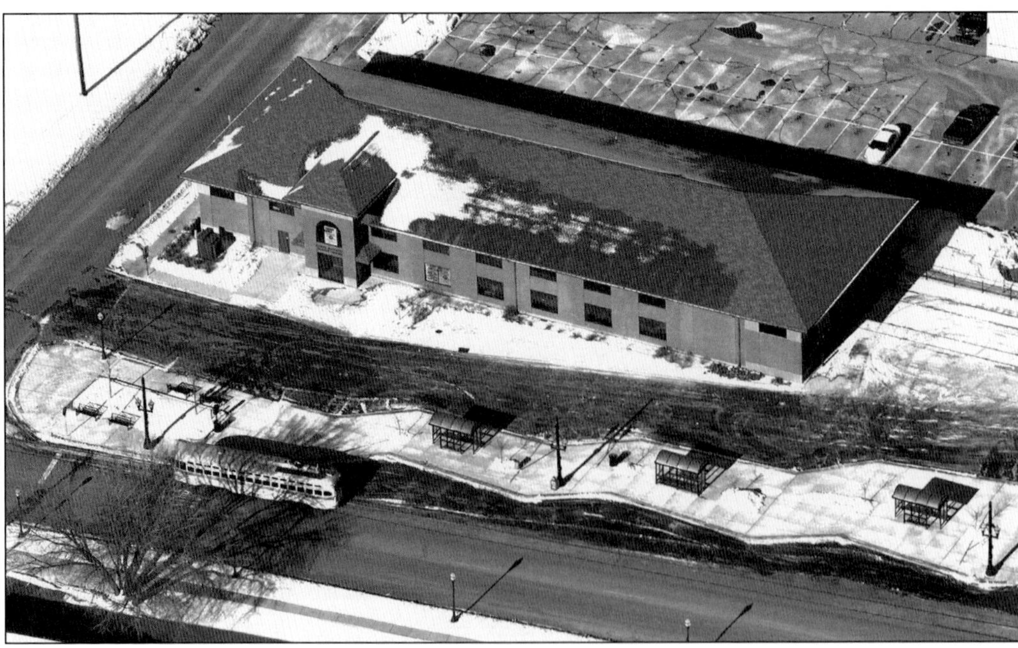

The Joseph McCarthy Transit Center is seen from this aerial view taken in February 2004. It is a Sunday afternoon, and the streetcar is facing west on Fifty-fourth Street at Eighth Avenue. The jagged sidewalk (on both sides) is where Kenosha city buses will terminate and await their departure times. In the upper right of the photograph, behind the carbarn, are two sets of tracks used to move cars in the out of the barn. (Photograph by THAP.)

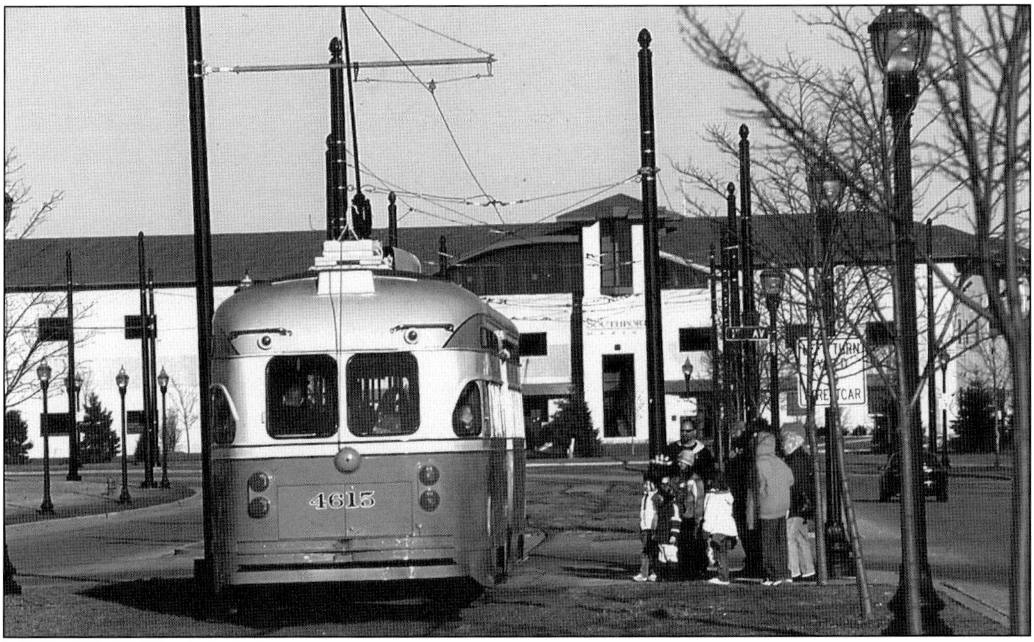

Looking east toward the new Southport Marina, PCC car No. 4615 glides to a stop at First Avenue on March 4, 2006. Painted bright traction orange and cream with a gray roof and black striping, the car is operating on private right-of-way in between the east and west lanes of Fifty-sixth Street. (Photograph by EB.)

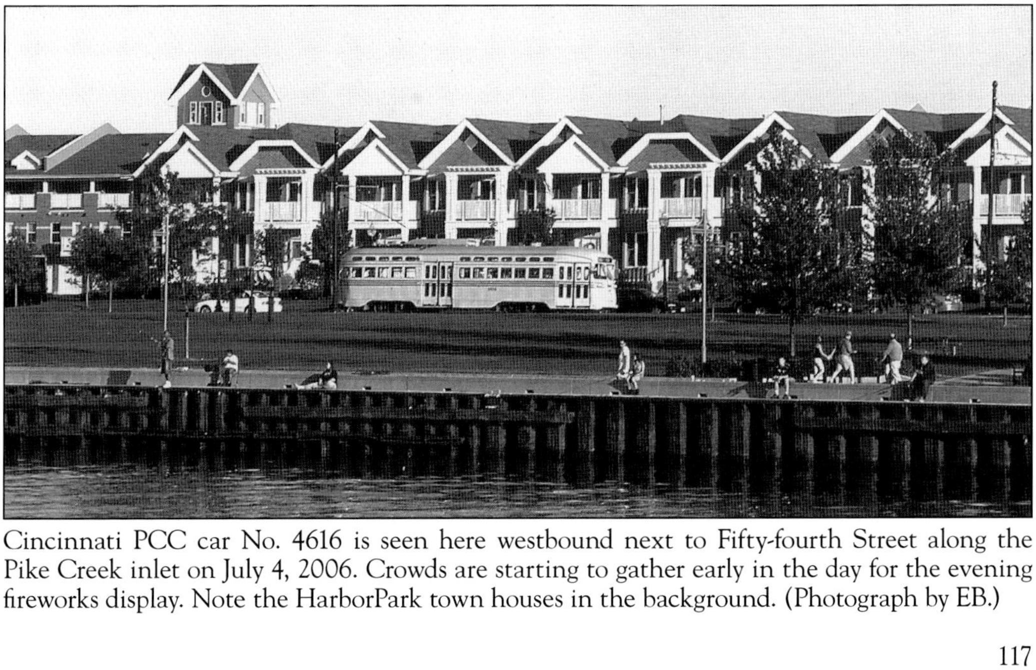

Cincinnati PCC car No. 4616 is seen here westbound next to Fifty-fourth Street along the Pike Creek inlet on July 4, 2006. Crowds are starting to gather early in the day for the evening fireworks display. Note the HarborPark town houses in the background. (Photograph by EB.)

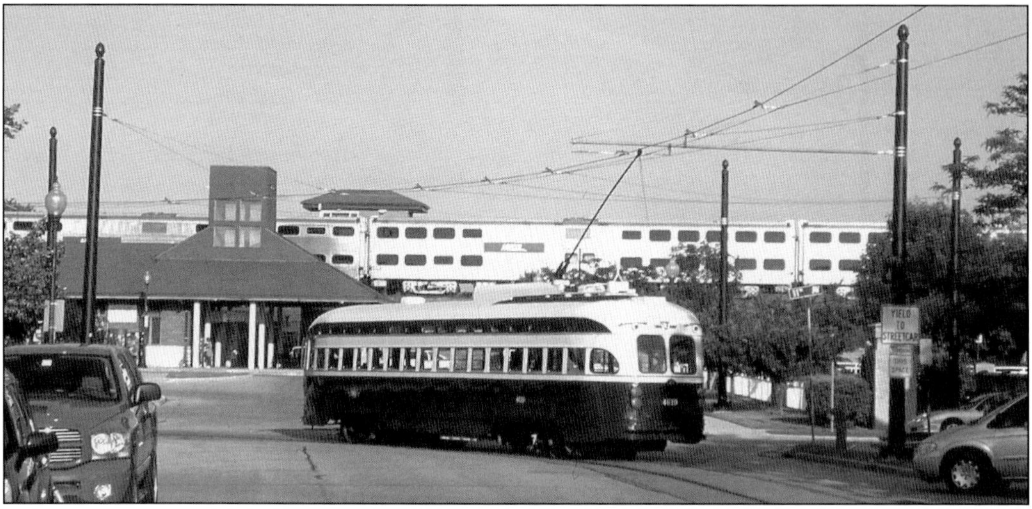

In July 2006, Kenosha Area Transit PCC car No. 4610, the Toronto car, turns the corner at Fifty-fourth Street and Eleventh Avenue. The Metra station and a commuter train consisting of new stainless steel, bi-level commuter cars await passengers traveling south. To the left, the elevator of this station can be seen and was built to accommodate persons with disabilities so they could reach the platform. (Photograph by DOE.)

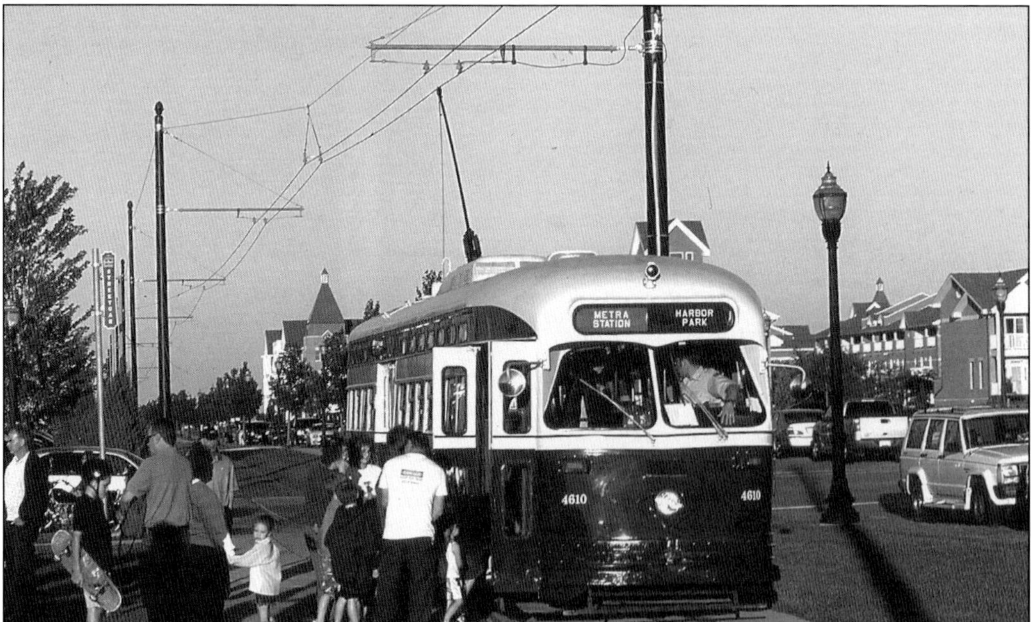

Crowds are gathering on August 30, 2006, for one of the many musical concerts that are held on the Kenosha lakefront. Standing along Fifty-fourth Street, westbound Kenosha Toronto PCC car No. 4610 is about to load passengers at Sixth Avenue. (Photograph by EB.)

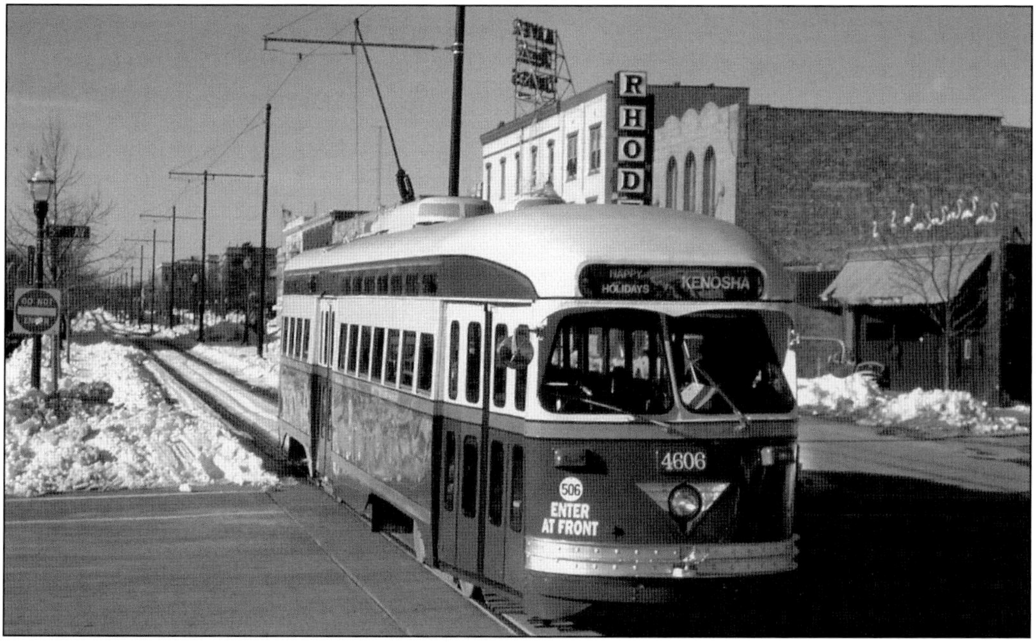

Fresh out of the shop after work to insure its mechanical reliability and with new doors, Kenosha Area Transit PCC car No. 4606 (Chicago) is seen here at Fifty-sixth Street and Fifth Avenue on December 9, 2006. Note the addition of silver paint on the front bumper and side rub rails. (Photograph by DOE.)

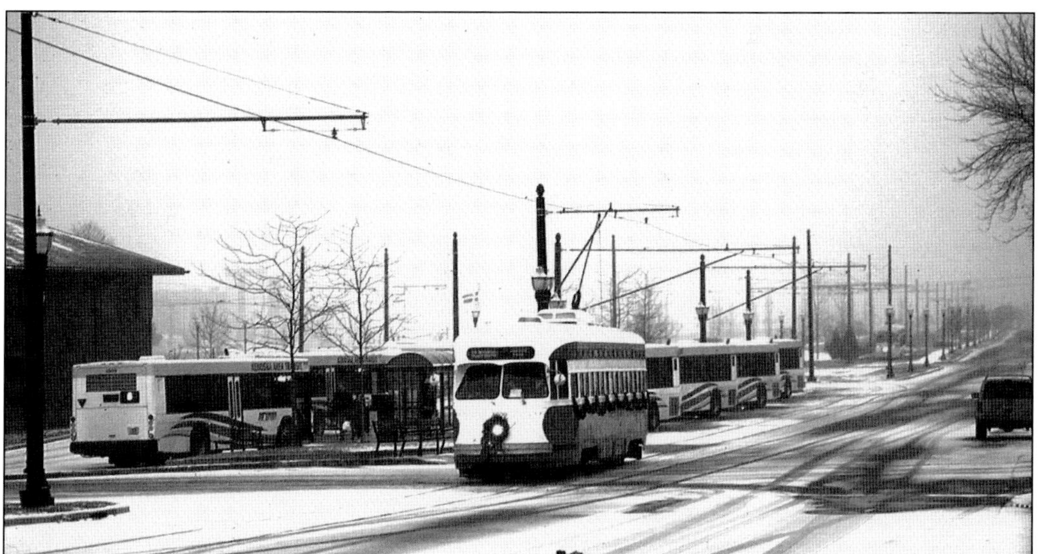

With the snow falling, Christmas-decorated PCC car No. 4609 starts to cross Eighth Avenue on December 3, 2005, looking east down Fifty-fourth Street. In the background, city buses can be seen awaiting their departure time, while the Cincinnati PCC car in the far background is crossing Sixth Avenue. Both streetcars are participating in the annual children's Christmas event, the Candy Cane Special. (Photograph by EB.)

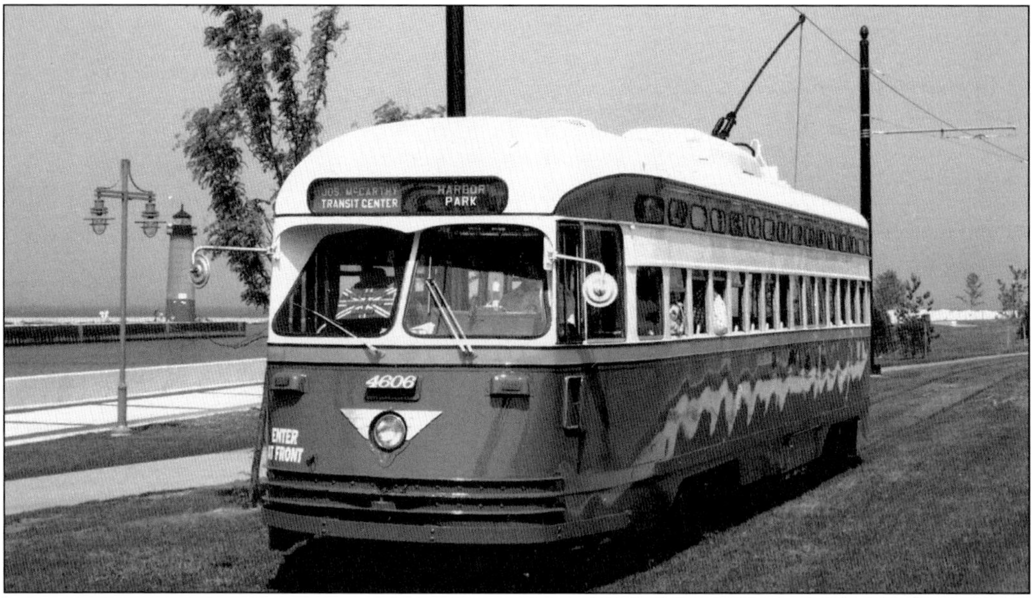

On the windshield, the Union Jack can be seen on this special excursion organized by John F. Doyle and Louis Rugani for their special guest Winstan Bond on July 24, 2002. Bond was the financial director of the National Tramway Museum at Crich in Derbyshire, England. The car is westbound, while the view looks northeast across the Pike Creek inlet to Lake Michigan. (Photograph by JFD, MS.)

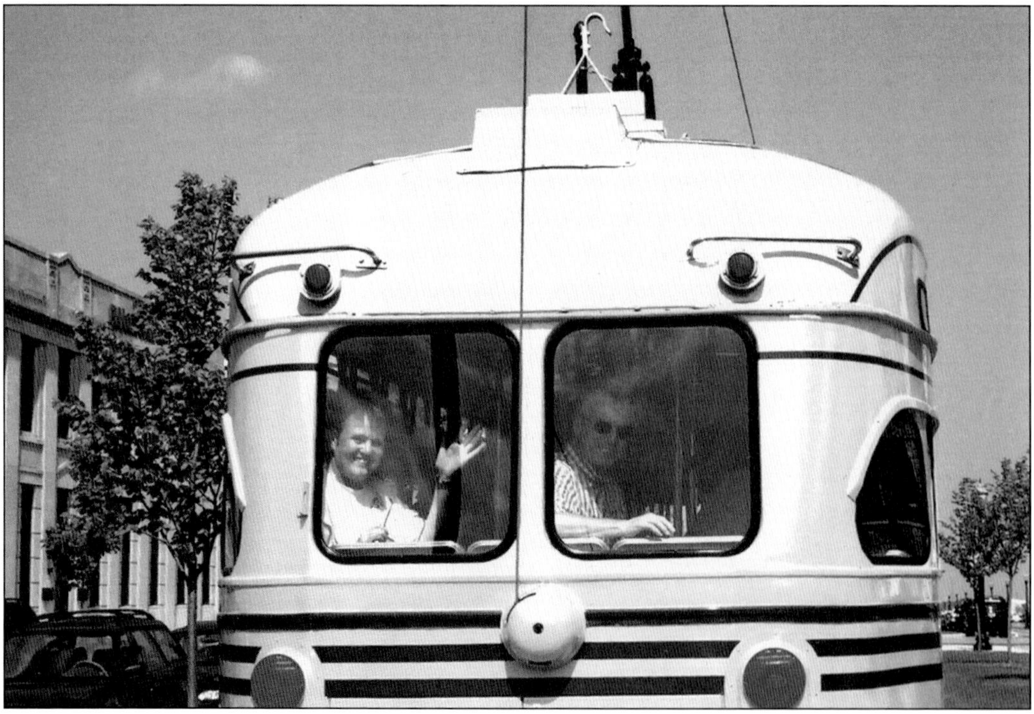

Gisela and Dieter Grimm from Immenhausen, a suburb of Kassel, Germany, wave to the photographer on June 5, 2003. The Cincinnati car is being used on this special excursion sponsored by John F. Doyle in honor of the Grimm's visit to Kenosha. (Photograph by DJD.)

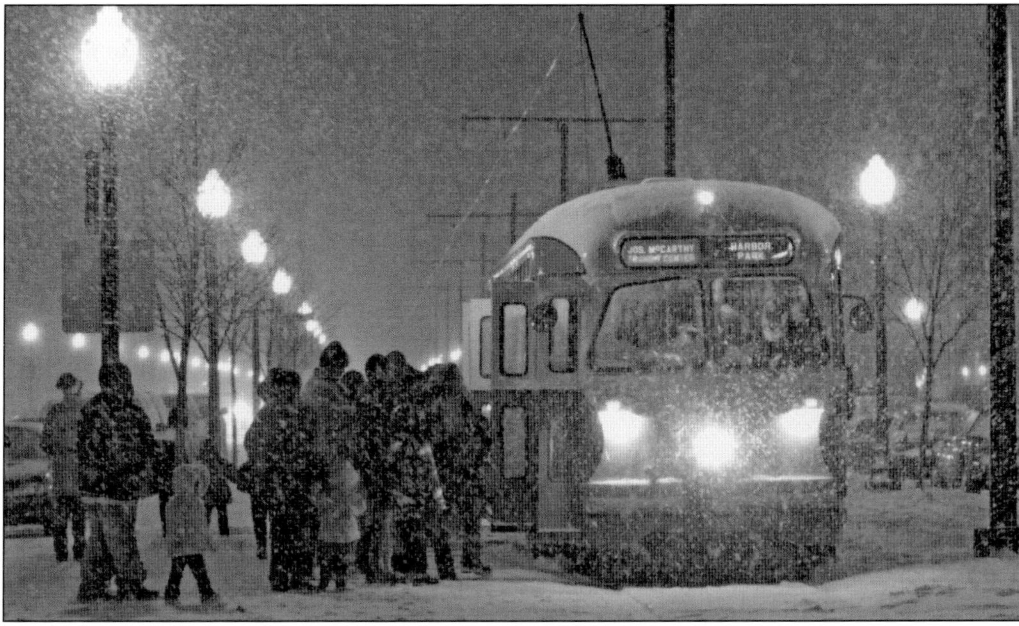

The snow is falling quickly, while the enchanted night has become almost silent. The voices of children and the muffled sound of the approaching streetcar are all that can be heard. Doors open out into the night. Children and parents clamor aboard into the warmth of the streetcar. Little hands are putting coins into the fare box, soon they will see Santa. The event is the Kenosha Candy Cane Special, December 3, 2005. (Photograph by EF.)

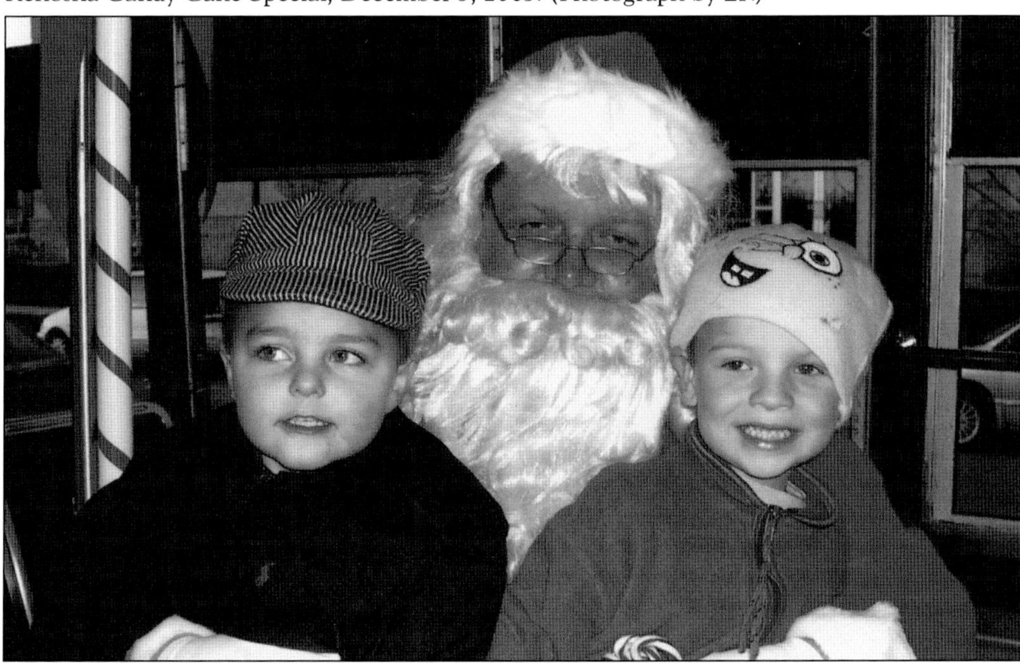

Little Benjamin Thomson and Jeffery Vitek of Western Springs, Illinois, are enjoying the candy canes given to them by Santa on December 4, 2004. Riding on a holiday-decorated Kenosha PCC streetcar, Santa (Edward Rosengren) listens patiently to the children's Christmas list. (Photograph by DJD.)

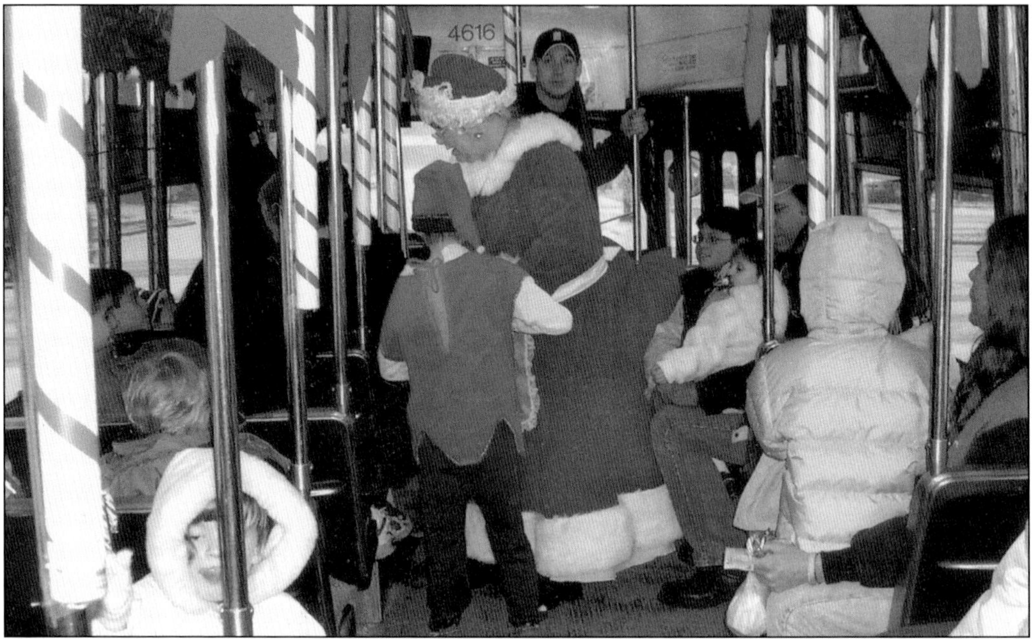

Mrs. Claus and an elf from the North Pole are passing out treats to the children on the Candy Cane Special on December 3, 2005. For this children's Christmas event, two Kenosha PCC streetcars are used: one with Santa and one with Mrs. Claus (Debbie Rosengren) and an elf (Trevor Rosengren). (Photograph by DJD.)

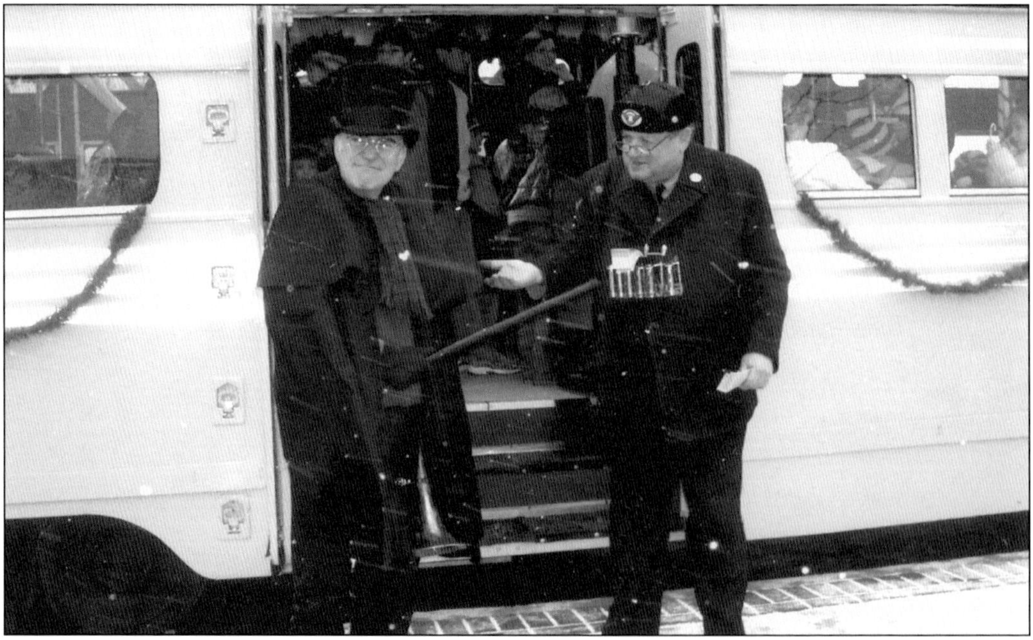

At the Kenosha Candy Cane Special on Saturday, December 3, 2005, John F. Doyle and Louis Rugani act out the following scene: "Come on Scrooge, you have to pay the twenty-five-cent fare. The children are laughing at you," Doyle, as the old-time conductor, said. "Bah hum bug, I'm not paying more than two pence, the twenty-five-cent fare is outrageous. I will take this matter up with the mayor," responded Rugani as Scrooge. (Photograph by DJD.)

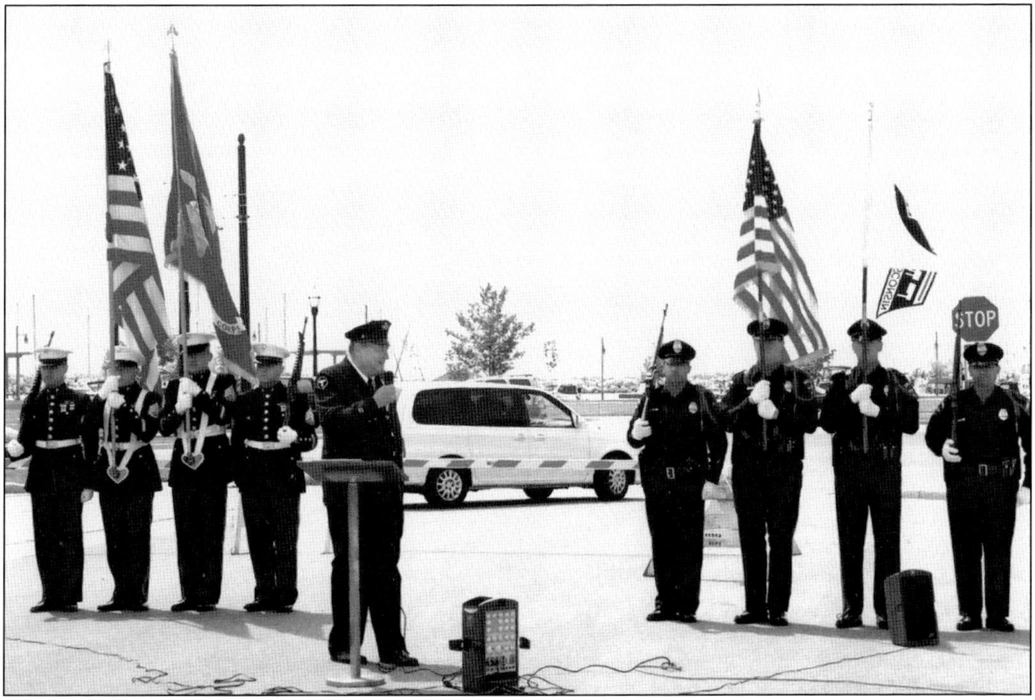

On June 14, 2003, in front of the Kenosha Public Museum, chairman of the Kenosha Streetcar Society John F. Doyle addresses the crowd at the centennial celebration of the beginning of streetcar service in Kenosha. Doyle is flanked by color guards of the United States Marine Corps and the Kenosha Police Department. (Photograph by DJD.)

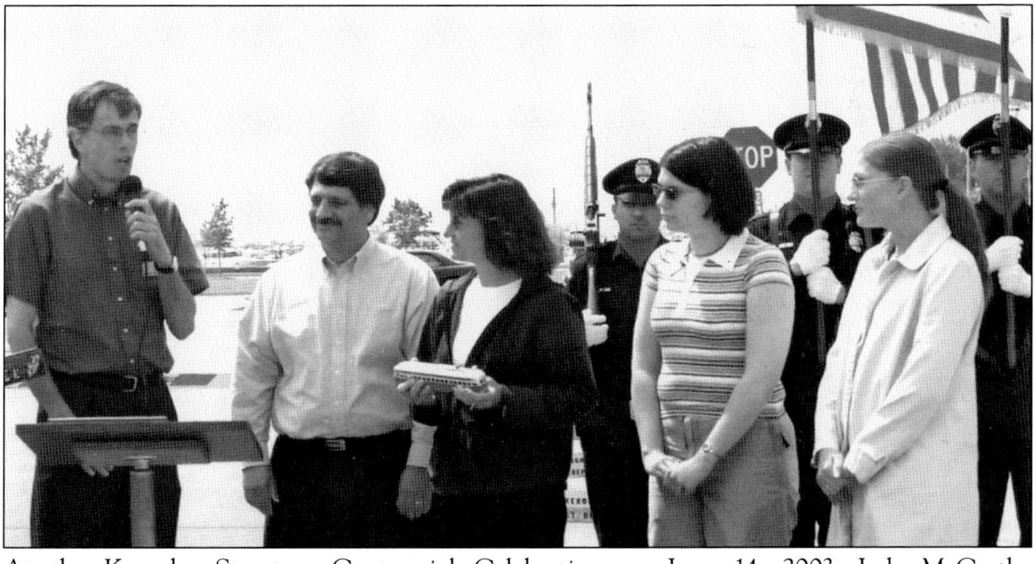

At the Kenosha Streetcar Centennial Celebration on June 14, 2003, Judy McCarthy holds a Kenosha model streetcar just given to her by Doyle (not pictured). John Bloner Jr., communications specialist for the city of Kenosha (far left), is about to introduce the mayor. Mayor John Antaramian will present a plaque to McCarthy in appreciation and honoring her late husband's service to Kenosha. Daughters Corey (second from right) and Kelly (far right) look on. (Photograph by DJD.)

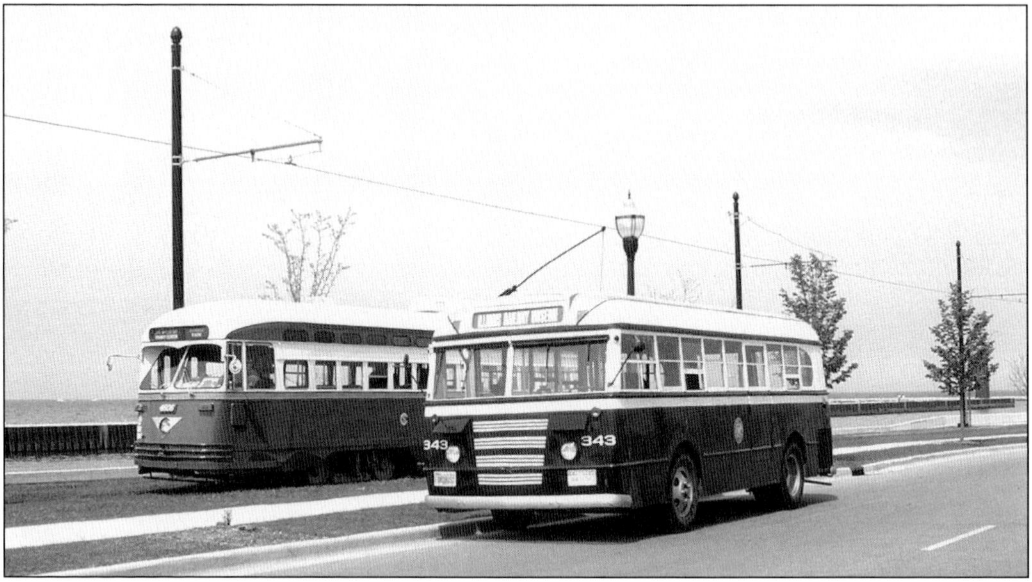

A Ford transit bus returns to Kenosha on June 14, 2003, for the Kenosha Streetcar Centennial Celebration. Ford produced hundreds of these small mechanical gas buses in an effort to help curb the shortage of transit buses during the war. Kenosha had 10 such buses with five being allocated by the Office of Defense in 1943. This bus painted in the blue and white livery of the Chicago and West Towns Railway is owned by the Illinois Railway Museum. (Photograph by JW.)

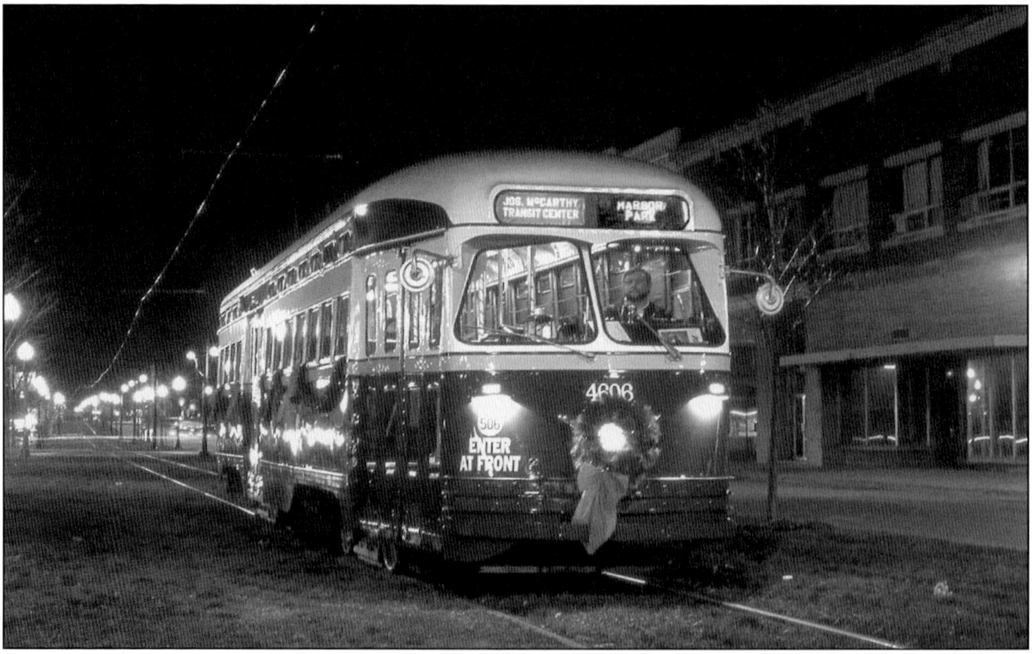

Louis Rugani and John F. Doyle sponsored the first two Santa Christmas specials with the City of Kenosha taking over in 2002. Renamed the Candy Cane Special, the event has become a very special treat for children. Here on December 8, 2004, PCC car No. 4606 is holiday decorated for the Candy Cane Special and is looking west down Fifty-sixth Street from Sixth Avenue. (Photograph by EB.)

The Kenosha Chicago PCC car No. 4606 is waiting to take crowds away after a spectacular July 4, 2005, fireworks display. This annual event is staged on Kenosha's lakefront. (Photograph by EB.)

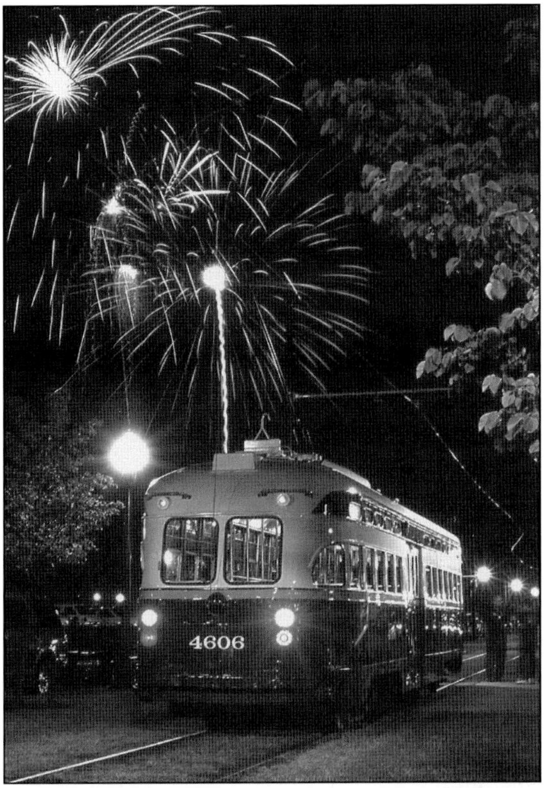

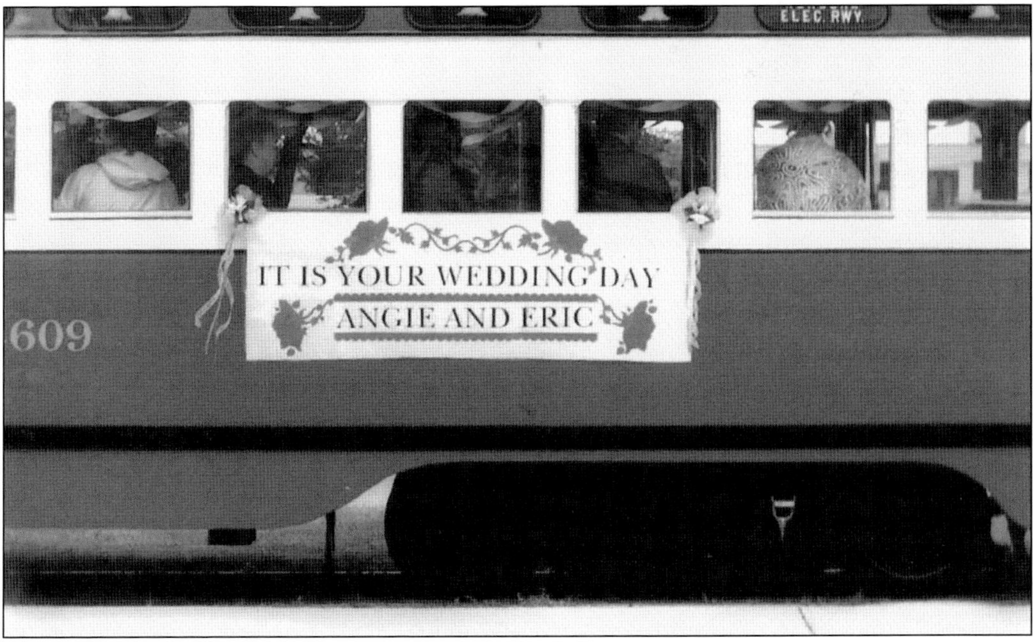

Starting off on the right track, a pre-wedding reception for bride Angela Abramski and groom Eric Bakke was held on the Kenosha Pittsburgh PCC streetcar on June 9, 2006. Kenosha streetcars also witnessed an onboard wedding and are ideal for birthday parties and other excursions. (Photograph by JK, KN, courtesy of JEW.)

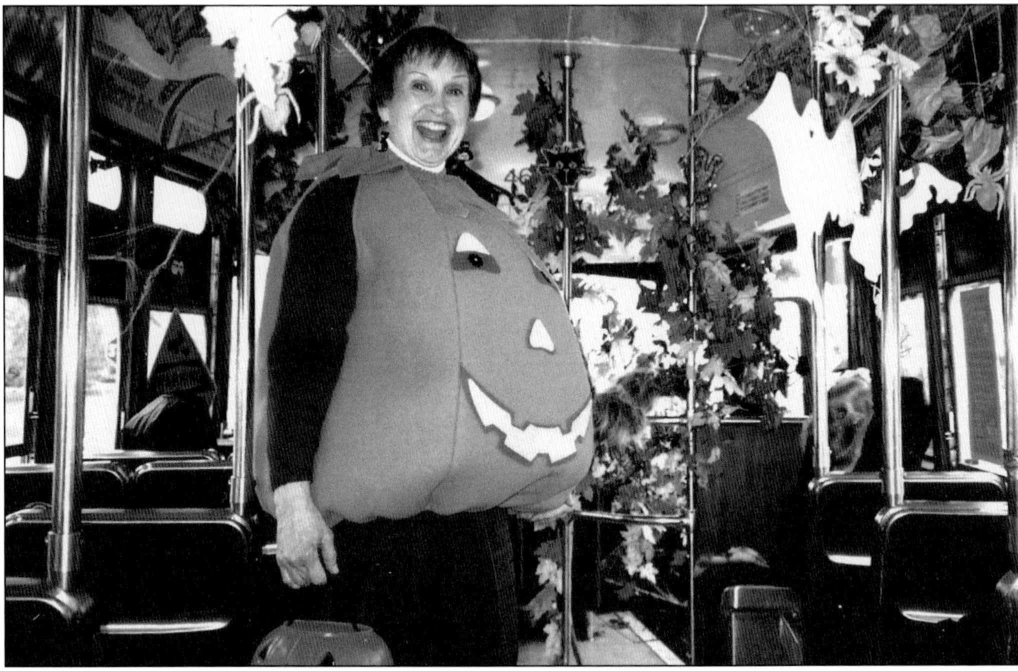

Kenosha Streetcar Society members volunteer to help for the many special events held involving Kenosha streetcars. Here board member and secretary Joyce Simons March is seen passing out candy on a special event car decorated for Halloween. (Photograph by GEK.)

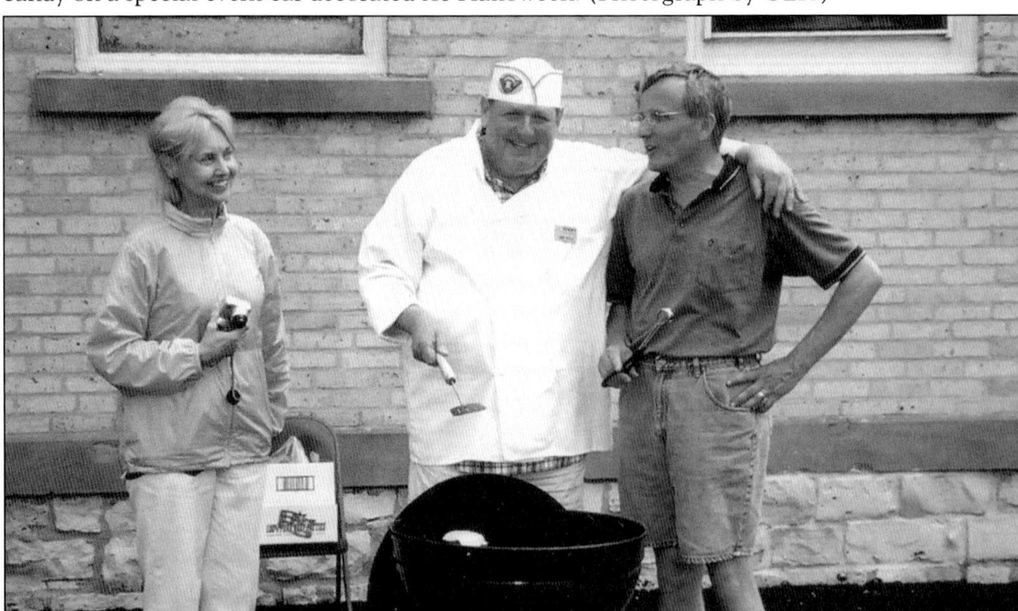

The Kenosha Streetcar Society holds many events throughout the year that include streetcar excursions, an Oktoberfest, a member Christmas party, and monthly movie and slide programs. "It's picnic time," on Saturday, June 12, 2004, as board members Roger Moddes and John F. Doyle are seen cooking hamburgers, while Diane J. Doyle looks on. Attending members also enjoyed a free streetcar ride pass for the day. (Photograph by GEK.)

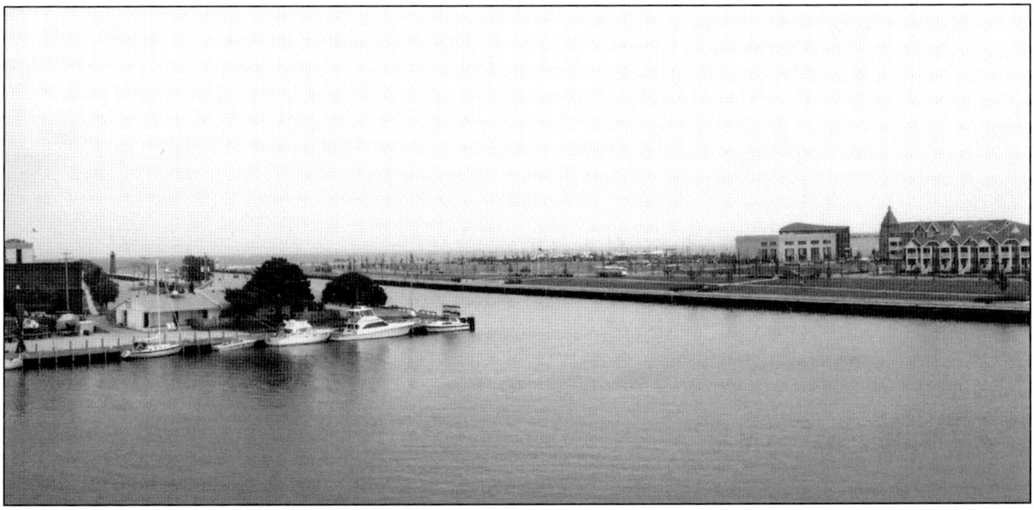

Looking across the Kenosha Harbor, the view shows HarborPark and Pike Creek inlet leading into the Kenosha Harbor from Lake Michigan on June 14, 2003. The streetcar paralleling the inlet is at Second Avenue. At one time, this area would be a scene of factories, railroads, and longshoremen loading cargo ships. (Photograph by DJD.)

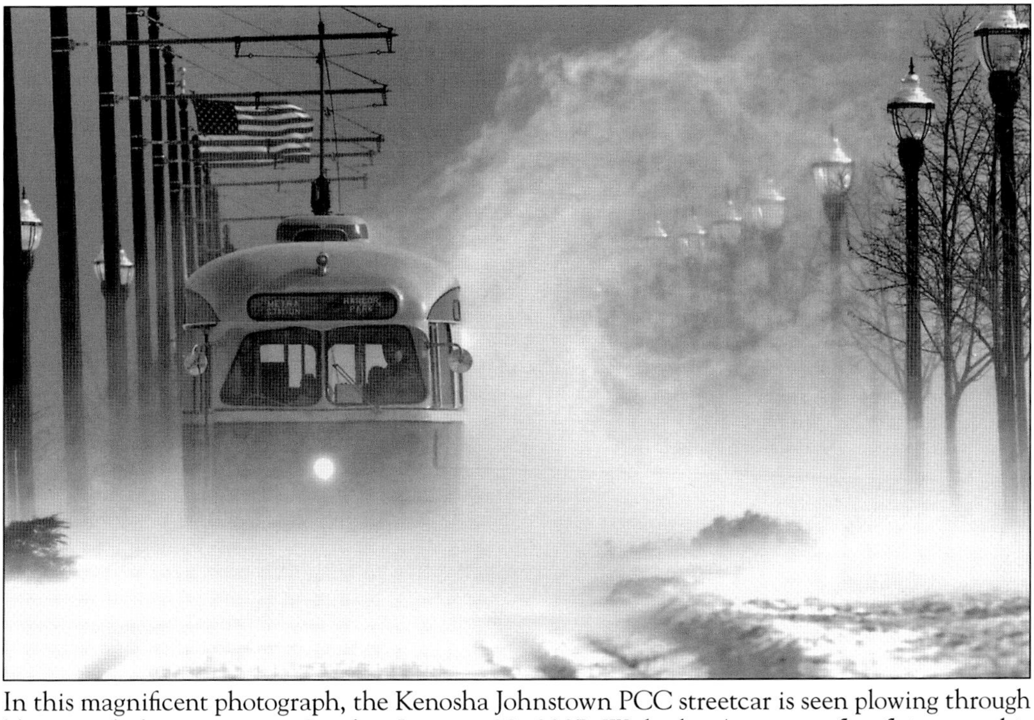

In this magnificent photograph, the Kenosha Johnstown PCC streetcar is seen plowing through blowing, drifting snow on Sunday, January 28, 2007. With the American flag flying on this beautiful winter day, this story ends. Hopefully the people of Kenosha will enjoy another 110 years of reliable and innovative transportation. (Photograph by PW, KN.)